EARLY ACHEBE

EARLY

ACHEBE

Bernth Lindfors

Africa World Press, Inc.

P.O. Box 1892
Trenton, NJ 08607

P.O. Box 48
Asmara, ERITREA

Africa World Press, Inc.

P.O. Box 1892
Trenton, NJ 08607

P.O. Box 48
Asmara, ERITREA

Copyright © 2009 Bernth Lindfors
First Printing 2009

Book design: Saverance Publishing Services
Cover design: Ashraful Haque

Library of Congress Cataloging-in-Publication Data

Lindfors, Bernth.
  Early Achebe / Bernth Lindfors.
      p. cm.
  Summary: Chiefly deals with the essays, stories, and novels published between 1951 and 1966 during the first phase of the writer's literary career.
  Includes bibliographical references and index.
  ISBN 1-59221-702-8 (hard cover) -- ISBN 1-59221-703-6 (pbk.) 1. Achebe, Chinua--Criticism and interpretation. I. Title.

  PR9387.9.A3Z815 2009
  823'.914--dc22

                                    2009013587

CONTENTS

ACKNOWLEDGEMENTS

Some of these essays have previously appeared in *African Literature Today, Ariel, Komparatistiche Hefte, The Literary Griot, Nigerian Field, Présence Africaine, Revue de Littérature Comparée*, and *Studies in Black Literature* as well as in various edited volumes and collections of my own writings. They are brought together here as a tribute to Chinua Achebe, Africa's finest novelist and most influential man of letters.

I am grateful to Guardian Newspapers Limited (Nigeria) for permission to reprint the caricatures by its staff artists, to David Levine and Kathy Hayes Associates for permission to reprint his sketch from the *New York Review of Books*, and to the *Daily Texan/Texas Student Media* for permission to reproduce the photo of Achebe taken during his lecture at The University of Texas at Austin in November 1969. Most of all, I wish to thank Chinua Achebe for allowing me to publish that lecture as well as excerpts from the interviews he gave on his first visit to Austin forty years ago.

INTRODUCTION

Much of this book deals with the essays, stories, and groundbreaking novels that Chinua Achebe published between 1951 and 1966. This was the first phase of his literary career, a phase that came to a rather abrupt end with the outbreak of the Nigerian civil war in 1967. In the years that followed he turned to shorter forms of creative expression—mainly poetry, short fiction, children's books, and literary criticism. He also kept busy by teaching at universities in Nigeria, the United States, and Canada, lecturing at conferences and symposia around the world, compiling anthologies of African writing, editing two journals, founding an Association of Nigerian Authors, and writing a book of acute political analysis, *The Trouble with Nigeria* (1983). He did not publish another novel until 1987, but this one, *Anthills of the Savannah*, served as a sequel to his earlier novels by depicting Africa under indigenous military rule. Since then Achebe has continued to remain active in a variety of capacities—writer, teacher, political pundit, and esteemed literary guru.

Yet it could be argued that the first four novels he wrote, before things fell apart in Nigeria, were the most influential of all his writings, for they transformed the way African literature was produced, consumed, studied, and taught not only in Africa but also in many other parts of the anglophone world. It has been said that Achebe invented the African novel. One could go still further and claim that his early novels changed the way people thought about Africa because they offered a convincing new interpretation of a whole continent's engagement with outside forces. Achebe, in four quick strokes, can be credited with having rewritten crucial chapters in Africa's colonial and postcolonial history.

To demonstrate his pervasive influence on others, I have included in this book several essays that discuss the impact his early fiction has had not only on fellow Nigerian writers and artists but also on teachers and critics of African literature at home and abroad. Today Achebe is the African writer most widely read in university and high school classrooms across the globe, so his influence on later generations is likely to continue to grow. *Things Fall Apart* is already regarded as an imperishable international classic.

A number of essays reprinted here were written in the 1960s and 1970s, when Achebe's works had not yet received the volume of attention and analysis they attracted in more recent decades. I have not attempted to update my own early writing by adding references to this impressive body of subsequent scholarship, for I felt that this would be anachronistic and would unnecessarily complicate my arguments, depriving them of their original simplicity and innocence. There has been much more sophisticated work done on Achebe's fiction by dozens of other critics in the past thirty years, but this book is not about what they have noticed or discovered. Rather, most of it is an effort to put on record some of my own initial responses to his first writings.

Chinua Achebe has very kindly agreed to allow me also to put on record a lecture he gave at The University of Texas at Austin in November 1969, when he was on the final leg of a month-long American speaking tour on behalf of Biafra. A few paragraphs from this lecture appeared in print afterwards in *Palaver: Interviews with Five African Writers in Texas*, ed. Bernth Lindfors, Ian Munro, Richard Priebe, Reinhard Sander (Austin: African and Afro-American

Research Institute, University of Texas at Austin, 1972), but the full lecture has never previously been published.

During the twenty-four hours Achebe spent in Austin in 1969, he gave a press conference, conducted two university classes, taped a half-hour television interview, delivered his lecture, and met with numerous students, faculty, and townspeople at an informal reception held in his honor. He was asked countless questions, and his responses to some of them round off this volume. The Nigerian-Biafran civil war was an important turning point in Achebe's literary career, so what he said then will help readers to understand better the evolution of his views on the role of the African writer in times of crisis. They will also learn a great deal from his candid reflections on his own early fiction.

LADIES AND GENTLEMEN
AT IBADAN

On Sunday, November 23, 1952, a group of young ladies from a local secondary school called St. Teresa's College staged a performance of the musical "Hiawatha" at University College Ibadan. The audience reaction apparently was far from courteous, and at least one sensitive undergraduate, embarrassed by the incivility of his peers, publicly rebuked them for displaying such boorish manners at a theatrical event. Here is his expostulation as it appeared in the *Bug*, a mimeographed bulletin published periodically by the students' union:

HIAWATHA

The behaviour of students during the performance of Hiawatha last Sunday was, quite frankly, disgraceful. Unintelligent and rude laughter, clapping and similar "pit" reactions are out of place in a University. They exasperate the few who are prepared to appreciate great works of art in a sober manner.

Those who cannot show proper response to art need not be blamed. But they should not disturb those who can. If a Shakespeare play is "caviare to the general" to them they should keep away from it.

Fortunately, Film companies provide "slapstick" for their boisterous taste.

NB. I understand that King Kong will be shown this week.

A.C. Achebe[1]

Albert Chinua Achebe was not the only student to be disturbed by the antics of such rowdy fellows at Ibadan. The following year there was a similar incident on campus and the *Bug* carried another complaint in the form of a letter to the editor.

DEAR EDITOR—

On Sunday 29th November, after the Musical Evening, Mr. Banbury asked me if some of the Artistes who sang native songs would oblige him by repeating them at the Smoking Concert after Hall III's formal dinner.

The ladies consented—I should say, in view of what happened, that they Condescended. For on that night was enacted the most sordid and disgraceful scene in the annals of this College. For no reason at all—they couldn't have been drunk with the tiny tots of beer—certain Isale-Eko type of Hooligans began to heckle the ladies before, during and after their songs.

And I must say right here that many gentlemen of Hall III disapproved of this behaviour. One of them even took down names of the chief hecklers for future reference. I have this list, and any one who wants to know the real hoodlums of Hall III can inspect this list at my place.

To continue, these ladies, for no fault in the world, were deliberately molested and embarrassed. I don't know what those fellows were doing, but I assure them that that isn't exactly how well-bred people behave. I repeat, that is <u>NOT</u> how well-bred people behave. I will end after the manner of Shakespeare: -

Oh Decency
Thou are locked in an iron chest
And men have lost its key
Bear with me,
My heart lies in degradation
    there with Third Hall
And I must pause till it comes
    back to me.

'Wole Soyinka[2]

Soyinka's remonstrance was not to go unchallenged. In the next issue of the *Bug* another student wrote:

A REPLY TO 'WOLE SOYINKA

Dear Editor—Wole's letter in your last issue of the "Bug" calls for serious comments. I am not holding brief for those members of Hall III who out of sheer involuntary lightheartedness cried "opposed" in the usual manner, as the ladies entered into the hall that evening. To many of us their coming was a pleasant surprise; for although we had no previous knowledge of it their contribution to the entertainment pro-gramme that night was 1st class and we thoroughly enjoyed it. I can say here again that were [*sic*] are very grateful.

However in showing his resentment for what he called the "sordid behaviour of hoodlums" and what not, I am afraid Wole himself has gone the "Isale Eko" way which he condemned. But knowing Wole's proclivity to histrionics I stop to wonder whether the "Wole-in-the-mood" is a character to be taken seri-ously.

Personally I do not think that a stock joke on the Campus could have hurt so much as to warrant the use of terms like ill-bred, hooligans e.t.c. against fellow students. It is only fair for me to suggest that Wole's scurrilous pen was inspired by a new brand of "TAKONISM"[3] that is yet to be classified and given a name. Otherwise the offence did not merit the torrent of invectives. This is even more so when it is realised that Wole himself was not present on the spot.

Of course no one would normally quarrel or bother about the right of mother-hen to defend her brood; but I want to stress that the use of BIL-LINGSGATE language in condemning an evil is itself an abomination. One expects that in an institution like this, decency both in words and actions should be the ideal. A cow is a good animal on the field but we turn her out of a garden.

Thank you.

(Monzi) Sesay[4]

Soyinka, of course, could not let this challenge go unanswered. Since the *Bug* was not to publish another issue until three weeks later, he replied in the *Eagle*,[5] a mimeographed newsletter he edited for the Progressive Party, a campus political organization that regularly lost student elections to its arch-rival, the Dynamic Party.

ON SESAY'S ESSAY

I wish to assure Mr. Sesay that as far as what he terms a "new brand of Takonism" is concerned, I'm quite incorrigible. I was a runner-up in the selection of "Gallant of the Year" and still intend to have a go at that title.

As for language, the whole question is whether the strength of my nib was too much for the offence. A matter of opinion, but one in which Sesay is absolutely disqualified to participate. What I mean is that it is only natural for a STINKINGRATE writer to detect BILLINGSGATE writing where it doesn't exist.

Sesay would rather I used a euphemism for 'hooligans'. Well, even hardened rogues hate to be called rogues, so, it only natural that Sesay should object to being termed a hooligan. But frankly, until he said so, I didn't know he was one of them.

Then there is Sesay's lack of honesty. Contrary to his statement, I never once used the term "ILL-BRED" in what I wrote. But of course, writers like Monzi always manufacture statements to strengthen their non-existent arguments.

"A cow", Monzi says, "is a useful animal...." Thanks for the compliment. But I will complete it this way—"...but a tse-tsay fly is a nuisance both to the cow and to other human beings."

"People—I beg your pardon—flies which buzz in glass houses...." Complete that one.

'Wole Soyinka

These letters and exchanges are interesting not only for the light they shed on the chivalrous young men who wrote them (Achebe characteristically sober but urbane; Soyinka characteristically lighthearted, witty, playfully disputatious, and mocking) but also for the illumination they provide on certain social interactions at a male-dominated African university campus in the 1950s. Women who put themselves on display in musical performances—Western or African—evidently were regarded as fair game for hecklers and "hooligans." Men who tried to protect such artistes from demeaning harassment were liable to be accused of championing women's rights or running for Gallant of the Year. It may be no accident that the two gentlemen at Ibadan who were willing to risk taking an unpopular stand in order to teach their fellows some manners later emerged as Africa's most articulate social critics.

NOTES

1. A.C. Achebe, "Hiawatha," *Bug* 4, no. 2 (November 29, 1952): 3.
2. Wole Soyinka, "Dear Editor," *Bug* 5, no. 1 (December 11, 1953): 11.
3. A student named S.A.N. Takon had written an article entitled "Give Our Female Undergraduates Their Rights" in the *Bug* 2, no. 5 (January 20, 1951): 5, and in the protracted correspondence that followed, the term "Takonism" was coined to refer to the position taken by Takon and other advocates of women's rights.
4. Monzi Sesay, "A Reply to 'Wole Soyinka," *Bug* 5, no. 2 (January 30, 1954): 7.
5. Wole Soyinka, "On Sesay's Essay," *Eagle* 3, no. 2 (January 30, 1954): 7.

For further information on such publications, see my "Popular Literature for an African Elite," *Journal of Modern African Studies* 12 (1974): 471-86.

UNDERGRADUATE WRITINGS

Chinua Achebe entered University College Ibadan in 1948 to study medicine but he did not last long as a science student. In an interview some years later he said, "When I left school I didn't really know what I wanted to do and medicine was very glamorous—it was either medicine or engineering—but I soon discovered that it wasn't really my cup of tea, so I changed."[1] More to his liking was the degree program in arts, which enabled him to study literature, history, and comparative religion. Yet though his decision to switch to arts cut him off entirely from the labs and glamour of the so-called "hard sciences," he seems to have retained a taste for the mind-expanding opportunities offered by these highly systematic disciplines. One of the first pieces he wrote for the *University Herald*, a campus publication issued by the students' union, was "An Argument Against the Existence of Faculties,"[2] in which he lamented the tendency of the university to narrow rather than broaden the education of its students by compelling them to choose between two separate and mutually exclusive streams of study. The tone of the article, suggested in its Wordsworthian epigraph, "Enough of Science and of Art," was no more than half-serious, but the serious half raised a legitimate question about curricular constraints in the degree programs offered at that time by Nigeria's only university. Since this essay has not been reprinted in any of the collections of Achebe's miscellaneous writings published to date,[3] it may be worthwhile to reproduce the entire text before commenting further on Achebe's complaints about forced academic specialization.

It is not yet realised by many people that the usual practice of cramping up students into water-tight compartments known as faculties is a reproach on civilisation. We hear so much today about freedom of this, that and the other, but never about freedom of academic pursuit. It is very distressing that a student should be condemned perpetually to weighing, measuring and looking at the back legs of toads, because of a very minor and venial sin—I mean the sin of having written "SCIENCE" on certain dotted lines when he first entered the college. For this alone, he is made to lead a dog's life, no change, no excitement.

I know one or two of these unfortunate students who would give anything to replace one of their subjects with, say, Latin. But here, they come up against academic intolerance. Latin is separated from Science by a huge wall on which is written (for the benefit of Science students): "*Warning! Arts Faculty Premises. Trespassers will not obtain a London Degree.*" Why should one not obtain a degree in Religious Studies, Applied Mathematics and Gynaecology if he wishes to do so? The reason is simple. We live in an age that is in love with tags and labels. We call History Arts and Chemistry Science, and then sit back lazily thinking we have fully accounted for these subjects.

I have long suspected that even though we all talk so glibly about Arts and Science, nobody can really differentiate between them. But I had no confidence then to translate this suspicion into print because, I said to myself, "men wiser and more learned than I probably know the difference." So my judgement was tempered by diffidence and the publication of the thesis was delayed.

Fortunately, the position is different now. I have discovered, in a rather curious way, that J.B. Bury in his inaugural lecture at Cambridge had said: "History is a Science, no less and no more." So it was just as I feared. Eminent professors are as confused in this matter as freshmen. History is Science. What then is Arts? We may appreciate this confusion better by coming nearer home (although it is customary in such discussions to maintain a considerable distance from home in the interest of our friends and relations). Coming nearer home, I say, we notice a rather curious situation in the Department of Mathematics. It is said that the Head of the Department represents the Arts Faculty on the Library Committee, while his second-in-command is the Dean of Science. We would all thank God that there is no real difference between Arts and Science. If there were, doctors would have had to deal with Schizophrenia on a departmental scale.

The point I wish to make is this: if there is so much confusion in the matter, is it not ridiculous that men whose boast it is that theirs is the Age of Reason, is it not extra-ordinary, I say, that these men should allow words of very doubtful meaning to stand in the way of students' freedom? "But surely," says one of my friends, "you believe such a thing as academic tradition. Why should one be allowed to take a degree in Botany, Greek and Phonetics? It has never been done." Academic tradition indeed! A mere euphemism for superstition.

Another specious argument that is often advanced in defence of faculties runs like this: *A faculty is a combination of related subjects e.g. Physics and Chemistry which become almost indistinguishable from each other in their upper reaches.* But only if we think deeply, we shall realize that *all* subjects are related.

Let us take two apparently different subjects such as History and Botany. I saw the other day in one of the lecture rooms the following botanical diagram:—

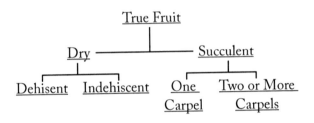

Now, every student of History sees immediately that this diagram has the same essential features as the family tree of the Duke of Lorraine whose policy was so important in the Habsburg-Valois Wars of the sixteenth century:

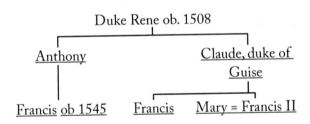

The only difference between these genealogical tables is that Anthony had only one son, while "Dry" apparently had a son and a daughter.

It is thus obvious that nothing can be said in defence of faculties. Let us, therefore, examine some of the points against them. In the first place, students in one faculty are now showing more and more interest in the affairs of other faculties. They realise that "perpendicular" education within the confines of one faculty is now out of date. They are bent on pulling down the walls that have for so long separated Arts from Science. (Those departments that have hitherto sat on those walls may do well to descend one way or the other before the final collapse. I refer, of course, to Geography and Mathematics.)

The restless desire for academic freedom may be seen in the way students discuss subjects outside their faculties with the utmost ease. A famous Arts student is reputed to have said that some plants were photographic while others suffered from photophobia. Another one was overhead [*sic*] explaining that it was dangerous to wear shorts at night because one might easily catch pneumonia of the legs. About the same time a Science student remarked that *The Doctor's Dilemma* was one of Shakespeare's famous novels.

The second argument may be illustrated by a short story. The different departments in a certain university were asked to send in their requisition for the year. One of them demanded an apparatus costing £3000. Another one thought a bit, and filled in "a box of chalk." Now, since the "chalk box" departments seem to be concentrated in one faculty, it means that very little is spent on a student in that faculty. Naturally, he will resent it.

We are told that the instinct of self-preservation is the strongest in man. This was perhaps true before money was invented. But certainly man's strongest instinct today is to get more than his money's worth. He is always striving to maintain a balance in his favour. If he is properly educated, he may learn to relinquish this balance; but that is as far as he can go. It means then that unless the "chalk-box" student is allowed to study at least one "expensive" subject, we may well expect a real crisis in the Universities.

Achebe's argument is neatly organized into three parts: (1) a preamble that states his position and asks the tantalizingly pertinent (and impertinent) question: "Why should one not obtain a degree in Religious Studies, Applied Mathematics and Gynaecology if he wishes to do so?"; (2) a critical investigation of two of the "specious" claims often advanced in defense of faculties; and (3) an examination of two of the points that can be raised against faculties. Each part is amply illustrated with colorful examples, some of which are so ridiculous that they do more to undercut Achebe's position than to support it. But Achebe's purpose was not to overwhelm his peers with rigorous reasoning; he preferred to amuse them by puncturing one absurdity with another, a rigid educational system with a systematically limp argument. The mirth generated by this double paradox served to reinforce his plea for abandoning bicameral faculties.

Achebe had spoken out a few months earlier against students who closed their minds to unfamiliar modes of mental exercise. He found such narrow-mindedness unworthy of university undergraduates. Writing in the *Bug* in response to a fellow student's complaints about a series of lectures in philosophy, he blended wit and mockery to make his point.

PHILOSOPHY

An article was published about lectures in Philosophy in the last issue of the Bug. It was written by Holy Devil. He said, inter alia, "these (lectures in philosophy) have progressed enough for us to be able to read a purpose into them." He then told us that we have been "swallowing without proper mastication these ideas which are in MY OPINION (capitals are mine) utterly un-progressive for certainly to philosophize in the absence of adequate knowledge...will produce...worthless philosophy."

This argument is, to say the least, muddled and illogical. Philosophy, says the Holy Devil is unprogressive because our knowledge (I suppose he means his knowledge) is inadequate. This to my mind, is the height of absurd reasoning. A lecture does not become 'unprogressive' because a devil in the audience has not enough knowledge to follow it. It will be "caviare to the general" as far as he is concerned, but certainly not unprogressive.

His warning against "swallowing without proper mastication"is unnecessary. He ought to credit us with a critical faculty. I strongly doubt whether we require a devil "come from hell" to make us think—philosophy implies thinking. What Holy Devil wants us to do is not really to *think* but to *suspect*—"to read a purpose into them." Dear Holy Devil, don't you think we can do without so much suspicion in this place? Of course when you said 'in my opinion,' you made it clear that your statements were couched in the language of devils. We mortals must undergo a mental somersault before we can understand "knowledge," "unprogressive" and such other terms used in your article. This is an unfortunate and inevitable circumstance arising from the difference in ideas and values as understood by men and by devils.

You are entitled to you views, Mr. Holy Devil, but please do not translate them into print in a community with such an overwhelming majority of human beings.

@@@@ ALBERT CHINUA ACHEBE @@@@@@
!!!!!!!--!!!!!!!!![4]

In this letter, as in his "Argument Against the Existence of Faculties," Achebe was defending the concept of a liberal education against those who would limit free inquiry or exposure to unfamiliar ideas. In the essay his target was an inflexible institutional structure imposed by the faculty and administration upon the students. In this letter he turned his fire on a fellow student who had ventured to grumble about philosophy lectures that were difficult for the ordinary undergraduate to comprehend. Achebe, in his delightfully urbane manner, was accusing students, faculty, and administrators of fostering anti-intellectualism on campus.

Achebe did not hesitate to "translate into print" his own views whenever he felt his community would benefit from them, even though his words might ring in some ears as "caviare to the general."[5] As a convert to the arts degree program, he was particularly sensitive to slights from science students and at least once rushed to the defense of arts students by attempting to turn the tables on a detractor who had ventured to criticize them for being "unscientific."

MR. OKAFOR versus ARTS STUDENTS

The time has passed when a man can take the whole field of knowledge for his province. On the other hand, too much departmentalization of university education can be a real danger. Mr. Ezelu Okafor is therefore right when he warns Arts Students against being "unscientific."

Unfortunately, Mr. Okafor's warning carries with it that absolute lack of humility with which a certain vocal group of science students is afflicted. These Science Students believe that they are as good as, if not better than, arts students, even in their own subjects. This belief is very often based on no more solid merit than a superficial acquaintance with literature of the Peter Cheyney type. Mr. Okafor who, one would have thought, should be above intermediate standard in English concludes his article thus: "it *shall* be of interest to know...." (a peculiar use of *shall*).

People like Mr. Okafor think that the greater their stock of technical terms, the better educated they are. He expects every arts student to know what *FEMUR* is. An English student might as well expect him to be able to account for the loss in English of inflexional endings in the middle English period. Perhaps he knows all about it.[6]

The tone of this piece and of another one on the same page of the *Bug* reproving unruly students for their rude behavior during a performance of the musical "Hiawatha" staged at the university by a neighboring girls' school,[7] is not quite as light as Achebe's earlier translations into print, but by this time he was only a year away from graduation so it may have been more appropriate for him to speak in the graver idiom of a campus elder. Caustic sobriety certainly was not the tenor of his initial contributions to campus publications.

Of course, we must remember that he came to the university with some experience in editing and writing for high school magazines. At Umuahia he had contributed to house organs and had assisted the faculty member entrusted with the responsibility of preparing the college annual for publication. Achebe has spoken of writing "little poems and things like that" at school.[8] This tradition of filling up pages with material that would entertain his fellow students was something he sought to carry on at University College Ibadan, so it is not surprising that some of his earliest published pieces as an undergraduate were entirely frivolous.

His first offering in the *University Herald*, and possibly his first work to appear in print at Ibadan, was a humorous sketch entitled "The Polar Undergraduate" which he later reprinted in *Girls at War and Other Stories*.[9] It deals with the tendency of some Ibadan students to stay awake much of the night and catch up on sleep during class lectures. Robert Wren, one of the few critics to comment on this essay, finds it "distinguished by stylistic ease and an amused (if not particularly amusing) misuse of mathematical symbolism."[10] David Carroll notes that much of the wit is "based on the application of a bizarre logic…to the classification of students."[11] Here are a few samples:

> The criterion for membership of this group [of polar undergraduates] has been summarized mathematically as, $20 < p \leq 24$, where p is the number of "sleepless" hours. Now, these sleepless hours may either occur in one stretch, or they may be broken up, and diversified by an interspersion, here and there, of small bits of sleep, Δs. In the latter instance, these small bits, when integrated, must not exceed four hours, i.e. the integral of delta s between limits minus infinity and nought is less than or equal to 4.…
>
> There is, however, a theory that has just been propounded, and which may throw light on polar undergraduates. It states that what matters in a University is not how many hours (p) we are wake; but the product of this quantity and our degree of alertness, (d). This product (dp) is fairly constant for all students, and p can only be increased at the cost of reduced mental and physical efficiency. This is the *Law of Conservation of Hours.*

Achebe, having perhaps already discovered that science was not his cup of tea, parodied mathematical formulations and natural laws in order to promulgate a pseudo-theory to explain a commonly observed biological phenomenon: that some student night owls slept by day. He also made oblique remarks about certain "compatriots" who had excelled in other spectacular behavioral aberrations—allusions that his reading audience would easily be able to decipher. This was fairly typical "in-house" undergraduate humor.

"The Polar Undergraduate" and "An Argument Against the Existence of Faculties," written at a time in his life when he was contemplating transferring from one academic faculty to another, reflect Achebe's allegiance to Two Cultures. He was a young man with an analytical bent groping toward free and creative expression. Here was a systematic logician deliberately perverting reason and indulging in high-spirited poetic license. Here was a medical student turned humorous essayist, a Scientist turned Artist.

In his next contribution to the *University Herald,* later reprinted in *Girls at War and Other Stories,* Achebe took his first step in the direction of recreating rural life. By this time (June 1951), well into his third year at Ibadan, he no doubt would have completed his transfer from science to arts, a fact that may account for the greater number of literary allusions and quotations in his prose. One hears echoes of Shakespeare, Wordsworth, and the King James Version of the Bible in this brief personal essay, called "In a Village Church."[12] Achebe, in the bemused manner of an avuncular yet detached participant, describes the little oddities he observed in a Sunday morning church service in a rural community. This may be a montage of memories gleaned from his childhood, when he was growing up in Ogidi as the son of a devout Christian convert who had become an evangelist and church teacher,[13] but it may also contain vignettes from some of his later experiences of organized religious activity elsewhere. Certainly it has a very genial and nostalgic tone, a benign air of commotion recollected in tranquility. Take this passage, for example:

> The seating arrangement inside the church was very simple. Men sat on the right, women on the left and the choir in front. This differentiation was not arbitrary but influenced very strongly the procedure of worship. Singing, for instance, followed very closely the seating pattern. Everybody seemed to agree that the organ was invented for the choir and such other young people as were yet inexperienced in the service

of God. As for the other groups, each sang lustily at its own pace. Obviously, the convention of starting the same verse at the same time was not recognised. The advantage of this system was that at any given time—from the beginning of the hymn to the ending of the same—there was always a voice to be heard. Inherent in the system, however, was one difficulty. The choir always got to the "Amen" when the women were just beginning the last verse, and men half way through it. But this was of very little consequence. The custom was that any group that finished before the others went in to help them in the true Christian fashion.

In this nicely orchestrated scene, and in others equally amusing, Achebe provides glimpses of a community caught in the flux of cultural transformation, when not everyone was responding to the same rhythm of events or even singing to the same tune. In other words, he captures in vivid images precisely the kind of societal confusion that was to become the hallmark of his novels.

Moreover, the relaxed detachment he achieved in depicting people and events that were very close to him physically yet distanced from him to some extent spiritually and intellectually enabled him to paint a memorable comic portrait that was both sympathetic and mildly satirical. The preacher sermonizing on the sacrifices required for the attainment of longevity, the bespectacled parishioner searching for the day's text in a tattered "antediluvian" Bible, and the snoring worshipper being awakened by the churchwarden toward the end of the service are introduced by Achebe in neat thumbnail sketches that illustrate absurd dimensions of the missionary enterprise in Africa. The essay is as much a comedy of colonial church manners as it is a reflective memoir recalling the picturesque grotesqueries of a changing world.

Achebe manages to find a way to make his reminiscences of a village church relevant to his university audience. The connecting link is sleep, the theme he had embroidered at length in "The Polar Undergraduate." The unconscious worshipper, he says,

> might be compared to undergraduates who go to the library for their siesta. The philosophy behind both actions is essentially the same. The religious atmosphere of the church blows through the minds of all worshippers, whether they are awake or asleep, looking at the preacher or at the nurses. In the same way, the library has its intellectual environment and breathes its knowledge on any one within reasonable distance of the shelves. This philosophy was sung by a famous poet many years ago.
>
> > "Nor less I deem that there are powers,
> > Which of themselves our minds impress,
> > That we can feed this mind of ours,
> > In a wise passiveness."
>
> A quiet village church is the best place on earth to learn philosophy.

Achebe's use of Wordsworth to round off his fanciful comparison is another example of "in-house" humor, but here it also has the functional strength of a proverb brought in at the right moment to reinforce and complete an argument. Even as an undergraduate essayist, Achebe sometimes displayed a crafted elegance of style that was unusually eloquent.

Up to this point in his academic career, Achebe apparently had not published any fiction. Indeed, in a BBC radio interview twenty years later, he recalled that he was so inexperienced and naïve as a young university student that he didn't even know what distinguished a short story from any other form of writing.

> I never learnt the craft of writing. When I went to school nobody talked about writing, nobody imagined there would be writers, so there was nobody who was ready to teach it. Now, an interesting thing happened when I was a student at Ibadan. I'd never written anything, really, and the English Department decided to have a competition in short story writing. And so we wrote short stories. I'd never written short stories, so I didn't know what short stories were supposed to be, really. I wrote what I thought was a short story and my teacher said "this is interesting, but it isn't quite a short story." So I said, "What is a short story? I'd like to know," and she never told me. So that's as much teaching as I got in writing.[14]

It is possible that one or two of the early essays Achebe published in the *University Herald*—particularly "In a Village Church," which has a narrative structure—may have been produced for this campus short story writing competition.

Achebe's first true short story in the *University Herald* appeared in May 1952 under the title "The Old Order in Conflict with the New." This was reprinted as "Beginning of the End" in *The Sacrificial Egg and Other Short Stories*, and was given yet another title, "Marriage is a Private Affair," when revised and reissued in *Girls at War and Other Stories*.[15] Several critics have commented on this story because it is built on a theme that Achebe later returned to in his second novel, *No Longer at Ease*,[16] the theme of love and marriage in modern Africa.

Nnaemeka, a well-educated young Igbo man living in Lagos, has become engaged to Nene, a young Ibibio woman brought up in that cosmopolitan city, but he is reluctant to break the news to his father for he knows that the old man expects him to marry within his own ethnic group. The father, though a devout Christian, still believes in following a number of traditional practices, including the custom that parents select suitable spouses for their children; in fact, he already has a girl in mind for his son and wants to begin negotiations with her parents as soon as Nnaemeka returns to the village on his next holiday. When Nnaemeka comes home and tells him that he intends to marry a girl of his own choosing, and not an Igbo girl at that, his father breaks off with him, even going so far as to return the wedding picture that Nnaemeka sends him six months later. Eight years pass and the old man refuses to change his attitude, but he suddenly is won over when Nene herself writes to ask if his two grandsons can come to the village with Nnaemeka to visit him. The news that he has grandchildren softens his heart and he feels remorse for having shut his door to members of his own family. Tradition thus ultimately crumbles in the face of persistent modernity.

The story obviously anticipates the love affair of Obi and Clara in *No Longer at Ease*, but there are significant differences that should be noted. First, Clara does not belong to another ethnic group; she is Igbo but an *osu*—someone considered an outcast in traditional Igbo society. Second, Obi's engagement to Clara is opposed by both his father and his mother, and he begins seriously to reconsider his intention to marry her when his mother threatens to commit suicide if the wedding occurs while she is still alive. But the most profound difference between the two family conflicts is in their resolution: Obi never marries Clara, and his story ends tragically, not happily.

Michael Echeruo sees the "unhappy ending of *No Longer at Ease* [as] important for it constitutes a real variation from the earlier story, and is quite possibly part of an intensification of Achebe's tragic disposition."[17] Robert Wren, in a similar vein, notes that

> The [earlier] story shows no sense of community
> with the past. Its theme is the freedom of the modern
> world created by urban (i.e., European) values. Tradi-
> tion has so little strength that the single idea, "grand-
> sons," crushes it....Marriage is not an affair of the
> family, of the community—it is "private." The whole
> thrust of Achebe's first two novels will say the oppo-
> site: that the clan is king, that nothing is private.[18]

To this one might add, as Wren is careful to do, that there is
a striking qualitative difference between Achebe's first short
story and his second novel; the writing in "The Old Order in
Conflict with the New" appears to be a rather crude, amateur
effort when set beside the easy narrative grace of *No Longer
at Ease*. Yet both works deal with a theme that Achebe evidently considered to be of crucial importance, for he devoted
nearly all of his fiction, early and late, to various aspects of it.
In stories as well as novels he explored the impact of cultural
change on the lives of representative Africans, attempting to
show "where the rain began to beat them."[19] Such elemental
matters as Love and Marriage were very stormy subjects in
African societies undergoing rapid Westernization.

But it may be misleading to suggest that Achebe's perspective on such issues shifted significantly between 1952
and 1960, the dates these two works were published. In an
interview with Ernest and Pat Emenyonu, Achebe empha-
sized that he didn't care to limit his fiction to examining only
one side of a question.

> I never will take the stand that the Old must win
> or that the New must win. If I wrote two stories in
> which the Old won in one, the New in the other,
> I would be quite happy. To me, that is the way life is.
> In Obi's story the marriage didn't come through
> because the woman is tabooed, and cult consider-
> ation, not tribe, is the primary issue. The fact that they

failed does not mean that I believe that all young men caught in such conflicts must go the way of Obi.

I never believe in taking firm positions and if I do two novels, I try to make sure that the same thing does not happen twice....The point is that no single truth satisfied me—and this is well founded in the Igbo world view. No single man can be correct all the time, no single idea can be totally correct. If you pick any proverb that seems to put forward a particular point of view, you can always find another one that seeks to contradict it.[20]

This statement appears to be borne out in Achebe's second and last short story published at Ibadan, a story that originally did not have a title but that he later decided to call "Dead Men's Path."[21] It provides another example of conflict between the Old and the New, but this time the Old wins. Michael Obi, a young man appointed headmaster of an unprogressive mission school, is determined to put his own educational ideas into practice and show others how a school should be run.

Ndume was backward in every sense of the word. Mr. Obi put his whole life in the work and his wife hers too. He had two aims (the other head masters had none, he said). A high standard of teaching was insisted upon and the school compound was to be turned into a place of beauty. Nancy's dream gardens soon came to life and blossomed. Beautiful hedges were planted and playgrounds were improved.

But one evening he is "scandalized" to see an old woman crossing the school compound, and when he learns that she is using an ancient footbath that connects the village shrine with the cemetery, he orders it closed off with hedges and barbed wire. An elderly priest of the earth deity calls upon him and asks him to reopen it, but he refuses. Two days later a young woman in the village dies in childbirth, and a diviner interprets her death as evidence that the ancestors are furious that their footpath has been desecrated. The next morning Michael Obi finds the school compound in ruins, the hedges torn up and the flowers trampled to death. The Old has reasserted its supremacy over the New.

Critics have disagreed over the position taken by Achebe in this story. G.D. Killam feels that "Achebe is impartial here; neither side is supported."[22] Robert Wren also regards the author's handling of events as nonjudgmental and deliberately enigmatic: "Who is right?...it has something no previous story by Achebe had: mystery. The old ways are allowed their due."[23] Michael Echeruo finds Achebe critical of both antagonists—"a superstitious but proud society—proud of the wisdom of its traditions—and an idealistic generation of star-gazers," yet Echeruo agrees that "for Achebe, the 'war of generations' is only an occasion for tragedy of a subtle kind. There has, in any case, been no resolution either way...of this war of the 'ages.'"[24] In sum, Achebe has contrived to maintain his neutrality, refusing to play favorites in a battle in which he sees wrong on both sides.

In opposition to these views are those expressed by David Carroll, who sees in Michael Obi's downfall

> a recurrent theme in Achebe's writing. Again and again in the fiction a simplified, dogmatic assertion of values achieves the opposite of what it intends by refusing to acknowledge any rival claims. The village priest, in contrast, suggests there is room for different ways—"Let the hawk perch and let the eagle also perch"—and in the story his voice is that of reasonableness.[25]

Achebe, in other words, was on the side of Tradition here because only that side had the good sense to speak in tolerant and levelheaded terms. The village priest was not the diehard fanatic that Michael Obi was.

Carroll's views are akin to those Achebe himself expressed in the interview cited earlier, and if one reads this story carefully, studying the revisions Achebe made before allowing the text to be reprinted in *Girls at War and Other Stories*, one can see that his sympathies lie more with the village priest than with Michael Obi. Here is the first version of the discussion between the two men with Achebe's subsequent deletions and revisions italicized:

> Three days later the village priest of Ani (*Earth Deity*) called on the headmaster. He was an old man and walked with a slight stoop. He carried a stout walking stick which he usually tapped on the floor, by way of emphasis, each time he made a new point in his argument. *At such a time a kindly twinkle would play across his eyes.*
>
> "*It has been brought to my notice,*" he said after the usual exchange of cordialities, "that our ancestral foot path has recently been closed...."
>
> "Yes," replied Mr. Obi. "We cannot allow people to make a highway of our school compound."
>
> "Look here, my son," said the priest bringing down his walking-stick, "this path *has been* here *from time immemorial.* The whole life of *the* village depends on it. Our dead relatives depart by it and our ancestors visit us by it. But *more* important perhaps, *our unborn babes cannot arrive any other way....*"
>
> "The whole purpose of our school, Mr. Obi *interrupted,* is to *show you the stupidity of such beliefs as you now hold.* Dead men do not require footpaths. The whole idea is just fantastic." *Contempt was quite visible on his face.*
>
> "What you say may be true," replied the priest, "but we follow the practices of our fathers. If you

re-open the path we shall have nothing to quarrel about." He rose to go.

"I am sorry," said the young headmaster. "But the school compound cannot be a thoroughfare. I would suggest your constructing another path skirting our premises. We can even get our boys to help in *constructing* it. I don't suppose *your* ancestors will find the detour *very* burdensome."

Now here is the revised version of this interaction with Achebe's interpolations and revisions italicized:

Three days later the village priest of *Ani* called on the headmaster. He was an old man and walked with a slight stoop. He carried a stout walking-stick which he usually tapped on the floor, by way of emphasis, each time he made a new point in his argument.

'*I have heard*,' he said after the usual exchange of cordialities, 'that our ancestral footpath has recently been closed…'

'Yes,' replied Mr. Obi. 'We cannot allow people to make a highway of our school compound.'

'Look here, my son,' said the priest bringing down his walking-stick, 'this path *was* here *before you were born and before your father was born*. The whole life of *this* village depends on it. Our dead relatives depart by it and our ancestors visit us by it. But *most* important, *it is the path of children coming in to be born…*'

Mr. Obi listened with a satisfied smile on his face.

'The whole purpose of our school,' *he said finally*, is to *eradicate just such beliefs as that*. Dead men do not require footpaths. The whole idea is just fantastic. *Our duty is to teach your children to laugh at such ideas.*'

'What you say may be true,' replied the priest, 'but we follow the practices of our fathers. If you re-open the path we shall have nothing to quarrel about. *What*

I always say is: let the hawk perch and let the eagle also perch. He rose to go.

'I am sorry,' said the young headmaster. 'But the school compound cannot be a thoroughfare. *It is against our regulations.* I would suggest your constructing another path, skirting our premises. We can even get our boys to help in *building* it. I don't suppose *the* ancestors will find the little detour *too* burdensome.

'I have no more words to say,' said the old priest, already outside.

Achebe removes the kindly twinkle from the old man's eyes but adds a proverb to his speech ("let the hawk perch and let the eagle perch") that reveals his open-mindedness; he is asking for peaceful coexistence and mutual respect, not deference or subservience to his own set of beliefs. He is willing to grant that what Michael Obi says "may be true," but he himself would rather say nothing at all than try to reform the younger man's fixed religious ideas. Michael Obi, on the other hand, is made to appear slightly less impetuous but somewhat more smug and disrespectful than he had been in the original version of the story. He does not interrupt the village priest but listens "with a satisfied smile on his face" before telling him that it is the duty of the school "to teach your children to laugh at such ideas" as the priest has put forward. Except for the smile, he no longer has contempt "visible in his face," but one hears more of it in his voice. He is uncompromising in his policy about the footpath, insisting that it "is against our regulations," even though it had been tolerated before. Such a pigheaded young man, foolishly believing he holds a monopoly on truth, is destined for well-deserved disaster.

And when disaster comes, Achebe makes it much more devastating than it had been in the original story. Initially, the "ruins" of Michael Obi's work consisted merely of some torn-up hedges and trampled flowers, followed *a few days later* by an inspection of the school by the *Government Supervisor*. In the revised version, many more hedges are destroyed, a school building is torn down, and

> that day, the white Supervisor came to inspect the school and wrote a nasty report on the state of the premises but more seriously about the "tribal war situation developing between the school and the village, arising in part from the misguided zeal of the new headmaster."

Achebe apparently wanted to underscore the humiliation of Michael Obi. Like Okonkwo in *Things Fall Apart*, this young headmaster was too proud and inflexible to survive in a situation calling for a modicum of compromise and accommodation.

One also sees in these revisions evidence of Achebe's maturation as a literary artist. This is particularly apparent in major stylistic alterations. For instance, he deftly Africanized the spoken idiom of the village priest, changing "It has been brought to my notice" to "I have heard"; "from time immemorial" to "before you were born and before your father was born"; and "our unborn babes cannot arrive any other way" to "it is the path of children coming in to be born." This eliminated the woodenness of the original dialogue, the pure Anglo-Saxon flavor of which seemed out of character for an African village priest. Of course, before making these revisions, Achebe had written all four of his novels, honing and perfecting his representation of African modes of speech. The first version of "Dead Men's Path" published in the *University Herald* shows him at the point at which he began his literary career; the version published in *Girls at War and Other Stories* reveals how far he had gone in twenty years. During that interval, the apprentice had become a master craftsman.

Achebe's university writings are thus worthy of careful scrutiny in any responsible study of his works, for they provide a record of the earliest germination of his talent, when he was, like so many of his classmates at Ibadan, an aspiring pencil-pusher rather than a proven man of the pen. His incipient literary ability, given encouragement at Ibadan, was to ripen and flower rapidly into a full-blown artistic genius in the years following graduation. Anyone wishing to chart the course of his career must begin at its earliest traceable point, even if the first recorded lines are rather faint and dull.[26] The Igbo have a saying that "a chick that will grow into a cock can be spotted the very day it hatches."[27] Future scholarship will have to examine these university writings to determine whether it was at University College Ibadan that Chinua Achebe first broke through an ordinary shell of immaturity to display recognizable signs of singular promise as an author. This is not a trivial academic question, for it could be argued that Achebe's hatching marked the birth of an entire literature.

NOTES

1. Cosmo Pieterse and Dennis Duerden, eds. *African Writers Talking: A Collection of Radio Interviews* (New York: Africana, 1972), 4.
2. *University Herald* 4, no. 1 (1951): 12-13.
3. These include *The Sacrificial Egg and Other Short Stories* (Onitsha: Etudo, 1962), *Girls at War and Other Stories* (London: Heinemann, 1972), *Morning Yet on Creation Day: Essays* (London: Heinemann, 1975), and *Hopes and Impediments: Selected Essays, 1965-1987* (London: Heinemann, 1988).
4. *Bug*, February 21, 1951, 5.
5. These appear to have been favorite phrases of his. He uses "translate into print" in both the "Argument Against the Existence of Faculties" and the "Philosophy" letter. He employs the Shakespearean "caviare to the general" (from *Hamlet*) in the "Philosophy" letter and in another letter cited in note 7.

6. *Bug*, November 29, 1952, 3.

7. Ibid. The text of this letter is reproduced in the chapter on "Ladies and Gentlemen of Ibadan."

8. Jim Davidson, "Interview with Chinua Achebe," *Meanjin* 1 (1980): 36.

9. *University Herald* 3, no. 3 (1950): 7; *Girls at War*, 48-51.

10. Robert Wren, *Achebe's World: The Historical and Cultural Context of the Novels* (Washington, DC: Three Continents Press, 1980), 14.

11. David Carroll, *Chinua Achebe*. 2nd ed. (New York: St. Martin's Press, 1980), 154.

12. *University Herald* 4, no. 2 (1951): 11; reprinted in *Girls at War*, 74-77.

13. Achebe describes his childhood in an autobiographical essay, "Named for Victoria, Queen of England," *New Letters* 40, no. 1 (1973): 15-22, and reprinted in *Morning Yet on Creation Day*, 65-70.

14. "Arts and Africa," *BBC African Service*, No. 249P (n.d.): 2; reprinted in part in *Echos du Commonwealth* 5 (1979-80): 181. It is interesting to note that of the four "slightly touched up" student pieces reproduced in *Girls at War and Other Stories* Achebe said, "I dare not call any of them stories" (ii).

15. *University Herald* 5, no. 1 (1952): 12-14; *The Sacrificial Egg*, 21-26; *Girls at War*, 20-28.

16. (London: Heinemann, 1960). For critical comments see, for example, Carroll, 155; Wren, 14-15; Michael Echeruo, "Introduction," *The Sacrificial Egg*, 3-4; G.D. Killam, *The Writings of Chinua Achebe*. Rev. ed. (London: Heinemann, 1977), 104-05; Austin J. Shelton, "Failures and Individualism in Achebe's Stories," *Studies in Black Literature* 2, no. 1 (1971): 7-8; and Karl-Heinz Böttcher, *Tradition und Modernität bei Amos Tutuola und Chinua Achebe: Grundzuge der westafrikanischen Erzahlliteratur englischer Sprache* (Bonn: Grundmann, 1974), 342-43.

17. Echeruo, "Introduction," 4.

18. Wren, *Achebe's World*, 14-15.

19. Chinua Achebe, "The Role of the Writer in a New Nation," *Nigeria Magazine* 81 (1964): 157.

20. Ernest and Pat Emenyonu, "Achebe: Accountable to Our Society," *Africa Report* 7, no. 5 (1972): 26-27.

21. "Short Story," *University Herald* 5, no. 2 (1952-53): 4-5; *The Sacrificial Egg*, 13-15; *Girls at War*, 78-82.

22. Killam, *The Writings of Chinua Achebe*, 104.
23. Wren, *Achebe's World*, 15.
24. Echeruo, "Introduction," 4-5.
25. Carroll, *Chinua Achebe*, 156.
26. Achebe also wrote at least one limerick at University College Ibadan; it appears in the *University Herald* 4, no. 3 (1951-52): 19, and runs as follows:

> There was a young man in our Hall
> Who said that because he was small
> His fees should be less
> Because he ate less
> Than anyone else in the Hall.

Two other poems on the following page in that issue, "Mr. Jones" and "Waste," have been attributed to Achebe in the Library of Congress's *Africa South of the Sahara: Index to Periodical Literature, 1900-1970* (Boston: G.K. Hall, 1971), but his name does not appear on the page so these attributions are uncertain. The unsigned editorials appearing in the *University Herald* 4, no. 3 (1951-52): 5, and 5, no. 1 (1952): 5, while Achebe was editor, may be attributed to him with greater confidence.

27. Okonkwo uses this expression in Achebe's *Things Fall Apart* (London: Henemann, 1958), 58.

FICTION AS HISTORY

Chinua Achebe is Nigeria's finest novelist. Reading his carefully composed works after the episodic narratives of his predecessors, Amos Tutuola and Cyprian Ekwensi, is like entering a well-tended garden after tramping through chaotic jungles and sordid city slums. One is immediately struck by the dignity and grace of his art. While Tutuola's fiction seems wildly spontaneous and Ekwensi's crudely contrived, Achebe's always appears disciplined and serene, the accomplished work of a mature artist who has thoroughly mastered his medium. Moreover, there is a profundity and high moral seriousness in his fiction that can only be found in writing of the very highest quality. A skillful raconteur like Tutuola and a facile journalist like Ekwensi simply do not belong in the same class with a gifted novelist like Achebe.

Their differences are apparent in the very titles of their books. Tutuola's titles are purely denotative, telling the reader who and what his books are about: *The Wild Hunter in the Bush of the Ghosts, The Palm-Wine Drinkard and His Dead Palm-Wine Tapster in the Deads' Town, My Life in the Bush of Ghosts, Simbi and the Satyr of the Dark Jungle, The Brave African Huntress, Feather Woman of the Jungle, Ajaiyi and His Inherited Poverty, The Witch-Herbalist of the Remote Town, Pauper, Brawler, and Slanderer.* Like many a traditional storyteller, Tutuola may feel a compulsion to preface his narrative with a brief statement if its subject. Ekwensi, who prefers shorter

titles, either names his books after his chief character(s)—
Jagua Nana, Iska, The Drummer Boy, People of the City—or
after an important object or event in the story—*The Leopard's
Claw, The Passport of Mallam Ilia, Yaba Roundabout Murder,
Trouble in Form Six*. Seldom has he used more imaginative
titles—*When Love Whispers, Burning Grass, Beautiful Feath-
ers*—and even on those occasions the titles did not adequately
represent the tales. Achebe's titles, in contrast, are aphoristic
summaries of his novels. Each one distils the reader's experience into a few memorable words that have the power to
evoke the emotional response felt while reading the novel. To
put it another way, each one is richly connotative, compress-
ing a wealth of associations into a pithy phrase. Achebe's titles
add an extra dimension to his fiction.

This is one of the triumphs of Achebe's art. He knows
how to achieve big effects economically by fastening on what
is most significant and setting it in a context that gives it a
wider application. He knows, in other words, how to univer-
salize the particular. When one of his heroes suffers a fall,
it is not just a personal tragedy or community tragedy but
also a calamity that has meaning and relevance for an entire
nation, indeed for an entire race. Yet it never falls short of
being a unique human tragedy, one with a discrete, self-sus-
taining life of its own. What sets Achebe so far above many
other African writers is his remarkable ability to add extra
dimensions of significance to his novels without compromis-
ing their individuality.

How Achebe managed to develop into such an excellent novelist is not completely clear. Certainly he does not
appear to have served a long apprenticeship as a writer. He
grew up in the small village of Ogidi (near Onitsha) where
his father was a teacher and principal in a mission school.
After completing primary school he went to Government
College Umuahia for his secondary education and then on
to University College Ibadan, where he had been awarded a
scholarship to study medicine. When he found that medi-

cine did not interest him, he switched to the Arts faculty so he could concentrate on English, history, and comparative religion. It was while he was at the university that he appears to have first started writing fiction.[1] In May 1952 (the same month that saw the publication of Tutuola's *The Palm-Wine Drinkard*) he published a short story, "The Old Order in Conflict with the New," in the *University Herald*. The title of the story is quite significant, for this is the theme—the devastation wrought upon the Old by the New—that preoccupies Achebe in much of his later fiction. His second short story, "Dead Men's Path," published eight months later in the same campus magazine, also dealt with the conflict between the Old and the New, but, as seen in the preceding chapter, this time the Old order triumphed. These early stories, though competently written and thematically related to his novels, do not compare in quality with the first chapters of *Things Fall Apart*, which he began thinking about writing while still at the university.[2] As an artist Achebe somehow managed to mature very rapidly.

His university literary training may have been an important stimulus. When asked in an interview if any particular author had influenced him, he replied,

> Perhaps [Joyce Cary] helped to inspire me, but not in the usual way. I was very angry with his book, *Mr. Johnson*, which was set in Nigeria. I happened to read this, I think, in my second year [at University College] and I said to myself: "This is absurd.... if somebody without any inside knowledge of the people he's trying to describe can get away with it, perhaps I ought to try my hand at it.[3]

When he did try his hand at it, he wrote a novel that many regard as the finest piece of fiction to have come out of Nigeria, Cary's internationally acclaimed *Mr. Johnson* notwithstanding.

Achebe's original intention was to write a Nigerian *Buddenbrooks*, a novel spanning several generations in a single Igbo family. Later he decided that this subject could be handled better in two novels, the second serving as a sequel to the first. He has said,

> My conception of the story was really a combination of the two books—it was one story originally, not even very long, and it covered the whole period of *Things Fall Apart* and *No Longer at Ease*. And having done it I immediately felt that it was not right—that the time covered was too long and therefore the story was going to be too thin. So what I did was simply mechanically to cut it in two and blow up the first part.[4]

It appears that he completed the manuscript of the original novel after graduating from the university in 1954 and taking a job as a radio broadcaster for the Nigerian Broadcasting Company. When he was sent to London in 1956 for an eight-month training course at the BBC, he took the manuscript with him, probably with the intention of looking for a publisher. By a lucky break he was spared the trouble. One of his teachers at the BBC happened to be a novelist, so, Achebe recalls,

> I rather diffidently went to him and asked him to look at my manuscript. He was very excited and passed it on to his publishers. So that was the start. They took it on.[5]

The novel was published by Heinemann on June 9, 1958, four years after Ekwensi's *People of the City*, six year's after Tutuola's *The Palm-Wine Drinkard*.

Things Fall Apart was very well received in both Europe and Africa and was available in an American edition and in German translation by the time Achebe's second novel,

No Longer at Ease, appeared in 1960. Shortly thereafter Heinemann Educational Books issued paperback editions of both novels to launch its African Writers Series, which was intended for use in African secondary schools. In 1964 Achebe's third novel, *Arrow of God*, appeared and drew praise from nearly every reviewer and critic. It was now clear to many that Achebe was an important African novelist. His fourth work, *A Man of the People*, published in 1966, established his reputation even more firmly.

Although all of Achebe's novels revolve around the same general theme—the human consequences of the collision of African and European cultures in Nigeria—they are not repetitive. Each one moves in a different direction, covering new ground and probing problems untouched by the others. Each is a completely self-contained work of art, yet taken together the four form a coherent tetralogy, the individual parts of which reinforce and illuminate one another. They are unified yet diversified, harmonious yet individually unique.

One way Achebe achieves this unusual synthesis is by placing each novel in a distinctive era in the recent past, *Things Fall Apart* and *Arrow of God* about a generation apart in pre-colonial and colonial days, *No Longer at Ease* and *A Man of the People* in more contemporary times, one just before political independence, the other a few years after independence had been achieved. And for each book he invents a language that is appropriate to the period and characters depicted. This combination of temporal variety and linguistic virtuosity yields both historical depth and social authenticity.

Achebe's critical writings confirm that he is an unusually perceptive and deliberate stylist. Speaking on the problems associated with the creation of an African literature in a non-African tongue, he once said,

> My answer to the question: *Can an African ever learn English well enough to be able to use it effectively in creative writing?* is certainly yes. If on the other

hand you ask: *Can he ever learn to use it like a native speaker?* I should say: I hope not. It is neither necessary nor desirable for him to be able to do so. The price a world language must be prepared to pay is submission to many different kinds of use. The African writer should aim to use English in a way that brings out his message best without altering the language to the extent that its value as a medium of international exchange will be lost. He should aim at fashioning out an English which is at once universal and able to carry his peculiar experience....I feel certain that the English language will be able to carry the weight of my African experience. But it will have to be a new English, still in communication with its ancestral home but altered to suit its new African surroundings.[6]

It is this "new English," this idiom "at once universal and able to carry his peculiar experience," that Achebe succeeded in creating in his novels. He gave the English language a new prose style.

Since linguistic innovations cannot be found in his early short stories, it must be assumed that Achebe began to Africanize his style in the course of writing *Things Fall Apart*—that is, between 1953 and 1956.[7] At first, perhaps out of consideration for foreign readers, he rarely introduced Igbo words into his fiction without immediately translating them. In *Things Fall Apart*[8] one frequently finds such sentences as

> The elders, or *ndichie*, met to hear a report of Okonkwo's mission. (10)
> His own hut, or *obi*, stood immediately behind the only gate in the red walls (11)
> At the most one could say that his *chi* or personal god was good. (23)

This man told him that the child was an *ogbanje*, one of those wicked children who, when they died, entered into their mothers' wombs to be born again. (68)

In *No Longer at Ease*,[9] which takes place in the city, Achebe used the same technique to explain Nigerian urban lingo.

He was playing his guitar *jeje*—quietly, soberly, unobtrusively, altogether in a law-abiding fashion. (113) "No be all drivers de reckless," said the good driver. "Dat one na foolish somebody. I give am signal make him no overtake but he just come *fiam*." The last word, combined with a certain movement of the arm meant *excessive speed*. (141)

However, in *Arrow of God*[10] Achebe began to make fewer concessions to non-Nigerian readers. Igbo words were left untranslated, and traditional customs and beliefs were seldom overtly explained. For many readers context provided the only clue to the meaning of passages such as this:

His *ikenga*, about as tall as a man's forearm and having two strong horns, jostled with the faceless *okposi* of the ancestors black with the blood of sacrifice, and his short personal staff of *ofo*. One of the rough, faceless *okposi* belonged to Nwafo. (6-7)

In his fourth novel, *A Man of the People*,[11] Achebe took another giant step toward artistic freedom by writing some of the dialogue in pidgin English. Again the uninitiated reader was left to his own resources in dealing with what confronted him on the printed page. Here are a few representative utterances:

"People wey de jealous the money gorment de pay
Minister no sabi say no be him one de chop am." (16)
"I no kuku mind the katakata wey de for inside." (16)
"I no go tell you lie girls for this una part sabi fine-o."
(17)
"E fool pass garri....Which person tell am no bobby
them de take do the thing?" (67)

Achebe's decision to use untranslated Igbo and unadul-
terated pidgin in his fiction is evidence of a significant change
in his orientation as a writer. Instead of continuing to act
primarily as an interpreter of African experience for readers
overseas, he apparently chose to turn in a new direction and
address himself more completely to his own people. He
could afford to do this because by 1964 his books were actually selling better at home than abroad.[12] But even if most of
his readers had remained British or American, he probably
would have continued to evolve a more uncompromisingly
African writing style. Achebe is not the sort of author who
is content to stand still or run in place, making no forward
progress. In each of his novels he attempts to explore fresh
territory and try out new techniques. Having pioneered in
the creation of an African prose style in English, he would
naturally have wanted to carry his linguistic experiments
further, regardless of who was reading his books.

Achebe's capacity for growth and change is demonstrated
in his handling of themes too. Some critics have accused him
of repeating himself, of telling the same story over and over
again,[13] but a close examination of what he has written reveals
the extraordinarily wide range of his humane interests and
moral concerns. So deep is his understanding of Nigerian
history and so broad his sympathy for all the human beings
who have lived and worked there that his novels may seem
repetitious in treatment even when they are most diverse in
theme. But they only *seem* repetitious. Actually Achebe alters
his voice in each one. As the historical period he chooses to

depict changes, so does his fiction. He is a chameleon-like chronicler.

In a 1964 lecture on "The Role of the Writer in a New Nation" Achebe spoke of the need for fictional recreations of the African past:

> The question is how does a writer recreate this past? Quite clearly there is a strong temptation to idealize it—to extol its good points and pretend that the bad never existed.
>
> When I think of this I always think of light and glass. When white light hits glass one of two things can happen. Either you have an image which is faithful if somewhat unexciting or you have a glorious spectrum which though beautiful is really a distortion. Light from the past passes through a kind of glass to reach us. We can either look for the accurate but maybe unexciting image or we can look for the glorious technicolour.
>
> This where the writer's integrity comes in. Will he be strong enough to overcome the temptation to select only those facts that flatter him? If he succumbs he will have branded himself an untrustworthy witness. But is not only his personal integrity as an artist which is involved. The credibility of the world he is attempting to recreate will be called to question and he will defeat his own purpose if he is suspected of glossing over inconvenient facts. We cannot pretend that our past was one long, technicolour idyll. We have to admit that like any other people's past ours had its good as well as its bad sides....I maintain that any serious African writer who wants to plead the cause of the past must not only be God's advocate; he must also do duty for the devil.[14]

This is an argument for objectivity, for accurate and honest depiction of the African past.

But notice that while Achebe insists on objectivity he also assumes that the writer will be committed to a point of view. He will "plead the cause of the past" in his fiction. In the same lecture Achebe stated that the "fundamental theme" of the African writer should be

> ...that African peoples did not hear of culture for the first time from Europeans; that their societies were not mindless but frequently had a philosophy of great depth and value and beauty, that they had poetry and above all, they had dignity. It is this dignity that many African peoples all but lost in the colonial period, and it is this that they must now regain. The worst thing that can happen to any people is the loss of their dignity and self-respect. The writer's duty is to help them regain it by showing them in human terms what happened to them, what they lost. There is a saying in Ibo that a man who can't tell where the rain began to beat him cannot know where he dried his body. The writer can tell the people where the rain began to beat them.[15]

To do this, he must be able to construct a convincing picture of the African past, one that will help his people overcome the inferiority complex they acquired during the colonial era. He must be a teacher totally committed to reversing prevailing notions about African history and the nature of African life before the coming of the white man. He must, in effect, be a revolutionary. On another occasion Achebe expressed it this way:

> Here, then, is an adequate revolution for me to espouse—to help my society regain its belief in itself and put away the complexes of the years of denigra-

tion and self-denigration....The writer cannot be expected to be excused from the task of re-education and regeneration that must be done. In fact he should march right in front.[16]

He should strive to heal his people by using his art to restore their self-confidence.

As for the European role in the African past, it should be exposed as candidly as possible for what it was. The "positive atrocity of racial arrogance and prejudice"[17] that the white man carried with him to Africa must be condemned but not his sincere, often self-sacrificing efforts to improve the quality of African life. Achebe admits "There have been gains—I am not one of those who would say that Africa has gained nothing at all during the colonial period. I mean this is ridiculous—we gained a lot."[18] The European presence in Africa must therefore be seen as a mixed blessing, an accident of history that had good as well as bad consequences for Africans. Its worst consequence was to persuade Africans that they were racially inferior to Europeans. Achebe has the sense to see that "It is too late in the day to get worked up about this or to blame others, much as they may deserve blame and condemnation. What we need to do is to look back and try to find out where we went wrong, where the rain began to beat us."[19] This requires examining the entire history of Africa's engagement with the outside world and calculating both the losses and the gains Africa derived from European colonialism. The writer must give credit where it is due yet cry out against injustice and mental oppression. He must learn to strike a balance between detached compassion and passionate protest.

Achebe, then, is a writer with an axe to grind but one who has enough self-discipline and clarity of vision to hone his criticism to a fine cutting edge so it become something more than a blunt political instrument. Instead of seeing the past in simplistic terms, as do some of his contemporaries, he recognizes and attempts to transcribe its complexity. He is objective yet committed, sympathetic yet morally severe. His aim is to expose the failure of Britain's "civilizing mission" in Africa and to present an undistorted view of African experience "not only for the enlightenment of our detractors but even more for our own education."[20] Achebe is a chronicler writing a new history of Africa.

After writing *Arrow of God*, Achebe decided to make a break with the past and concern himself exclusively with contemporary issues. "It is clear to me," he said, "that an African creative writer who tries to avoid the big social and political issues of the contemporary Africa will end up being completely irrelevant."[21] Achebe's search for relevance led him to describe independent Nigeria just as he saw it—"a cesspool of corruption and misrule."[22] His earlier novels dealing with the impact of Europe on Igbo village life had not been without social relevance at the time they were written, but Achebe recognized that "the things that preoccupied us three or four years ago [are] no longer that important. In Africa, three years is a long time. Things are changing so fast that you must run awfully hard just to keep up. Ten years ago we were not independent, and things that seemed important to us then are no longer so today."[23] Achebe has kept pace with the times by responding to the changing preoccupations of his society. Initially he was a reconstructionist dedicated to creating a dignified image of the African past; later he became an angry reformer crusading against the immorality and injustices of the African present. His novels thus not only chronicle seventy years of Nigerian history but also reflect the dominant African intellectual concerns of his day.

For this reason one suspects his novels with have enduring significance. Later generations of readers will find in them an interpretation of African experience that is characteristic of its time. The compassionate evocations of Igbo village life, the graphic depictions of mid-twentieth-century Lagos, the brilliantly drawn characters will probably speak with as much power then as they do now, eloquently recalling crucial moments in that confused era in Nigeria's past which began with the arrival of the first white man and ended with the outbreak of civil war. Achebe's novels appear destined to remain classics of African literature.

NOTES

1. As mentioned in the previous chapter, Achebe has spoken of writing "little poems and things like that" at Government College Umuahia, but he may not have written any fiction while there.

2. See his comment on Joyce Cary below. In the afterword to an American edition of this novel (New York: McDowell, Obolensky, 1959), 216, Achebe said, "In the university I was definitely certain that I would write novels, and the story of *Things Fall Apart* began to form vaguely in my mind. When in the end I settled down to write it I did not need any kind of draft."

3. Lewis Nkosi, "Interview with Chinua Achebe," *Africa Report* 9, no. 7 (July 1964): 20.

4. Robert Serumaga, "Chinua Achebe Interviewed by Robert Serumaga," *Cultural Events in Africa* 28 (March 1967): iii.

5. Tony Hall, "I Had to Write on the Chaos I Foresaw," *Sunday Nation* (Nairobi), January 15, 1967, 15.

6. Chinua Achebe, "The English Language and the African Writer," *Moderna Språk* 58 (1964): 444-46; *Transition* 18 (1965): 29-30.

7. It should be remembered that by 1956 three of Tutuola's books were available. It is conceivable that Achebe may have noticed the influence of the Yoruba language on Tutuola's unorthodox handling of English.

8. *Things Fall Apart* (London: Heinemann, 1958).

9. *No Longer at Ease* (London: Heinemann, 1960).

10. *Arrow of God* (London: Heinemann, 1964).

11. *A Man of the People* (London: Heinemann, 1966).

12. In "The Novelist as Teacher," *New Statesman*, January 29, 1965, 161, Achebe said, "Last year the pattern of sales of *Things Fall Apart* in the cheap paperback edition was as follows: about 800 copies in Britain, 20,000 in Nigeria; and about 2,500 in all other places. The same pattern was true also of *No Longer at Ease*."

13. See, for example, Charles Larson, "Things Fall Further Apart—New African Novels," *CLA Journal* 10 (1966): 64-67.

14. Chinua Achebe, "The Role of the Writer in a New Nation," *Nigeria Magazine* 81 (1964): 158.

15. Ibid., 157.

16. Achebe, "The Novelist as Teacher," 162.

17. Achebe, "The English Language and the African Writer," 442 and 28.

18. Serumaga, "Chinua Achebe Interviewed," ii.

19. Achebe, "The Novelist as Teacher," 161.

20. Achebe, "The Role of the Writer," 158.

21. Chinua Achebe, "The African Writer and the Biafran Cause," *Conch* 1, no. 1 (1969): 8.

22. Ibid., 11.

23. M. Felton, "An Interview with Chinua Achebe," *Spectrum* (Lagos), 1, no. 1 (1967): 4. There is every indication that Achebe would have continued writing political fiction had the Nigerian-Biafran war not intervened. In the interview with Tony Hall, "I Had to Write on the Chaos I Foresaw," 15, he said, "Right now…my interest in the novel is politics. *A Man of the People* was not just a flash in the pan. This is the beginning of a new phase for me, in which I intend to take a hard look at what we in Africa are making of independence—but using Nigeria which I know best."

THE PALM-OIL WITH WHICH ACHEBE'S WORDS ARE EATEN

Among the Igbo the art of conversation is regarded very highly,
and proverbs are the palm-oil with which words are eaten.

CHINUA ACHEBE

Chinua Achebe is a writer well known throughout Africa and even beyond. His fame rests on solid personal achievements. As a young man of twenty-eight he brought honor to his native Nigeria by writing *Things Fall Apart*, the first novel of unquestioned literary merit from English-speaking West Africa. Critics tend to agree that no African novelist writing in English has yet surpassed Achebe's achievement in *Things Fall Apart*, except perhaps Achebe himself. It was published in 1958 and Achebe has written four novels and won several literary prizes since. During this time his reputation has grown like a bush-fire in the harmattan. Today he is regarded by many as Africa's finest novelist.

If ever a man of letters deserved his success, that man is Achebe. He is a careful and fastidious artist in full control of his art, a serious craftsman who disciplines himself not only to write regularly but also to write well. He has that sense of decorum, proportion, and design lacked by too many contemporary novelists, African and non-African alike. He is also a committed writer, one who believes that it is his duty to serve his society. He feels that the fundamental theme with which African writers should concern themselves is

> that African peoples did not hear of culture for the first time from Europeans; that their societies were not mindless but frequently had a philosophy of great depth and value and beauty, that they had poetry and, above all, they had dignity.[1]

Each of Achebe's novels[2] sheds light on a different era in the recent history of Nigeria. *Things Fall Apart* (1958) is set in a traditional Igbo village community at the turn of the century when the first European missionaries and administrative officials were beginning to penetrate inland. In *Arrow of God* (1964) the action takes place in a similar environment about twenty-five years later, the major difference being that the missionaries and district officers have by this time become quite firmly entrenched. Achebe switches to an urban scene in *No Longer at Ease* (1960) in order to present a picture of the life of an educated Nigerian in the late nineteen-fifties. He brings the historical record up to postcolonial times in *A Man of the People* (1966), a devastating political satire that ends with a military coup. And in *Anthills of the Savannah* (1987) he focuses on the military elites who had ruled Nigeria and many other African countries after the collapse of democratically elected regimes. Achebe's novels read like chapters in a biography of his people and his nation since the coming of the white man.

What gives each of Achebe's novels an air of historical authenticity is his use of the English language. He has developed not one prose style but several, and in each novel he is careful to select the style or styles that will best suit his subject. In dialogue, for example, a Westernized African character will never speak exactly like a European character nor will he speak like an illiterate village elder. Achebe, a gifted ventrilo-quist, is able to individualize his characters by differentiating their speech. Of course, any sensitive novelist will try to do this, but most novelists do not face the problem of having to represent in English the utterances of a character who is speaking another language. To resolve this problem, Achebe has devised an African vernacular style[3] that simulates the idiom of Igbo, his native tongue. One example of this style will suffice. In *Arrow of God* a chief priest tells one of his sons why it is necessary to send him to a mission school.

> I want one of my sons to join these people and be my eye there. If there is nothing in it you will come back. But if there is something there you will bring home my share. The world is like a Mask dancing. If you want to see it well you do not stand in one place. My spirit tells me that those who not befriend the white man today will be saying *had we known* tomorrow. (55)

In an article on "English and the African Writer," Achebe demonstrates that he could have written this passage in a different style:

> I am sending you as my representative among those people—just to be on the safe side in case the new religion develops. One has to move with the times or else one is left behind. I have a hunch that those who fail to come to terms with the white man may well regret their lack of foresight.[4]

Achebe comments, "The material is the same. But the form of the one is *in character* and the other is not. It is largely a matter of instinct, but judgement comes into it too."[5]

Achebe's use of an African vernacular style is not limited to dialogue. In *Things Fall Apart* and *Arrow of God*, novels set in a traditional society, the narrative is studded with proverbs and similes that help to evoke the cultural milieu in which the action takes place. In *No Longer at Ease* and *A Man of the People*, on the other had, one finds the language of the narrative more cosmopolitan, more Westernized, more suited to life in the city. Here are some similes drawn from narrative portions of *Things Fall Apart* (TFA) and *Arrow of God* (AOG):

> ...like a bush-fire in the harmattan. (TFA, 1)
> ...like pouring grains of corn into a bag full of holes. (TFA, 19)
> ...as if water had been poured on the tightened skin of a drum. (TFA, 42)
> ...like a yam tendril in the rainy season. (TFA, 45)
> ...like the snapping of a tightened bow. (TFA, 53)
> ...as busy as an ant-hill. (TFA, 100)
> ...like the walk of an Ijele Mask lifting and lowering each foot with weighty ceremony. (AOG, 84)
> ...like a grain of maize in an empty goatskin bag. (AOG, 100)
> ...as one might pull out a snail from its shell. (AOG, 118)
> ...like a bad cowry. (AOG, 146)
> ...like a lizard fallen from an iroko tree. (AOG, 242)
> ...like the blue, quiet, razor-edge flame of burning palm-nut shells. (AOG, 274)

Now here are some similes drawn from narrative portions of *No Longer at Ease* (NLAE) and *A Man of the People* (AMOP):

> ...as a collector fixes his insect with formalin. (NLAE, 1)
> ...swivelling their hips as effortlessly as oiled ball-bearings. (NLAE, 18)

...like a giant tarmac from which God's aeroplane
   might take off. (NLAE, 24)
...like an enchanted isle. (NLAE, 28)
...like the jerk in the leg of a dead frog when a current
   is applied to it. (NLAE, 137)
...like a panicky fly trapped behind the windscreen.
   (NLAE, 149)
...as a dentist extracts a stinking tooth. (AMOP, 4)
...like that radio jingle advertising an intestinal worm
   expeller. (AMOP, 29)
...as I had been one day, watching for the first time
   the unveiling of the white dome of Kilimanjaro
   at sunset. (AMOP, 45)
...as those winged termites driven out of the earth by
   late rain dance furiously around street lamps and
   drop panting to the ground. (AMOP, 51)
...like a slowed up action film. (AMOP, 145)
...like a dust particle in the high atmosphere around
   which the water vapour of my thinking formed
   its globule of rain. (AMOP, 146)

In the urban novels one also finds similes drawn from village
life, but in the novels set entirely in traditional society one
fines no similes drawn from urban experience. This is altogether fitting, for Achebe's urban characters have lived in
villages, but most of the characters in his village novels have
had little or no exposure to cities. Here again we see Achebe
using judgment and instinct to select the type of imagery
that is appropriate to the time, place, and people he is trying
to picture. It is Achebe's use of appropriate language that
lends an air of historicity to his novels.

I have taken time to comment on Achebe's artistry
because the argument I intend to pursue is based on the
premise that he is an exceptional literary artist. I believe that
he is both a conscious and an unconscious artist, that he has
an instinct for knowing where things belong and a talent for

putting them there, and that he possesses a shrewd sense of what is *in character* and what is not. All these qualities are displayed in his deliberate search for an appropriate language for each novel, a style that will not only suit his subject and evoke the right cultural milieu but will also help to define the moral issues with which the novel is concerned.

It is my contention that Achebe, a skillful artist, achieves an appropriate language for each of his novels largely through the use of proverbs. Indeed, Achebe's proverbs can serve as keys to an understanding of his novels because he uses them not merely to add touches of local color but to sound and reiterate themes, to sharpen characterization, to clarify conflict, and to focus on the values of the society he is portraying. Proverbs thus provide a "grammar of values"[6] by which the deeds of a hero can be measured and evaluated. By studying Achebe's proverbs we are better able to interpret his novels.

Things Fall Apart is the story of Okonkwo, a famous warrior and expert farmer who has risen from humble origins to become a wealthy and respected leader of his clan. His entire life has been a struggle to achieve status, and he has almost attained a position of preeminence when he accidentally kills a kinsman. For this crime he must leave his clan and live in exile for seven years. When he returns at the end of the seventh year, he finds that things have changed in his home village. White missionaries have established a church and have made a number of converts. White men have also set up a court where the district commissioner comes to judge cases according to a foreign code of law. Okonkwo tries to rouse his clan to take action against these foreigners and their institutions. In a rage he kills one of the district commissioner's messengers. When his clan does not support his action, he commits suicide.

Okonkwo is pictured throughout the novel as a wrestler. It is an appropriate image not just because his life has been a ceaseless struggle for status, but also because in the eyes of his people he brings about his own downfall by challenging too powerful an adversary. This adversary is not the white man, but rather Okonkwo's *chi*, his personal god or guardian spirit.[7] Okonkwo is crushed because he tries to wrestle with his *chi*. The Igbo have a folktale about just such a wrestler.

> Once there was a great wrestler whose back had never known the ground. He wrestled from village to village until he had thrown every man in the world. Then he decided that he must go and wrestle in the last of spirits, and become champion there as well. He went, and beat every spirit that came forward. Some had seven heads, some ten; but he beat them all. His companion who sang his praise on the flute begged him to come away, but he would not. He pleaded with him but his ear was nailed up. Rather than go home he gave a challenge to the spirits to bring out their best and strongest wrestler. So they sent him his personal god, a little, wiry spirit who seized him with one hand and smashed him on the stony earth.[8]

Although this tale does not appear in *Things Fall Apart*, there is sufficient evidence in the novel to suggest that Okonkwo is being likened to one who dares to wrestle with a spirit. A hint is contained in the first paragraph of the opening chapter that tells how Okonkwo gained fame as a young man of eighteen by throwing an unbeaten wrestler "in a fight which the old men agreed was one of the fiercest since the founder of their town engaged a spirit of the wild for seven days and seven nights" (1). And later, when Okonkwo commits the sin of beating one his wives during the sacred Week of Peace, "...people said he had no respect for the gods of his clan. His enemies said his good fortune had gone to his head. They called him the little bird *nza* who so far forgot himself after a heavy meal that he challenged his *chi*" (26).

Achebe uses proverbs to reinforce the image of Okonkwo as a man who struggles against his *chi*. Notice in the following passage how skillfully this is done:

> Everybody at the kindred meeting took sides with Osugo when Okonkwo called him a woman. The oldest man present said sternly that those whose palm-kernels were cracked for them by a benevolent spirit should not forget to be humble. Okonkwo said he was sorry for what he had said, and the meeting continued.
>
> But it was really not true that Okonkwo's palm-kernels had been cracked for him be a benevolent spirit. He had cracked them himself. Anyone who knew his grim struggle against poverty and misfortune could not say he had been lucky. If ever a man deserved his success, that man was Okonkwo. At an early age he had achieved fame as the greatest wrestler in all the land. That was not luck. At the most one could say that his *chi* or personal god was good. But the Ibo people have a proverb that says when a man says yes his *chi* also says yes. Okonkwo said yes very strongly; so his *chi* agreed. And not only his *chi* but his clan too, because it judged a man by the work of his hands (22-23).

When Okonkwo returns from exile, he makes the mistake of believing that if he says yes strongly enough, his *chi* and his clan will agree. No doubt he should have known better. He should have accepted his years in exile as a warning from his *chi*. In his first months of exile he had come close to understanding the truth:

> Clearly his personal god or *chi* was not made for great things. A man could not rise beyond the destiny of his *chi*. The saying of the elders was not true—that

if a man said yea his *chi* also affirmed. Here was a
man whose *chi* said nay despite his own affirmation.
(117)

However, as the years of exile pass, Okonkwo's fortunes
improve and he begins to feel "that his *chi* might now be
making amends for the past disaster"(154). He returns to his
clan rich, confident, and eager to resume his former position
of leadership. When he finds his village changed, he tries to
transform it into the village it had once been. But although he
says yes very strongly, his *chi* and his clan say nay. Okonkwo
the wrestler is at last defeated.

Quite a few of the proverbs that Achebe uses in *Things
Fall Apart* are concerned with status and achievement:

> ...the sun will shine on those who stand before it
> shines on those who kneel under them. (5)
> ...if a child washed his hands he could eat with kings.
> (6)
> ...a man who pays respect to the great paves the way
> for his own greatness. (16)
> The lizard that jumped from the high iroko tree to
> the ground said he would praise himself if no
> one else did. (18)
> ...you can tell a ripe corn by its look. (18)
> I cannot live on the bank of a river and wash my
> hands with spittle. (148)
> ...as a man danced so the drums were beaten for
> him. (165)

Such proverbs tell us much about the values of Igbo society,
values by which Okonkwo lives and dies. Such proverbs also
serve as thematic statements reminding us of some of the
major motifs of the novel—e.g., the importance of status,
the value of achievement, the idea of man as shaper of his
own destiny.

Sometimes in Achebe's novels one finds proverbs expressing different views of the same subject. Examined closely, these proverbs can provide clues to significant differences in outlook or opinion that set one man apart from others. For example, there are a number of proverbs in *Things Fall Apart* comparing parents to their children. Most Igbos believe that a child will take after his parents, or as one character puts it, "When mother cow is chewing grass its young ones watch its mouth" (62). However, Okonkwo's father had been a failure, and Okonkwo, not wanting to be likened to him, had striven to make his own life a success. So impressive were his achievements and so rapid his rise that an old man was prompted to remark, "Looking at a king's mouth, one would think he never sucked at his mother's breast" (22). Okonkwo believed that one's ancestry was not as important as one's initiative and will power, qualities that could be discerned in a child at a very early age. "A chick that will grow into a cock," he said, "can be spotted the very day it hatches" (58). He had good reason for thinking so. He himself had achieved much as a young man, but his own son Nwoye had achieved nothing at all.

> How could he have begotten a woman for a son? At Nwoye's age, Okonkwo had already become famous throughout Umuofia for his wrestling and his fearlessness.
>
> He sighed heavily, and as if in sympathy the smouldering log also sighed. And immediately Okonkwo's eyes were opened and he saw the whole matter clearly. Living fire begets cold, impotent ash. He sighed again, deeply. (138)

It is worth noting that in complaining about Nwoye's unmanliness, Okonkwo says, "A bowl of pounded yams can throw him in a wrestling match" (57). All the proverbs here are working to characterize Okonkwo and to set him apart from other men, especially from his father and son. The proverbs reveal that no one, least of all Okonkwo himself, considers him an ordinary mortal; rather, he is the sort of man who would dare to wrestle with his *chi*.

Obi Okonkwo, who is Okonkwo's grandson and the hero of Achebe's second novel, *No Longer at Ease*, is a very different kind of person. When he returns from studies in England, he is an honest, idealistic young man. He takes a high-paying job in the civil service but soon finds that his salary is not sufficient to meet the financial demands made upon him. He also gets involved with a woman his parents and clan despise. In the end he his caught taking bribes and is sent to prison.

Obi is an unheroic figure, a good man who slides rather than falls into evil ways. His actions are ignoble and unworthy. When he begins taking bribes, he tries to satisfy his conscience by refusing to take them from people he knows he cannot help. Kinsmen who attend his trial cannot understand why he took such risks for so little profit; one says, "I am against people reaping where they have not sown. But we have a saying that if you want to eat a toad, you should look for a fat and juicy one" (6). But Obi lives by half-measures, by resolute decisions mollified by irresolute actions. He falls in love with Clara, a woman whose unusual ancestry Obi's parents look upon with horror, and he wants to marry her. A friend warns him not to pollute his lineage: "What you are going to do concerns not only yourself but your whole family and future generations. If one finger brings oil it soils the others" (75). Obi, feeling he must free himself from the shackles of tradition, becomes engaged to Clara but later yields to parental pressure and breaks off with her. When she reveals she is pregnant, he arranges for her to get an abortion. More shameful, at least in the eyes of his clan, is Obi's refusal to return home for his mother's funeral, an action that leads one dismayed clansman to suggest that Obi is rotten at the core: "A man may go to England, become a lawyer or doctor, but it does not change his blood. It is like the bird that flies off the earth and lands on an ant-hill. It is still on the ground" (160). Obi never gets off the ground, never reaches heroic heights, never stops swallowing undernourished toads.

Helping to set the tone of the story are a great number of proverbs that comment on or warn against foolish and unworthy actions. Besides those already mentioned, one finds:

> He that fights for a ne'er-do-well has nothing to show for it except a head covered in earth and grime. (5)
>
> The fox must be chased away first; after that the hen might be warned against wandering into the bush. (5)
>
> ...he replied that a man who lived on the banks of the Niger should not wash his hands with spittle. (10, 135)
>
> ...like the young antelope who danced herself lame when the main dance was yet to come. (11)
>
> When a new saying gets to the land of empty men they lose their heads over it. (48)
>
> A person who has not secured a place on the floor should not begin to look for a mat. (60)
>
> Shall we kill a snake and carry it in our hand when we have a bag for putting long things in? (80)
>
> ...digging a new pit to fill up an old one. (108)
>
> ...a man should not, out of pride and etiquette, swallow his phlegm. (156)
>
> ...the little bird *nza* who after a big meal so far forgot himself as to challenge his *chi* to single combat. (163)
>
> A man does not challenge his *chi* to a wrestling match. (40)

The last two proverbs cited here may remind us of Okonkwo, but no one could mistake Obi for his grandfather. Okonkwo erred by daring to attempt something he did not have the power to achieve; this makes him a tragic hero. Obi erred by stooping to take bribes; this makes him a crook. To put it in proverbial terms, Okonkwo wrestles his *chi*, Obi swallows a toad. It is not only the stupidity but the contemptibility of Obi's ways that many of the proverbs in the novel help to underscore.

An important theme in *No Longer at Ease* is the conflict between old and new values. Obi's people tax themselves mercilessly to raise funds to send him to England for university training. The "scholarship" they award him is to be repaid both in cash and in services when he finishes his studies. They want him to read law so that when he returns, he'll be able to handle all their land cases against their neighbors. They expect a good return on their investment because Obi is their kinsman; they have a saying that "he who has people is richer than he who has money" (79). Obi, however, immediately asserts his self-will by choosing to read English instead of law. When he returns, he starts to pay back the loan but refuses to allow his kinsmen to interfere with his personal life. He especially resents their efforts to dissuade him from marrying Clara. Having adopted Western values Obi believes that an individual has the right to choose his own wife. It is this that brings him into conflict with his parents and kinsmen. Obi's Western education has made him an individualist, but his people still adhere to communal values.[9]

Obi's people attach great importance to kinship ties, and their beliefs regarding the obligations and rewards of kinship are often revealed in their proverbs. Even when a prodigal son like Obi gets into trouble, they feel it is necessary to help him: "a kinsman in trouble had to be saved, not blamed; anger against a brother was felt in the flesh, not in the bone" (5). They also have a song that cautions:

He that has a brother must hold him to his heart,
For a kinsman cannot be bought in the market,
Neither is a brother bought with money. (129)

Certainly it would be very wrong to harm an in-law for "a man's in-law was his *chi*" (46). And conflict within the clan should be avoided, for in unity is strength: "If all snakes lived together in one place, who would approach them?" (81). Those who prosper are expected to help those who are less fortunate: "when there is a big tree small ones climb on its back to reach the sun" (96). But all the burdens should not fall on one man: "it is not right to ask a man with elephantiasis of the scrotum to take on small pox as well, when thousands of other people have not yet had their share of small diseases" (99). Obi accepts some of the values expressed in these proverbs, but his own individualistic attitude is probably best summed up in the saying, "Ours is ours but mine is mine" (32). Obi's problem lies in having to make choices between the old values and the new, between "ours" and "mine."

Ezeulu, the hero of Achebe's third novel, *Arrow of God*, is faced with a similar problem. As chief priest of a snake cult he is committed to traditional ways, but just to be on the safe side he sends one of his sons to a mission school to "be [his] eye there" and to learn the white man's ways. This action draws criticism from some of the leaders of the clan, criticism that rapidly mounts into angry protest when the Christianized son is caught trying to kill a sacred python. Ezeulu also falls afoul of the district officer by refusing to accept an official appointment as paramount chief of his village. For this he is thrown into prison for two months. When he returns to his village, he envisions himself as an avenging arrow in the bow of his god, an instrument by which his god intends to punish his people. Ezeulu therefore refuses to perform certain rituals that must be performed before new yams can be harvested. This precipitates a crisis that results in the destruction of Ezeulu, his priesthood, and his religion.

To understand Ezeulu one must comprehend his deep concern over the way his world is changing. This concern is expressed both in his decision to send one of his sons to a mission school and in the proverbs he uses to justify his decision. He tells his son that a man must move with the times: "I am like the bird Eneke-nti-oba. When his friends asked him why he was always on the wing he replied: 'Men of today have learnt to fly without perching.'...The world is like a Mask dancing. If you want to see it well you do not stand in one place" (55). Months later Ezeulu reminds his son that he must learn the white man's magic because "a man must dance the dance prevalent in his time" (234). Ezeulu explains his decision to the village elders by comparing the white man to a new disease: "A disease that has never been seen before cannot be cured with everyday herbs. When we want to make a charm we look for the animal whose blood can match its power; if a chicken cannot do it we look for a goat or a ram; it that is not sufficient we send for a bull. But sometimes even a bull does not suffice, then we must look for a human" (165). Ezeulu's son is to be the human sacrifice that will enable the clan to make medicine of sufficient strength to hold the new disease in check. In other words, Ezeulu decides to sacrifice his son in order to gain power to cope with the changing times.

The question is whether Ezeulu's action is an appropriate response to the problem. Some elders think it is not and blame Ezeulu for bringing new trouble to the village by taking so improper a step. The importance that Ezeulu's people attach to appropriate action is reflected in many of the proverbs in the novel. For example:

> If the lizard of the homestead neglects to do the things for which its kind is known, it will be mistaken for the lizard of the farmland. (20-21)
> ...let us first chase away the wild cat, afterwards we blame the hen. (122)

We do not by-pass a man and enter his compound.
(138)
We do not apply an ear-pick to the eye. (138)
...bale that water before it rises above the ankle.
(156, 197)
When a masked spirit visits you you have to appease
its footprints with presents. (190)
...a traveller to distant places should make no
enemies. (208)
...a man of sense does not go on hunting little bush
rodents when his age mates are after big game.
(209)
He who sees an old hag squatting should leave her
alone; who knows how she breathes? (282)

Sending a son to a mission school is regarded by some elders
as a highly inappropriate action for a chief priest to take, no
matter what his motivation.

Ezeulu's enemies interpret his deed as a gesture of friendship toward the white man. Thus, when the district commissioner rather curtly commands Ezeulu to appear in his
office within twenty-four hours and Ezeulu call the elders
together to ask if they think he should heed the summons,
one unfriendly elder replies in no uncertain proverbs that
Ezeulu must either suffer the consequences of friendship
with the white man or do something to end the friendship.

...does Ezeulu think that their friendship should
stop short of entering each other's houses? Does he
want the white man to be his friend only by word of
mouth? Did not our elders tell us that as soon as we
shake hands with a leper, he will want an embrace?...
What I say is this...a man who brings ant-ridden
faggots into his hut should expect the visit of lizards.
But if Ezeulu is now telling us that he is tired of the
white man's friendship our advice to him should be:

> You tied the knot, you should also know how to undo it. You passed the shit that is smelling; you should carry it away. Fortunately the evil charm brought in at the end of a pole is not too difficult to take outside again. (177-78)

It is worth noting that the proverb about bringing ant-ridden faggots home is quoted twice by Ezeulu himself. He uses it to reproach himself when his mission-educated son is found trying to kill a sacred python (72). Here, momentarily at least, Ezeulu seems willing to accept responsibility for the abomination. Ezeulu uses the proverb a second time when a friend accuses him of betraying his people by sending his son to the white man's school. Ezeulu counters by pointing out that he did not bring the white man to his people; rather, his people brought the white man upon themselves by failing to oppose him when he first arrived. If they wish to blame someone, they should blame themselves for meekly submitting to the white man's presence and power. "The man who brings ant-ridden faggots into his hut should not grumble when lizards begin to pay him a visit" (163). This is a key proverb in *Arrow of God* for it enunciates a major theme: that a man is responsible for his actions and must bear their consequences.

But in addition to being responsible for his actions, a man is also expected to act responsibly. This idea is conveyed in another key proverb that is used four times in the novel: "an adult does not sit and watch while the she-goat suffers the pain of childbirth tied to a post" (258, cf. 21, 31, 189). Ezeulu uses this proverb twice to reprimand elders for encouraging the village to fight a "war of blame" against a neighboring village. He reminds them that elders must not neglect their duty to their people by acting irresponsibly. It is quite significant that this same proverb is used later by the elders to rebuke Ezeulu for failing to perform the ritual that will permit new yams to be harvested (258). The elders suggest that Ezeulu is doing nothing to prevent or relieve the suffering of his people. They urge him to do his duty by performing the necessary ritual. They urge him, in other words, to act responsibly.

Ezeulu answers that he has a higher responsibility, for his god, Ulu, has forbidden him to perform the ritual. The elders then say that if Ezeulu will perform the ritual, they themselves will take the blame for it: "...if Ulu says we have committed an abomination let it be on the heads of the ten of us here. You will be free because we have set you to it, and the person who sets a child to catch a shrew should also find him water to wash the odour from his hand. We shall find you the water" (260). Ezeulu answers, "...you cannot say: do what is not done and we shall take the blame. I am the Chief Priest of Ulu and what I have told you is his will not mine" (260-61). Ezeulu sincerely believes that he is the instrument of a divine power, "an arrow in the bow of his god" (241). When his actions bring disaster upon himself and his people, he does not feel responsible but rather feels betrayed by his god.

> Why, he asked himself again and again, why had Ulu chosen to deal thus with him, to strike him down and cover him with mud? What was his offence? Had he not divined the god's will and obeyed it? When was it ever heard that a child was scalded by the piece of yam its own mother put in its palm? What man would send his son with a potsherd to bring fire from a neighbour's hut and then unleash rain on him? Who ever sent his son up the palm to gather nuts and then took an axe and felled the tree? (286).

Tortured by these questions, Ezeulu finally goes mad.

The elders come to regard Ezeulu as a man who brought tragedy upon himself by failing to recognize his own limitations. In order to act appropriately and responsibly, a man must know his limitations. This idea finds expression in many of the proverbs in the novel:

> ...like the little bird, *nza*, who ate and drank and challenged his personal god to a single combat. (17)
>
> ...no matter how strong or great a man was he should never challenge his *chi*. (32)
>
> The man who carries a deity is not a king. (33)
>
> A man who knows that his anus is small does not swallow an udala seed. (87, 282)
>
> ...only a foolish man can go after a leopard with his bare hands. (105)
>
> The fly that struts around on a mound of excrement wastes his time; the mound will always be greater than the fly. (282)

To sum up, Ezeulu, in trying to adjust to the changing times, takes certain inappropriate actions that later lead him to neglect his duties and responsibilities. Not knowing his limitations, he goes too far and plunges himself and his people into disaster.

Achebe's fourth novel, *A Man of the People*, is set in post-colonial Nigeria and takes as its hero a young schoolteacher, Odili Samalu. Odili, who tells his own story, is moved to enter politics when his mistress is seduced by Chief the Honourable M.A. Nanga, M.P. and Minister of Culture. Odili joins a newly formed political party and prepares to contest Nanga's seat in the next election. He also tries to win the affection of Nanga's fiancée, a young girl Nanga is grooming as his "parlour wife." In the end Odili loses the political battle but manages to win the girl. Nanga loses everything because the election is so rough and dirty and creates such chaos in the country that the Army stages a coup and imprisons every member of the Government.

In Nanga, Achebe has created one of the finest rogues in Nigerian fiction. Claiming to be a "man of the people," Nanga is actually a self-seeking, grossly corrupt politician who lives in flamboyant opulence on his ill-gotten gains. He is fond of pious platitudes—"Not what I have but what I do is my kingdom" (2); "Do the right and shame the Devil" (12)—but his ruthless drive for money and power is far from pious. When criticized, he accuses his critics of "character assassination" and answers that "no one is perfect except God" (75). He frequently complains of the troubles and burdens that Government Ministers have to bear and readily agrees when someone remarks, "Uneasy lies the head that wears the crown" (68). Nanga has enormous power that he is willing to use to help others provided that they in turn help him. In a country in which "it didn't matter *what* you knew but *who* you knew" (19), Nanga obviously was a man to know.

The maxims quoted here help to characterize Nanga and his world. They are sayings borrowed from a foreign culture and are as often misapplied and abused as are the manners and institutions that have been borrowed from Europe and transplanted in contemporary Africa. Nanga quotes these maxims but does not live by them; similarly, he gives lip service to democratic elections but does everything in his power to subvert and manipulate them. Detribalized but imperfectly Westernized, adhering to no systematic code of values, Nanga battles to stay on top in a confused world. He is one of the most monstrous offspring produced by the tawdry union of Europe and Africa, and his misuse of non-African mottoes and maxims exposes not only his own insincerity and irresponsibility but also the moral chaos in the world in which he lives.

Odili, a more thoroughly Westernized African, is man of far greater virtue and integrity. His narrative is sprinkled with imported metaphors and proverbial expressions—e.g., "kicked the bucket" (28), "pass through the eye of a needle" (63), "one stone to kill two birds with" (152), "attack…is the best defence" (162), "a bird in the hand" (165)—but he always uses them appropriately. Whatever he says can be trusted to be accurate and honest. Somehow Odili has managed to remain untainted amidst all the surrounding corruption, and his clear vision provides an undistorted view of a warped society.

Contemporary Nigeria is, after all, the real subject of the novel. What sort of society is it that allows men like Nanga to thrive while men like Odili suffer? Some important clues are provided in the novel. In contemporary Nigeria one must, for example, be circumspect:

> ...the proverbial traveler-to-distant-places who must not cultivate enmity on his route. (1)
> ...when one slave sees another cast into a shallow grave he should know that when the time comes he will go the same way. (40)
> ...if you respect today's king, others will respect you when your turn comes. (70)
> ...if you look only in one direction your neck will become stiff. (90)

But one must not be unduly inquisitive:

> ...naked curiosity—the kind that they say earned Monkey a bullet in the forehead. (153)
> The inquisitive eye will only blind its own sight. (164)
> A man who insists on peeping into his neighbour's bedroom knowing a woman to be there is only punishing himself. (164)

One should take advantage of opportunities ("if you fail to take away a man's sword when he is on the ground, will you do it when he gets up...?" 103); capitalize on good fortune ("[would] a sensible man...spit out the juicy morsel that good fortune placed in his mouth?" 2); and avoid wasting time on trivialities ("like the man in the proverb who was carrying the carcass of an elephant on his head and searching with his toes for a grasshopper" 80). Most important of all, one must be sure to get one's share. Like the world of Obi Okonkwo in *No Longer at Ease*, this is a world in which "ours is ours but mine is mine" (140).

One must not only get one's share, one must also consume it. Eating is an important image in the novel. Politicians like Nanga tell their constituents, "Our people must press for their fair share of the national cake" (13). Those who stand in the way of such hungry politicians are branded as "the hybrid class of Western-educated and snobbish intellectuals who will not hesitate to sell their mothers for a mess of pottage" (6). These intellectuals, Nanga says, "have bitten the finger with which their mother fed them" (6). Although some people believe that God will provide for everyone according to His will ("He holds the knife and He holds the yam" 102), the politicians know that the fattest slices of the national cake along with the richest icing will go to the politicians who hold the most power. This is the reason why elections are so hotly contested. In these elections people are quite willing to support a corrupt politician like Nanga in the belief that if he remains well fed, he may let a few crumbs fall to his constituents. When someone like Odili protests that such politicians are using their positions to enrich themselves, the people answer cynically, "Let them eat,…after all when white men used to do all the eating did we commit suicide?" (161). Besides, who can tell what the future may bring?: "…who knows? It may be your turn to eat tomorrow. Your son may bring home your share" (162). It is not surprising that Odili sums up this era as a "fat-dripping, gummy, eat-and-let-eat regime…a regime which inspired the common saying that a man could only be sure of what he had put away safely in his gut or, in language ever more suited to the times: 'you chop, me self I chop, palaver finish'" (167).

The reason such an era comes to an end is that the politicians make the mistake of overeating, of taking more than their share. In proverbial terms, they take more than the owner can ignore. This key proverb is used four times in the novel. Twice it is applied to a miserly trader who steals a blind man's stick: "Josiah has taken away enough for the owner to notice," people say in disgust. "Josiah has now removed enough for the owner to see him" (97). Odili later reflects on the situation and the proverb:

> I thought much afterwards about that proverb, about the man taking things away until the owner at last notices. In the mouth of our people there was no greater condemnation. It was not just a simple question of a man's cup being full. A man's cup might be full and none the wiser. But here the owner knew, and the owner, I discovered, is the will of the whole people. (97)

In the middle of his campaign against Nanga, Odili wishes that "someone would get up and say: 'No, Nanga has taken more than the owner could ignore!'" (122). But it is only after much post-election violence and an army takeover that Odili's wish comes true. Not until such upheavals result in the establishment of a new order do people openly admit that Nanga and his cohorts "had taken enough for the owner to see" (166).

Thus, in *A Man of the People*, as in Achebe's other novels, proverbs are used to sound and reiterate major themes, to sharpen characterization, to clarify conflict, and to focus on the values of the society Achebe is portraying. By studying the proverbs in a novel, we gain insight into the moral issues with which that novel deals. Because they provide a *grammar of values* by which the actions of characters can be measured and evaluated, proverbs help us to understand and interpret Achebe's novels.

Achebe's literary talents are clearly revealed in his use of proverbs. One can observe his mastery of the English language, his skill in choosing the right words to convey his ideas, his keen sense of what is *in character* and what is not, his instinct for appropriate metaphor and symbol, and his ability to present a thoroughly African world in thoroughly African terms. It is this last talent that enables him to convince his readers "that African peoples did not hear of culture for the first time from Europeans; that their societies were not mindless but frequently had a philosophy of great depth and value and beauty, that they had poetry and, above all, they had dignity."[10]

NOTES

1. Chinua Achebe, "The Role of the Writer in a New Nation," *Nigeria Magazine* 81 (June 1965): 157.

2. *Things Fall Apart* (London: Heinemann, 1958); *No Longer at Ease* (London: Heinemann, 1960); *Arrow of God* (London: Heinemann, 1964); *A Man of the People* (London: Heinemann, 1966); *Anthills of the Savannah* (London: Heinemann, 1987). All quotations are from these editions.

3. I discuss this at greater length in "African Vernacular Styles in Nigerian Fiction," *CLA Journal* 9 (1966): 265-73. See also Gerald Moore, "English Words, African Lives," *Présence Africaine* 54 (1965): 90-101; Ezekiel Mphahlele, "The Language of African Literature," *Harvard Educational Review* 34 (Spring 1964): 298-305; and Eldred Jones, "Language and Theme in *Things Fall Apart*," *Review of English Literature* 5, no. 4 (October 1964): 39-43.

4. *Transition* 18 (1965): 30. The same article appears in *Moderna Språk* 58 (1964): 438-46.

5. Ibid.

6. I have borrowed this phrase from Melville J. Herskovits, who once said, "...the total corpus of the proverbs of Africans, as with proverb-users in other societies, is in a very real sense their grammar of values." *Dahomean Narrative* (Evanston: Northwestern University Press, 1958), 56. For another discussion of Achebe's proverbs, see Austin J. Shelton, "The 'Palm-Oil' of Language: Proverbs in Chinua

Achebe's Novels," *Modern Language Quarterly* 30, no. 1 (1969): 86-111.

7. There has been some controversy about the meaning of "chi." See Austin J. Shelton, "The Offended *chi* in Achebe's Novels," *Transition* 13 (1964): 36-37, and Donatus Nwoga, "The *chi* Offended," *Transition* 15 (1964): 5. Shelton prefers to translate this concept as "God within," but Nwoga, an Igbo, supports Achebe's translation of it as "personal god." Victor C. Uchendu, an Igbo anthropologist, describes *chi* as "the Igbo form of guardian spirit" (*The Igbo of Southeast Nigeria* [New York: Holt, Rinehart and Winston, 1965], 16). I have followed Achebe and Uchendu here.

8. Quoted from Achebe's *Arrow of God*, 31-32. A variant of this tale can be found in Cyprian Ekwensi, *Ikolo the Wrestler and Other Ibo Tales* (London: Nelson, 1947), 34-37. Another variant appears in F. Chidozie Ogbalu, *Niger Tales* (Aba, Nigeria: African Literature Bureau, n.d.), 9-11.

9. This theme is discussed by Obiajunwa Wali in "The Individual and the Novel in Africa," *Transition* 18 (1965): 31-33.

10. Achebe, "The Role of the Writer," 1.

THE BLIND MEN AND THE
ELEPHANT

There is a famous story about six blind men encountering an elephant for the first time. Each man, seizing on the single feature of the animal that he happened to have touched first, and being incapable of seeing it whole, loudly maintained his limited opinion on the nature of the beast. The elephant was variously like a wall, a spear, a snake, a tree, a fan, or a rope, depending on whether the blind men had first grasped the creature's side, tusk, trunk, knee, ear, or tail.[1]

I have referred to this fable because I believe it epitomizes the problem of every critic who is confronted with a new work of art, especially one that comes out of a culture different from his own. It is impossible for him to see the thing whole. He may inspect it with the greatest curiosity and scholarly care, counting its parts, studying its structure, analyzing its texture, probing its private recesses, measuring its real and symbolic dimensions, and trying to weigh its ultimate significance, but he will never master all its complexity, never understand everything that makes it live and move as an independent artistic creation. He simply cannot help but perceive it from his own limited point of view that has been conditioned by his previous cultural experiences. In a desperate effort to make some sense of unfamiliar lines and contours he may resort to comparisons with other forms he knows quite well, drawing parallels where oblique coincidences happen to intersect. The elephant thus becomes a wall, a spear, a snake, a tree, a fan, a rope. And the blind men bicker about the accuracy of their perceptions while truth stands huge and unrecognized in their midst.

The native critic, it has been argued, is better equipped than anyone else to appreciate the creative genius of his own culture. He is the only one who can grab the elephant by the tail and still look him straight in the eye. He is able to achieve this partly because he was born and bred closest to the beastly truth and partly because his upbringing has endowed him with superior insight into the workings of his society, the ground upon which this truth stands. Yet it would seem obvious that anyone so close to what he is viewing would have trouble viewing it in a larger context and assessing it with the kind of dispassionate objectivity that rational aesthetic evaluation requires. Indeed, if all interpretation were left to native critics, truth might be sought principally on a local level, its universal dimensions all but forgotten. Common sense just does not allow a single tribe of critics to claim a monopoly on clear vision. Every individual will have his blind spots, and some critics—native as well as foreign—will be much blinder than others.

This is why any literature needs all the criticism it can get. Only by glimpsing truth from a variety of perspectives are we able to comprehend its complexities and ambiguities. Only by comparing different views of the same subject can we arrive at a valid conception of what it really looks like. If we choose to stand still and see everything through rose-colored spectacles, we will have a narrow, tainted vision of reality. Our image of the elephant will be incomplete and distorted by our bias.

If we could learn to accept the fact that no individual—not even the author himself—is capable of telling the whole truth and nothing but the truth about a literary work, we would then be in a better position to evaluate the contribution a critic makes to our understanding of that work. We would not expect perfection, for we would realize that literary criticism is a fickle and uncertain art in which no-one has the final word. There are never any right or wrong answers as in elementary mathematics or physics; there are only good and bad arguments based on different interpretations of the same data.

The critic who ventures to criticize other critics must therefore not only be aware of his own perceptual limitations and guard against acute astigmatism and myopia, but he must also take pains to build a sound case for his particular point of view. It is not enough for him to swagger and shout insults at everyone who sees things differently. He must be sure of his footing before he casts his spear, and he must aim carefully if he wants to hit his target squarely. Above all, he must refrain from launching irrelevant personal attacks for his quarrel is not with men but with their ideas. One cannot restore a blind man's vision by flogging him.

To illustrate polar extremes of good and bad metacriticism (defined here as criticism of literary criticism) one need look no farther than *African Literature Today* 5 (1971). I will select two articles, both of which happen to challenge views I expressed in earlier issues of the same journal. Ernest Emenyonu, in a provocative essay entitled "African Literature: What does it take to be its critic?" (1-11) takes me to task for having a low opinion of Cyprian Ekwensi's art, [2] and Gareth Griffiths, in "Language and Action in the Novels of Chinua Achebe" (88-105), questions my assertions about Achebe's use of proverbs.[3] Let us look at Emenyonu's complaints first.

Emenyonu obviously admires Ekwensi both as a literary artist and as a man. He knows him personally, has interviewed him extensively about his life and writings, and is convinced that "both the characters and settings of his novels are truly African" (7). He also seems persuaded that if I and other "Western critics" only knew Ekwensi personally, would take the trouble to interview him extensively about his life and writings, and would try to become acquainted with the diverse African peoples and places upon which he bases his novels, then we too would be genuinely impressed with his literary genius. Indeed, until we are willing to make this investment in intimacy, we are incapable of judging him fairly, for "even well-intentioned minds" will be misled by "inadequate information" (4). Any of Ekwensi's close friends and associates would presumably be a better critic of his works than a total stranger who has never met him socially. To bolster his argument, Emenyonu offers bits and pieces of biographical data which are intended to help us understand and appreciate Ekwensi's craftsmanship. Some of this information can be found on dust jackets of Ekwensi's novels and would be very difficult for anyone remotely interested in his work to overlook. The fact that Ekwensi has had a varied career as a "teacher, a journalist, a forestry officer, a pharmacist, a broadcaster, a features producer, a film writer, a dramatist, a national director of Information Services, head of a national broadcasting corporation, and a diplomat" is too well known to bear repeating, but the sequence in which he held these jobs while developing as a writer is, as Emenyonu rightly maintains, of vital importance to any investigation of his literary evolution. It therefore seems odd that Emenyonu should reject my attempts "to prove something about the gap between Ekwensi's publication dates and the actual dates when the author wrote the works" (6). I was not, as he states later, "trying to assess Ekwensi's artistic growth from the chronological order of the publication of his works" (7) but rather from the chronological order in which the works were *written*. In other words, I was attempting to do precisely what Emenyonu himself insists the responsible critic must do: establish a factual basis for generalizations about an author's development. It is true I had no way of knowing that "the raw materials for *People of the City* had been collected as far back as 1947" (7),[4] but I knew from delving into Ekwensi's background that the book had been written on a brief boat trip to England. However, according to three printed sources based on early interviews with the author,[5] this trip took place in 1951, not 1953 as Emenyonu claims! If Emenyonu is so intent on setting the biographical record straight, one wishes he would make an effort to verify the "facts" he collected from Mr. Ekwensi.

Another surprising inconsistency in Emenyonu's argument is his unwillingness to accept certain kinds of biographical evidence. That Ekwensi has been influenced by many types of Western literature is a fact that even Ekwensi himself would not dispute. Indeed, in 1964 he published an autobiographical essay entitled "Literary Influences on a Young Nigerian"[6] in which he cited no fewer than twenty Western writers who had made some impact on him. In interviews he has mentioned still others as being "always present in my imagination when I write."[7] It therefore seems very peculiar that my efforts to document the extent of Ekwensi's debt to certain of these sources should be treated by Emenyonu with scornful sarcasm. Why are some well-established biographical facts admissible and others not? Emenyonu would have us believe that

> *the only thing that should be known* about Ekwensi in this regard is that he had an early overpowering and almost compulsive interest in reading, especially fiction. So possessed was Ekwensi by this trait that even while his teachers were solving mathematical equations on the blackboard, Ekwensi was preoccupied with novels hidden between his legs beneath his desk. (6. Italics mine)

If this interesting bit of gossip is truly the "only thing that should be known" about Ekwensi's reading habits, why should anyone do any further research on the subject? Emenyonu seems to want to set rigid limits on certain kinds of biographical inquiry even while demanding that critics do their utmost to learn everything there is to know about the life and times of the author.

Curiously enough, some of the statements Emenyonu makes do more to support my contentions about Ekwensi than they do to refute them. For instance, his remark that "any other West African who went through the unfortunately British dominated educational system read virtually the same titles as Ekwensi" (6), reveals that Ekwensi was more profoundly influenced by certain books than were his contemporaries who had equal access to them. Otherwise, why would not more authors in British West Africa have written like Rider Haggard, Robert Louis Stevenson and Edgar Wallace? Why was Ekwensi the only one who produced juvenile adventure fiction of this indelible stamp? The answer seems to be that the others outgrew their interest in popular schoolboy classics while Ekwensi was still strongly under their spell, at least in the earliest phase of his career. There may be better explanations, but however one chooses to interpret the evidence, the fact remains that Ekwensi copied familiar foreign models which other African writers consciously or unconsciously eschewed. As an imitator of Western adolescent adventure fiction, he was unique.

What is more bizarre about Emenyonu's argument is his assumption that there is some kind of conspiracy among Western critics to denigrate the works of African authors who opt to write about "the Africa of today, under the influence of today's economic pressures, politics, and conflict of values" (6). He asserts that most Western critics prefer novels and plays set deep in the bush because these works reflect "African primitive ways" and therefore yield the type of ethnographic and sociological data that people ignorant of contemporary African realities are invariably looking for (2). If an African author defies the expectations of these prejudiced critics by writing about modern times, he is branded un-African, and if he happens to write well, he is immediately suspected of having some Western literary blood in his veins and the critics begin a frantic search for his European or American ancestors (2-3). One wonders if Emenyonu really believes in the malevolent bogeymen he has termed "Western critics" in this imaginative scenario, or if he is merely trying to erect a racial barrier behind which he can hide suspect defensive criticism. For the strategy is quite clever. If we accept Emenyonu's premises and endorse his demonology, we are then forced to conclude (1) that any non-African who finds fault with an African literary work set in "the Africa of today" is a narrow-minded primitivist with his heart in the jungle, and (2) any non-African who seeks to identify traces of Western influence in an African novel, play, or poem is a hardened racist incapable of explaining African literary creativity in any other way. The *deus ex machina* in this black and white morality play is of course the African critic whom Emenyonu heralds as "more disposed to offer [his] views on an African work solely to help the reader towards gaining a *proper perspective* of the author and the realities of his work" (10. Italics mine). Only a blind man of a special hue can see the elephant properly and tell the world what it really looks like!

More disturbing than the latent xenophobia underlying Emenyonu's argument is his tendency to tar many Western critics with the same brush. I cannot pretend to know as much about the motives and morals of Anne Tibble, A.G. Stock, and Austin Shelton as Emenyonu claims to know, but I can at least answer some of the charges he levels at me. First, I want to assure him that I am not hopelessly infatuated with village novels depicting "African primitive ways." I happen to think that the urban novels of Soyinka, Armah, and Awoonor are among the best to have come out of Africa; I prize them not because they are "modern" in setting, theme, and technique, but because they are extraordinarily perceptive and beautifully written. I admire Achebe's rural novels for the same reason: they are elegant works of art. Secondly, my interest in African literature is more literary than anthropological, sociological, or racialistic. I do not particularly care what Africans choose to write about so long as they write well. Thirdly, I do not believe that "a Peace Corps sojourn, a spell of field work in Africa, a conference in African literature, a graduate student-ship in African literature in a Western university, any of these is enough to qualify one as an authority on African literature" (10). Nor do I believe that "African literature in all its rami-fications represents a mere appendage to British or French literature since most of the African writers write chiefly in English or French"(1). I am sure these notions are as repugnant to me as they are to Emenyonu. Finally, my effort to detect foreign (and native!) influences on Ekwensi's writing was not a back-handed maneuver to explain away his successes but a straightforward attempt to account for his failures. I sincerely doubt that I will think more highly of Ekwensi as a literary artist "as soon as [he] writes a novel about black magic, ritual, medicine men, mud and thatched huts, banana leaves, palm trees and rolling rivers" (6-7). After all, Ekwensi tried this years ago in at least two of his school readers—*Juju Rock* and *The Leopard's Claw*—and in sections of *Jagua Nana*.

All these points would have been clear to Emenyonu if he had been able to suppress his fears about Western critics plotting the overthrow of modern African literature or if he had simply known me and my critical writings better. Why should the courtesy of elementary biographical research be extended only to creative writers and not to critics?

One legitimate answer to this question is that biographi-cal research really doesn't matter at all because it is totally irrelevant to literary evaluation. A writer must be judged by what he writes, not by how he lives. Interviews and other forms of biographical inquiry may be interesting ways to collect personal information about an author but they are not substitutes for intelligent appraisal of his works. This applies to novelists as well as critics. The fact that Ekwensi was a poor student of mathematics does not make him a great writer. The fact that he has had a diversified career does not guarantee that his novels will be successful. Although we cannot prevent fascinating personal revelations from conditioning our attitude towards an artist, we should never allow them to determine our response to his art. Literary biography must not usurp the function of literary criticism.

Following this train of thought, one is tempted to go a step further and postulate that the least reliable critics are likely to be those who know an author personally, for their feelings towards him as a man will subvert their critical objectivity. It would be very difficult for any close friend or lifelong enemy of an artist to view his art with scholarly detachment. Even those who know him only slightly are apt to hold firm opinions about him which will color their reactions to what he creates. This is one of the great dangers of conducting biographical research with a tape recorder. The interviewer who interrogates the author face to face is bound to come away with a vivid impression of his character and personality, and this impression will linger and influence him when he sits down to evaluate the writer's work. If we accept Emenyonu's dictum that African literature "should be looked at objectively or not at all" (10), logic dictates that we must reject all criticism by friends, acquaintances, and interviewers of African authors. *Ergo*, we must reject Emenyonu's assessment of Ekwensi.

I admit this is an extreme position and not one which I would choose to defend with my last drop of ink. I happen to believe that biographical research is a valid and useful mode of literary investigation and that interviews are essential for eliciting an author's conception of his own work. But I do not believe that biographical criticism provides all the answers to problems of literary interpretation nor that it even necessarily raises the most meaningful questions about an author and his books. For the biographical critic is as limited in vision as anyone else and as prone to see the universe from a single point of view. If he is not aware that the author he is studying is equally crippled in insight and perception, then he is likely to be rather arrogant in his assertions, insisting that there is only one *proper perspective* on the truth. He will not realize that he and the author are only two blind men among many who seek to explain the mystery of the elephant by viewing it from a certain angle.

Before leaving this subject, let me say that I agree with Emenyonu that too little biographical research has been done on African authors, but I am not inclined to blame this deficiency primarily on Western critics. It seems to me that African scholars are in the best position to do this type of research, especially if they share a common cultural heritage with a prominent author.

As far as metacriticism is concerned, I hope it is clear that I am not arguing that critics should avoid challenging opinions with which they disagree. Critical debates are necessary not only to correct misinformation but also, more vitally, to clarify points of view that are in conflict. Metacriticism justifies itself only by contributing something new and original to literary interpretation.

An example of good metacriticism is Gareth Griffiths's "Language and Action in the Novels of Chinua Achebe," which argues that Achebe's verbal artistry is far more subtle and complex than is generally recognized, even by critics who admire his excellence as a stylist. Griffiths points out that because Achebe is a master of irony and ambiguity, one cannot accept every statement in his fiction at its face value. There are likely to be extra nuances of meaning embedded in a word, phrase, or sentence, depending on where, when, how, why, and by whom it is uttered. This is especially true of proverbs, which must be studied in context before their full significance can be understood and appreciated.

Griffiths therefore takes issue with my contention that Achebe's proverbs, examined in isolation, provide a "grammar of values" by which the deeds of characters can be measured and evaluated. Griffiths insists we must watch how these proverbs operate within the larger lexicon of rhetoric built into the novels before we can attach moral meaning to them. The proverbs cannot be trusted to deliver only one message; their environment and semantic elasticity may give them strange new shapes, abnormal connotations. Moreover, Achebe himself is at pains to prove that the old "proverbial culture itself...no longer provides a valid morality [because] the proverbial universe is no longer intact (93)...the moral universe of the proverbs with its sequence of appropriate actions and responses has disintegrated along with the society which produced it" (97). By employing proverbs ironically, Achebe thus reinforces a major historical point central to all his novels.

This is a persuasive argument, and I am willing to accept most of it without question. Griffiths has exposed serious limitations in my approach to Achebe's proverbs and has offered an attractive alternative mode of analysis that he demonstrates can yield significant insights into the nature of Achebe's genius as a writer. His penetrating observations on "proverbial patterning" and aesthetic distance help to advance our understanding of the extraordinarily complex web of social and linguistic relationships that Achebe creates in his fiction. Yet I am not entirely convinced that Griffiths's analytical procedures are basically different from my own or that they always lead him in the best direction. Proverbs are perhaps too slippery to be grasped by one hand, no matter how deft and dexterous that hand might be.

In examining Achebe's proverbs out of context, I was attempting to study them as independent resonators of moral ideas that gained amplification through frequency of sounding. The more often a particular note was heard, the more important it became in the total concert of meaning Achebe was orchestrating. The context didn't matter so much as the repeated occurrence of the same sound throughout the artistic performance, because it was through constant bombardment that the composer communicated major moral ideas to his audience.

My method of analysis could hardly be called original. Anyone who has spent time tracking down "image clusters" in a Shakespearean play, dominant symbols in a poem, or recurring motifs in a novel has done essentially the same kind of work. It involves extracting the data from the text, organizing it into logical categories, and then commenting on the significance of its patterns. It is basically an inductive technique requiring that the investigator examine a large quantity of evidence before venturing to draw conclusions.

Griffiths rejects context-free proverb analysis as inadequate because it fails to consider the "total linguistic structure" in which the proverbs are set (96). He prefers a method that will take into account unstated as well as stated truths, submerged as well as surface meanings. So he chooses to scrutinize the artist's words in context to see how their significations are changed by their surroundings. He is still looking for Achebe's moral message. He is still using an inductive method. The major difference between his approach and mine is that he is trying to read Achebe's meaning from a larger "grammar of values" imbedded in the novels.

To do this, he must examine the same proverbs that I examined and decide when Achebe is speaking straight and when he is talking through his *alter ego*, his ironic mask, or his hat. This is not an easy job, and the great virtue of Griffiths's essay is that he usually argues well and convincingly. But there are times when what he says neither invalidates nor differs much from what I said, even though he apparently thinks our statements are at odds. For instance, he objects to my classification of the proverb "Shall we kill a snake and carry it in our hand when we have a bag for putting long things in?" as a comment or warning "against foolish and unworthy actions." Clearly, in the context, the proverb does not warn against foolish or unworthy actions; in fact it is used by the old man at the Umuofia Progressive Union meeting to justify an unworthy action, or rather to justify an action which in terms of the tribal code is acceptable but in terms of the public morality to which Obi's position exposes him is a crime (97-98).

I would argue, also from the context, that the old man cites this proverb to condemn the foolishness of not approaching a fellow Umuofian for a special favor, particularly when he is in a good position to grant it. The old man wants Obi to use his influence to help find suitable employment for a "countryman" who has just lost his job at the Post Office. It would be foolish, indeed unworthy, of the Umuofia Progressive Union *not* to appeal to Obi, their brother in the senior service, to take the small steps necessary to remedy their compatriot's misfortune. As the old man puts it in another proverb, "that is why we say that he who has people is richer than he who has money."[8]

Griffiths is correct to note the irony of the situation—a proverbial plea for sane, responsible action is being perverted to justify an unworthy action—but this irony is visible only to the reader, not to the loyal members of the Umuofia Progressive Union. As Griffiths himself states, the proverb recommends "an action which in terms of the tribal code is acceptable." We see it differently because we stand with Achebe outside the moral universe of the average urban Umuofian, savoring its paradoxical immorality. The fact that we are in a position to appreciate a new cutting edge to an old saw does not in any way hinder the saw from continuing to operate on its original plane of significance. Indeed, the kernel notion of a "foolish and unworthy action" is amplified as much by ironic negation as by constant affirmation. The proverb still reverberates with all the appropriate thematic and moral overtones. The din is merely augmented by the mocking echo we now hear behind each articulation of the key idea. So while Griffiths is justified in calling our attention to contextual ironies that give a proverb new dimensions of meaning, he has no right to insist that we forget all the older truths it continues to convey. For these truths may endure and even prevail in the end. If *No Longer at Ease* is not a novel about foolish, unworthy actions *and their ironic consequences*, then what is it about?

Throughout his essay Griffiths pleads for recognition of the "relativity" of proverbial wisdom, pointing out that many proverbs are capable of yielding different meanings in different situations and that some become quite ambiguous if not absurd when undercut by deliberate irony. This is a good point, and one wishes Griffiths were willing to recognize a similar "relativity" in literary criticism, for sometimes he begs the question of interpretation by assuming that his opinion on a controversial text is right and others are wrong. For instance, his discussion of *A Man of the People* is based on Arthur Ravenscroft's premise that Odili is an "unreliable" hero who, in Griffiths's words,

> struggles, as far as he is able, to act up to the ideals he proposes, but despite his intentions he is betrayed time and time again into self-deception and hypocrisy. He tells his story defensively, as if half-aware of his plight, and organises his material and his comment to justify his action and its outcome. But his efforts only serve to emphasise the gap between intention and achievement. We are simultaneously made aware of the double-standards he operates when judging his own actions and those of others, and of the tragic innocence necessary to continue such self-deceptions successfully. (99-100)

Griffiths goes on to say that Achebe succeeds in creating an "ironic novel of high distinction" by deliberately withdrawing Odili's "capacity for honest self-appraisal" (100).

This interpretation of Odili, a further elaboration of what I would term the "Ravenscroft heresy"[9] in Achebe studies, is almost the reverse of what the author actually intended in creating his hero. If I may lapse into the somewhat uncomfortable role of biographical critic for a moment and quote what Achebe said when answering students' questions after a lecture at The University of Texas at Austin, I think the crux of the problem will be clear. Asked what his "outlook on Odili was" and whether he intended him "as an object of satire, even burlesque," Achebe answered

> Well, I like that young man. He was idealistic, he was naive, he was this and he was that, but I think he was also basically honest, which makes a difference. He was very honest. He knew his own shortcomings; he even knew when his motives were not very pure. This puts him in a class worthy of attention, as far as I'm concerned.[10]

Now if an artist views his hero as a very honest man who knows his own shortcomings, and critics tend to see the same character as a self-deceiving anti-hero incapable of honest self-appraisal, then something must be wrong either with the artist's art or with the critics' response to it. How else can the discrepancy be explained? One could perhaps try to prove that the artist was not fully aware of what he was doing, that his conception of his hero was largely an unconscious or intuitive one, and that he actually managed to create a character more complicated and therefore far more interesting than he had intended. Or one could perhaps take the opposite tack and criticize the critics for over-reacting to particular traits or deeds of the hero and consequently misinterpreting his role in the novel. Either way the discrepancy would be accounted for as a failure of perception on someone's part. One would simply have to decide whether it was the artist or the critic who was a bit obtuse.

A reasonable alternative to this sort of exegetical witch-hunt would be an approach which recognized the validity of various interpretations of the same work of art, a relative approach in matters of aesthetic discrimination. Such an alternative would acknowledge that blind men are blind in different ways and none can be expected to see much beyond what is nearest to him. The literary artist is just another interpreter of the elephant who happens to be in a position to view things from the inside. This makes his perceptions no more valid or legitimate than those of any other critic. What really count are not the reactions of a single man but the accumulated impressions of generations of visually handicapped spectators. Only then will we be able to see the truth in the largest possible perspective.

If we adopt this relative approach to literary criticism, we come to realize that the stated opinions of Achebe, Griffiths, Emenyonu, and Lindfors on a given book are of no consequence in and of themselves but that they begin to assume importance when they are in substantial agreement or disagreement with what others think and say about the same book. The crucial points at issue become clear only through rational debate which focuses on the ideas rather than the personalities of the debaters. This is where Griffiths proves himself a better metacritic than Emenyonu. Instead of arguing *ad hominem*, Griffiths quarrels with the basic critical assumptions upon which my case rests and then offers another way of looking at the same data which is so perceptive and revealing that I am forced to admit the cogency of his point of view. Unlike other metacritics who would have us close our eyes so they can guide us, Griffiths tries to teach us a new way of seeing. He appears to realize that metacriticism, though a blind man's art, should be concerned with providing the clearest possible vision of literary realities.

The moral of this essay is that good metacriticism emanates from the intellect, not from the spleen, and always has as its ultimate aim a true illumination of a work of art.

NOTES

1. John Godfrey Saxe, "The Blind Men and the Elephant," *New Nation English: Book Five (B)*, ed. Etim Akaduh, et al (London: Nelson, 1968), 94-96.

2. For my views on Ekwensi, see "Cyprian Ekwensi: An African Popular Novelist," *African Literature Today* 3 (1969): 2-14.

3. For my views on Achebe's use of proverbs, see "The Palm-Oil with which Achebe's Words are Eaten," *African Literature Today* 1 (1968): 3-18, reprinted in the previous chapter.

4. In an interview recorded in 1962 Ekwensi speaks of *People of the City* as "a little thing I turned out based on a number of short stories I wrote for Radio Nigeria." The "raw materials" had thus apparently been processed at least once before Ekwensi transmuted them into a novel. See "Cyprian Ekwensi," *African Writers Talking: A Collection of Radio Interviews*, ed. Cosmo Pieterse and Dennis Duerden (London: Heinemann; New York: Africana, 1972), 78.

5. *West Africa*, October 21, 1961, 1,157; *West African Review*, June 1956, 553, 555; *Drum*, June 1952, 14.

6. *Times Literary Supplement*, June 4, 1964, 475-76.

7. "Entretien avec l'écrivain nigerien Cyprian Ekwensi," *Afrique* 24 (1963): 51.

8. Chinua Achebe, *No Longer at Ease* (London: Heinemann, 1960), 79.

9. See Arthur Ravenscroft, "African Literature V: Novels of Disillusion," *Journal of Commonwealth Literature* 6 (1969): 120-23.

10. "Interview with Chinua Achebe," *Palaver: Interviews with Five African Writers in Texas*, ed. Bernth Lindfors, et al (Austin, Texas: African and Afro-American Research Institute, 1972), 9.

ACHEBE'S PROVERBS:
AN INVENTORY

Many critics have commented on Achebe's use of traditional Igbo proverbs in his fiction. What follows here is
an attempt to list and annotate all the non-English proverbs,
proverb variants, proverbial phrases, maxims, and other sen-
tentious sayings in his first four novels. Cross-references have
been provided for items that appear in more than one novel.

To discriminate between proverbs and other types of
aphorisms, I have been guided by William Bascom who dis-
tinguishes "proverbs from 'proverbial phrases' or metaphorical comparisons, and from maxims or mottoes like 'Honesty
is the best policy' which can be applied only in the literal
sense. Proverbs, which are the most important type of apho-
rism in Africa, have a deeper meaning than is stated literally,
a meaning which can be understood only through analysis of
the social situations to which they are appropriate." ("Folklore Research in Africa," *Journal of American Folklore* 77
[1964]: 16).

NOVELS

First editions of *Things Fall Apart* (TFA), *No Longer at Ease*
(NLAE), *Arrow of God* (AOG), and *A Man of the People*
(AMOP)

LIST OF WORKS CITED

Basden, G.T. *Among the Ibos of Nigeria*. London: Cass, 1966.

Egudu, Romanus. "Ojebe Poetry," *Black Orpheus* 21 (April 1967): 7-14.

Epelle, Kiea. *Our Folk Lore and Fables*. Lagos: Public Relations Department, n.d.

Fox, A.J. *Uzuakoli: A Short History*. London: Oxford University Press, 1964.

Jeffreys, M.D.W. "Some Ibo Proverbs," *Folklore* 67 (September 1956): 168-69.

Leonard, Major A.G. *The Lower Niger and its Tribes*. London: Macmillan, 1906.

Nwanodi, G. Okogbule. "Ibo Proverbs," *Nigeria Magazine* 80 (March 1964): 61-62.

Shelton, Austin J. "The 'Palm-Oil' of Language: Proverbs in Chinua Achebe's Novels." *Modern Language Quarterly* 30 (1969): 86-111.

Thomas, Northcote W. *Anthropological Report on the Ibo-Speaking Peoples of Nigeria*. Pts. 3 and 6. London: Harrison and Sons, 1913-14.

Uchendu, Victor C. *The Igbo of Southeast Nigeria*. New York: Holt, Rinehart and Winston, 1965.

Ward, Ida C. *An Introduction to the Ibo Language*. Cambridge: Heffer, 1936.

OTHER WORKS CONSULTED

Burdo, Adolphe. *Niger et Bénué: Voyage dans l'Afrique Centrale*. Paris: E. Plon, 1880.

Green, M.M. "The Unwritten Literature of the Igbo-speaking People of South-Eastern Nigeria," *Bulletin of the School of Oriental and African Studies* 12, pts. 3 & 4 (1948): 838-46.

_____. "Sayings of the Okonko Society of the Igbo-speaking People," *Bulletin of the School of Oriental and African Studies* 21, pt. 1 (1958): 157-73.

_____. *Igbo Village Affairs*. London: Cass, 1964.

Henderson, Richard N. and Helen Kreider Henderson. *An Outline of Traditional Ibo Socialization*. Ibadan: Institute of Education, University of Ibadan, 1966.

Okafor-Omali, Dilim. *A Nigerian Villager in Two Worlds*. London: Faber and Faber, 1965.

Schmidt, Nancy Jeanne. "An Anthropological Analysis of Nigerian Fiction." Ph.D. dissertation, Northwestern University, 1965.

Talbot, P. Amaury. *The Peoples of Southern Nigeria*. Vols. 1-4. London: Milford, 1926.

Walters, Justine Q. "Igbo Aphorisms in the Novels of Chinua Achebe." Master's thesis, University of California, Berkeley, 1967.

Watson, Linville F. "Northern Ibo Social Stratification and Acculturation." Ph.D. dissertation, University of Pennsylvania, 1953.

PROVERBS

Things Fall Apart
1. ...whenever he saw a dead man's mouth he saw the folly of not eating what one had in one's lifetime. (2) Shelton 88
2. He who brings kola brings life. (3) NLAE 6
3. ...proverbs are the palm-oil with which words are eaten. (4) Leonard 70, Thomas 3.3

4. ...the sun will shine on those who stand before it shines on those who kneel under them. (5) AMOP 98
5. ...if a child washed his hands he could eat with kings. (6) Uchendu 19, Shelton 89
6. When the moon is shining the cripple becomes hungry for a walk. (8)
7. Let the kite perch and let the egret perch too. If one says no to the other, let his wing break. (15-16) Nwanodi 61, AMOP 138
8. ...a man who pays respect to the great paves the way for his own greatness. (16) NLAE 21, AMOP 70, Shelton 89
9. A toad does not run in the daytime for nothing. (17) Whenever you see a toad jumping in broad daylight, then know that something is after its life. (180) Fox 88, AOG 25, 171, 254
10. ...an old woman is always uneasy when dry bones are mentioned in a proverb. (17) Shelton 88
11. The lizard that jumped from the high iroko tree to the ground said he would praise himself if no one else did. (18) AOG 143, Thomas 3:25, 6:22, Shelton 89-90
12. Eneke the bird says that since men have learnt to shoot without missing, he has learnt to fly without perching. (18) Eneke the bird was asked why he was always on the wing and he replied: "Men have learnt to shoot without missing their mark and I have learnt to fly without perching on a twig." (181) AOG 55
13. ...you can tell a ripe corn by its look. (18) AOG 156
14. Looking at a king's mouth,...one would think he never sucked at his mother's breast. (22) Shelton 90
15. ...those whose palm-kernels were cracked for them by a benevolent spirit should not forget to be humble. (22) Shelton 90

16. ...when a man says yes his *chi* says yes also. (23) ...if a man said yea his *chi* also affirmed. (117) AOG 33, Shelton 90

17. ...the little bird *nza* who so far forgot himself after a heavy mean that he challenged his *chi*. (26) NLAE 163, AOG 17, Shelton 91

18. A chick that will grow into a cock can be spotted the very day it hatches. (58)

19. A child's fingers are not scalded by a piece of hot yam which its mother puts into its palm. (59) AOG 286, Shelton 91

20. It is like Dimragana, who would not lend his knife for cutting up dog-meat because the dog was taboo to him, but offered to use his teeth. (61)

21. When mother-cow is chewing grass its young ones watch its mouth. (62) AOG 213

22. ...as the dog said, "If I fall down for you and you fall down for me, it is play." (64) AMOP 140

23. A baby on its mother's back does not know that the way is long. (90) Fox 88, Thomas 3:7

24. ...if one finger brought oil it soiled the others. (112) NLAE 75, AOG 231, Ward 206, Epelle 2, Thomas 3:24

25. Never kill a man who says nothing. (124)

26. There is nothing to fear from someone who shouts. (125)

27. Living fire begets cold, impotent ash. (138)

28. I cannot live on the bank of a river and wash my hands with spittle. (148) NLAE 10

29. An animal rubs its itching flank against a tree, a man asks his kinsman to scratch him. (149)

30. A child cannot pay for its mother's milk. (149)

31. ...as a man danced so the drums were beaten for him. (165)

32. We must bale this water now that it is only ankle-deep...(181) Basden 283, Jeffreys 168, AOG 156, 197, Thomas 3:4.

No Longer at Ease

33. ...anger against a brother was felt in the flesh, not in the bone. (5) Shelton 97

34. He that fights for a ne'er-do-well has nothing to show for it except a head covered in earth and grime. (5)

35. The fox must be chased away first; after that the hen might be warned against wandering into the bush. (5) AOG 122, Shelton 97

36. ...if you want to eat a toad you should look for a fat and juicy one. (6) Shelton 98

37. ...the proverb of the house rat who went swimming with his friend the lizard and died from cold, for while the lizard's scales kept him dry the rat's body remained wet. (6) Ward 203, Shelton 98

38. He that brings kola brings life. (6) TFA 3

39. An only palm-fruit does not get lost in the fire. (6) Thomas 6:58, Shelton 96

40. You have the yam and you have the knife; we cannot eat unless you cut us a piece. (9) AOG 119, AMOP 102

41. ...a man who lived on the banks of the Niger should not wash his hands with spittle. (10) It was like having a river and yet washing one's hands with spittle. (135) TFA 148

42. Do not be in a hurry to rush into the pleasures of the world like the young antelope who danced herself lame when the main dance was yet to come. (11) Shelton 92

43. ...if you pay homage to the man on top, others will pay homage to you when it is your turn to be on top. (21) TFA 16, AMOP 70

44. Ours is ours, but mine is mine. (32) AMOP 140, Shelton 96

45. ...the power of the leopard resided in its claws. (33)

46. ...a man does not challenge his *chi* to a wrestling match. (40) AOG 32, Shelton 93

47. ...a man's in-law was his *chi*. (46)

48. When a new saying gets to the land of empty men they lose their heads over it. (48) Shelton 92-93

49. You cannot plant greatness as you plant yams or maize. (54)

50. The great tree chooses where to grow and we find it there, so it is with the greatness of men. (54)

51. A person who has not secured a place on the floor should not begin to look for a mat. (60)

52. The eye is not harmed by sleep. (71)

53. If one finger brings oil it soils the others. (75) TFA 112, AOG 112, Ward 206, Epelle 2, Thomas 3:24, Shelton 94

54. ...he who has people is richer than he who has money. (79) Shelton 97

55. Shall we kill a snake and carry it in our hand when we have a bag for putting long things in? (80) Shelton 93

56. If all snakes lived together in one place, who would approach them? (81) Shelton 97

57. A debt may get mouldy, but it never decays. (82) Our people have a saying that a debt may get mouldy but it never rots. (96) Shelton 93

58. ...when there is a big tree small ones climb on its back to reach the sun. (96)

59. The start of weeping is always hard. (97)

60. ...it is not right to ask a man with elephantiasis of the scrotum to take on small pox as well, when thousands of other people have not had even their share of small diseases. (98-99) Shelton 94

61. ...the proverb about digging a new pit to fill up an old one. (108)
62. No petrol, no fire. (113)
63. ...clothes and oil were not kinsmen. (127)
64. ...when a coward sees a man he can beat he becomes hungry for a fight. (137) Thomas 6:32, Shelton 95
65. ...a man should not, out of pride and etiquette, swallow his phlegm. (156) Shelton 94
66. ...the words of encouragement which the bedbug was said to have spoken to her children when hot water was poured on them all. She told them not to lose heart because whatever was hot must in the end turn cold. (158) Thomas 3:32
67. Wherever something stands, another thing stands beside it. (159) Shelton 98
68. It is like the bird that flies off the earth and lands on an anthill. It is still on the ground. (160) AOG 283, Thomas 3:37
69. ...like the little bird *nza* who after a big meal so far forgot himself as to challenge his *chi* to single combat. (163) TFA 26, AOG 17
70. The most horrible sight in the world cannot put out the eye. (167)

Arrow of God
71. When a woman marries a husband she should forget how big her father's compound was. (12)
72. A woman does not carry her father's *obi* to her husband. (12)
73. We often stand in the compound of a coward to point at the ruins where a brave man used to live. (13)
74. The man who has never submitted to anything will soon submit to the burial mat. (13) Shelton 99

75. When a handshake goes beyond the elbow it becomes another thing. (283) Shelton 103
76. ...like the little bird, *nza*, who ate and drank and challenged his personal god to single combat. (17) TFA 26, NLAE 163, Shelton 100
77. Wisdom is like a goatskin bag; every man carries his own. (19) Shelton 101
78. If the lizard of the homestead neglects to do the things for which its kind is known, it will be mistaken for the lizard of the farmland. (20-21)
79. When an adult is in the house the she-goat is not left to suffer the pains of parturition on its tether. (21) ...when an adult is in the house the she-goat is not left to bear its young from the tether. (31) ...when an elder is in the house the she-goat is not left to produce its young in tether. (189) ...an adult does not sit and watch while the she-goat suffers the pain of childbirth tied to a post. (258) Ward 207, Nwanodi 61, Shelton 99-100
80. ...a boy sent by his father to steal does not go stealthily but breaks the door with his foot. (22) Thomas 3:44
81. When we hear a house has fallen do we ask if the ceiling fell with it? (22) ...when the roof and walls of a house fall in, the ceiling is not left standing. (105)
82. ...when a man of cunning dies a man of cunning buries him. (24) Thomas 6:42
83. ...a toad does not run in the day unless something is after it. (25) ...a toad does not run in the daytime unless something is after it. (171, 254) TFA 17, 180, Fox 88
84. The reed we were blowing is now crushed. (31)
85. ...no matter how strong or great a man was he should never challenge his *chi*. (32) NLAE 40
86. The fly that has no one to advise it follows the corpse into the grave. (32) The fly that has no one to advise him follows the corpse into the ground...(282) Shelton 100

87. ...let the slave who sees another cast into the shallow grave know that he will be buried in the same way when his day comes. (32) AMOP 40, Shelton 100

88. The man who carries a deity is not a king. (33)

89. If a man says yes his *chi* also says yes. (33) TFA 23, 117, Shelton 101

90. ...when we see a little bird dancing in the middle of the pathway we know that its drummer is in the near-by bush. (48)

91. ...like a leper. Allow him a handshake and he wants an embrace. (51) ...as soon as we shake hands with a leper he will want an embrace. (177) Shelton 102

92. The inquisitive monkey gets a bullet in the face. (53) AMOP 153, Shelton 104

93. ...like the bird Eneke-nti-oba. When his friends asked him why he was always on the wing he replied: "Men of today have learnt to shoot without missing and so I have learnt to fly without perching." (55) TFA 18, 181, Shelton 102

94. The world is like a Mask dancing. If you want to see it well you do not stand in one place. (55) Shelton 103

95. ...whatever music you beat on your drum there is somebody who can dance to it. (56) ...whatever tune you play in the compound of a great man there is always someone to dance to it. (124)

96. ...the lizard that ruined his own mother's funeral...(60, 276) The lizard who threw confusion into his mother's funeral rite did he expect outsiders to carry the burden of honouring his dead? (155) ...like the lizard in the fable who ruined his mother's funeral by his own hand. (287) Egudu 11, Shelton 104

97. A coward may cover the ground with his words but when the time comes to fight he runs away. (60)

98. Unless the wind blows we do not see the fowl's rump. (72) Shelton 105

99. …a man who brings home ant-infested faggots should not complain if he is visited by lizards. (72) The man who brings ant-infested faggots into his hut should not grumble when lizards begin to pay him a visit. (163) …a man who brings ant-ridden faggots into his hut should expect the visit of lizards. (178) Shelton 104

100. …the very thing which kills mother rat prevents its little ones from opening their eyes. (74) The very thing which kills Mother Rat is always there to make sure that its young ones never open their eyes. (283) Thomas 3:41

101. An old woman is never old when it comes to the dance she knows. (86) AMOP 75

102. A man who knows that his anus is small does not swallow an *udala* seed. (87) He who will swallow *udala* seeds must consider the size of his anus. (282)

103. The man who sends a child to catch a shrew will also give him water to wash his hand. (87) …the person who sets a child to catch a shrew should also find him the water to wash the odour from his hand. (260) Shelton 106

104. Did you expect what the leopard sired to be different from the leopard? (91)

105. When Suffering knocks at your door and you say there is no seat left for him, he tells you not to worry because he brought his own stool. (105)

106. Only a foolish man can go after a leopard with his bare hands. (105) AMOP 127

107. …the very house he has been seeking ways of pulling down has caught fire of its own will. (106) The house he has been planning to pull down has caught fire and saved him the labour. (266) AMOP 115

108. The stranger will not kill his host with his visit; when he goes may he not go with a swollen back. (106)

109. The death that will kill a man begins as an appetite. (110)

110. He forgot the saying of the elders that if a man sought for a companion who acted entirely like himself he would live in solitude. (114)

111. You have the yam and you have the knife. (119) NLAE 9, AMOP 102

112. You do not expect me to provide the snuff and also the walking around, to give you a wife and find you a mat to sleep on. (119)

113. The only medicine against palm wine is the power to say no. (121)

114. ...let us first chase away the wild cat, afterwards we blame the hen. (122) NLAE 5

115. ...a boy who tries to wrestle with his father gets blinded by the old man's loin cloth. (123) Thomas 3:20

116. ...a woman who began cooking before another must have more broken utensils. (123)

117. ...when we see an old woman stop in her dance to point again and again in the same direction we can be sure that somewhere there something happened long ago which touched the roots of her life. (123)

118. We do not by-pass a man and enter his compound. (138)

119. The time a man wakes up is his morning. (138)

120. We do not apply an ear-pick to the eye. (138) Epelle 2, Thomas 3:26

121. ...greeting in the cold harmattan is taken from the fire-side. (140)

122. ...a man who visits a craftsman at work finds a sullen host. (140)

123. ...like the lizard who fell down from the high iroko tree without breaking any bone and said that if nobody else thought highly of the feat he himself did. (143) TFA 18, Thomas 3:25, 6:22

124. ...the flute player must sometimes stop to wipe his nose. (149)
125. ...even the smallest child in a man's compound knew its mother's hut from the others. (152)
126. A ripe maze can be told merely by looking at it. (156) TFA 18
127. The fellow does not fall where his body might be picked up. (156) AMOP 135
128. ...wanting to bale the water before it rises above the ankle. (156) ...they must bale the water while it was still only ankle-deep. (197) TFA 181, Basden 283, Jeffreys 168, Thomas 3:4, Shelton 105
129. The offspring of a hawk cannot fail to devour chicks. (158)
130. The fly that perches on a mound of dung may strut around as long as it likes, it cannot move the mound. (161) The fly that struts around on a mound of excrement wastes his time: the mound will always be greater than the fly. (282) Shelton 101
131. ...when two brothers fight a stranger reaps their harvest. (162) ...when brothers fight to death a stranger inherits their father's estate. (275)
132. ...a man who does not know where the rain started to beat him cannot know where he dried his body. (163) Shelton 105-06
133. A disease that has never been seen before cannot be cured with ordinary herbs. (165) Shelton 103
134. When we want to make a charm we look for the animal whose blood can match its power...(165)
135. ...a man who has nowhere else to put his hand for support puts it on his own knee. (165)
136. ...no matter how many spirits plotted a man's death it would come to nothing unless his personal god took a hand in the deliberation. (169)

137. ....a snake is never as long as the stick to which we liken its length. (169)
138. ...you must expect foreigners to talk through the nose. (170) ...strangers talk through the nose. (170)
139. ....an animal more powerful than *nte* was caught in *nte's* trap. (174) ...a thing greater than *nte* had been caught in *nte's* trap. (275)
140. ....if you thank a man for what he has done he will have strength to do more. (175)
141. ....when a man sees a snake all by himself he may wonder whether it is an ordinary snake or the untouchable python. (176) A common snake which a man sees all alone may become a python in his eyes...(283)
142. Unless the penis dies young it will surely eat bearded meat. (176) Thomas 6:74
143. When hunting day comes we shall hunt in the backyard of the grass-cutter. (176)
144. You tied the knot, you should also know how to undo it. (178)
145. You passed the shit that is smelling; you should also carry it away. (178)
146. Fortunately the evil charm brought in at the end of a pole is not too difficult to take outside again. (178)
147. When a masked spirit visits you you have to appease its footprints with presents. (190)
148. A fowl does not eat into the belly of a goat. (193) AMOP 140
149. ....until a man wrestles with one of those who make a path across his homestead the others will not stop. (198) Thomas 6:37
150. They had taken away too much for the owner not to notice. (198) AMOP 97, 122, 166
151. Who would swallow phlegm for fear of offending others? How much less swallow poison? (203) ...it's the

fear of causing offence that makes men swallow poison. (204)

152. A woman cannot place more than the length of her leg on her husband. (207)

153. The young he-goat said that but for his sojourn in his mother's clan he would not have learnt to stick up his upper lip. (207)

154. ....a traveller to distant places should make no enemies. (208) AMOP 1

155. ....a man of sense does not go on hunting little bush rodents when his age mates are after big game. (209)

156. ....if the rat could not run fast enough it must make way for the tortoise. (209) If the rat cannot flee fast enough let him make way for the tortoise! (286)

157. ....the stone rarely succeeds like the eye in hitting the mark. (210)

158. Every lizard lies on its belly, so we cannot tell which has a belly-ache. (211) Thomas 6:34

159. ....a woman who carries her head on a rigid neck as if she is carrying a pot of water will never live for long with any husband. (212)

160. ....there are more ways than one of killing a dog. (213)

161. ....when mother-cow is cropping giant grass her calves watch her mouth. (213) TFA 62

162. The wife who had seen the emptiness of life had cried: Let my husband hate me as long as he provides yams for me every afternoon. (216)

163. ....foolish for a man to spit out a morsel which fortune had placed in his mouth...(216) AMOP 2

164. A man might pick his way with the utmost care through a crowded market but find that the hem of his cloth had upset and broken another's wares; in such a case the man, not his cloth, was held to repair the damages. (217)

165. Whoever puts the other down…will strip him of his anklet. (221) …whoever throws the other down will strip him of his anklet. (241)
166. Wherever the flame goes out now I shall put the torch away. (226)
167. …if one finger brought oil it messed up the others. (231) TFA 112, NLAE 75, Ward 206, Epelle 2, Thomas 3:24
168. …like the puppy in the proverb which attempted to answer two calls at once and broke its jaw. (232)
169. …a man must dance the dance prevalent in his time. (234) …a man must dance the dance prevailing in his time. (266) Shelton 103-04
170. Why should a man be in a hurry to lick his fingers; was he going to put them away in the rafter? (240)
171. Do you know what happens when two elephant fight? (240-01) Epelle 2
172. …the noise even of the loudest events must begin to die down by the second market week. (242)
173. A man who asks questions does not lose his way…(255) Epelle 2, Thomas 3:18, 35
174. How do you carry a man with a broken waist? (259)
175. …he whose name is called again and again by those trying in vain to catch a wild bull has something he alone can do to bulls. (280)
176. The thing that beats the drum for *ngwesi* is inside the ground. (282)
177. Darkness is so great it gives horns to a dog. (282)
178. He who built a homestead before another can boast more broken pots. (282)
179. It is *ofo* that gives rain-water power to cut dry earth. (282)
180. The man who walks ahead of his fellows spots spirits on the way. (282)

181. Bat said he knew his ugliness and chose to fly by night. (282)
182. When the air is fouled by a man on top of a palm tree the fly is confused. (282)
183. An ill-fated man drinks water and it catches in his teeth. (282)
184. Even while people are still talking about the man Rat bit to death Lizard takes money to have his teeth filed. (282) Thomas 6:50
185. He who sees an old hag squatting should leave her alone; who knows how she breathes? (282)
186. White Ant chews *igbegulu* because it is lying on the ground; let him climb the palm tree and chew. (282)
187. The sleep that lasts from one market day to another has become death. (283)
188. The man who likes the meat of the funeral ram, why does he recover when sickness visits him? (283)
189. The mighty tree falls and the little birds scatter in the bush...(283)
190. The little bird which hops off the ground and lands on an anthill may not know it but is still on the ground...(283) NLAE 160, Thomas 3:37
191. The boy who persists in asking what happened to his father before he has enough strength to avenge him is asking for his father's fate...(283) Thomas 3:41
192. The man who belittles the sickness which Monkey has suffered should ask to see the eyes which his nurse got from blowing the sick fire...(283)
193. When death wants to take a little dog it prevents it from smelling even excrement. (283)
194. Give me a sharp boy even though he breaks utensils in his haste. (283)
195. ....a man is like a funeral ram which must take whatever beating comes to it without opening its mouth; only the

silent tremor of pain down its body tells of its suffering. (286)

196. When was it ever heard that a child was scalded by the piece of yam its own mother put in its palm? (286) TFA 59

197. What man would send his son with a potsherd to bring fire from a neighbour's hut and then unleash rain on him? (286)

198. Who ever sent his son up the palm to gather nuts and then took an axe and felled the tree? (286)

A Man of the People

199. ...the proverbial traveler-to-distant-places who must not cultivate enmity on his route. (1) AOG 208

200. ...if you thought that a sensible man would spit out the juicy morsel that good fortune placed in his mouth. (2) AOG 216

201. ...when poor man done see with him own eye how to make big man e go beg make e carry him poverty de go je-je. (16)

202. ...it is better the water is spilled than the pot broken. (32)

203. ...when one slave sees another cast into a shallow grave he should know that when the time comes he will go the same way. (40) AOG 32

204. A man who has just come in from the rain and dried his body and put on dry clothes is more reluctant to go out again than another who has been indoors all the time. (42)

205. ...if you respect today's king others will respect you when your turn comes. (70) TFA 16, NLAE 21

206. When an old woman hears the dance she knows her old age deserts her. (75) AOG 86

207. ...like the man in the proverb who was carrying the carcass of an elephant on his head and searching with his toes for a grasshopper. (80) Leonard 73

208. ...if you look only in one direction your neck will become stiff. (90)

209. ...it is only when you are close to a man that you can smell his breath. (94)

210. Some people's belly is like the earth. It is never so full that it will not take another's corpse. (97) Shelton 107

211. ...removed enough for the owner to see him. (97) ...taking things away until the owner at last notices. (97) ...taken more than the owner could ignore! (122) ...taken enough for the owner to see. (166) Shelton 108

212. ...when those standing have not got their share you are talking about those kneeling. (98) TFA 5

213. He holds the knife and He holds the yam. (102) NLAE 9, AOG 119

214. ...if you fail to take away a strong man's sword when he is on the ground, will you do it when he gets up...? (103)

215. ...setting fire to a house that was due for demolition and saving someone's labour. (115) AOG 106, 266

216. ...a man who avoids danger for years and then gets killed in the end has wasted his care. (123)

217. Man no fit fight tiger with empty hand. (127) AOG 105

218. When a mad man walks naked it is his kinsman who feels shame, not himself. (132) Ward 205, Shelton 108-09

219. A mad man may sometimes speak a true word...but you watch him, he will soon add something to it that will tell you his mind is still spoilt. (135)

220. ...why don't you fall where your pieces could be gathered? (135) AOG 156

221. If Alligator comes out of the water one morning and tells you that Crocodile is sick can you doubt his story? (136)

222. ...the hawk should perch and the eagle perch, whichever says to the other *don't*, may its own wing break. (138) TFA 15-16, Nwanodi 61

223. ...what one dog said to another. He said: "If I fall for you this time and you fall for me next time then I know it is play not fight." (140) TFA 64

224. A goat does not eat into the hen's stomach no matter how friendly the two may be. (140) AOG 193

225. Ours is ours but mine is mine. (140) NLAE 32

226. ...if the very herb we go to seek in the forest now grows at our very back yard are we not saved the journey? (141)

227. ...like a babe cutting its first tooth: anyone who wants to look at our new tooth should know that his bag should be heavy. (141)

228. ...there are only two things you can do with yam—if you do not boil it, you roast it. (143)

229. ...a man of worth never gets up to unsay what he said yesterday. (152)

230. ...naked curiosity—the kind that they say earned Monkey a bullet in the forehead...(153) AOG 53

231. The inquisitive eye will only blind its own sight. (164)

232. A man who insists on peeping into his neighbour's bedroom knowing a woman to be there is only punishing himself. (164)

233. ...a man could only be sure of what he had put away safely in his gut...(167)

234. ...you chop, me self I chop, palaver finish. (167)

MAXIMS, PROVERBIAL PHRASES, AND OTHER SENTENTIOUS SAYINGS

Things Fall Apart

1. When a man is at peace with his gods and ancestors, his harvest will be good or bad according to the strength of his arm. (14)
2. ...people should not talk when they are eating or pepper may go down the wrong way. (39)
3. ...*jigida* and fire are not friends. (63)
4. ...what is good in one place is bad in another place. (65) ...what is good among one people is an abomination with others. (125) Thomas 6:54
5. It is not bravery when a man fights with a woman. (83) AOG 77
6. There is no story that is not true. (125)
7. Never make an early morning appointment with a man who has just married a new wife. (126)
8. We are better than animals because we have kinsmen. (149)
9. A man who calls his kinsmen to a feast does not do so to save them from starving. (150)
10. When we gather together in the moonlit village ground it is not because of the moon. Every man can see it in his own compound. (150)
11. ...the outsider who wept louder than the bereaved. (165) NLAE 78
12. It is good that a man should worship the gods and spirits of his fathers. (170)
13. An Umuofia man does not refuse a call. (172)
14. Worthy men are no more. (178)

No Longer at Ease

15. A kinsman in trouble had to be saved, not blamed. (5)

16. Women and music should not be dated. (27)
17. ...the kind of English they admired if not understood; the kind that filled the mouth, like the proverbial dry meat. (32)
18. Our people have a long way to go. (36, 69)
19. ...to believe such a thing was to chew the cud of foolishness. It was putting one's head into a cooking pot. (48) AOG 265, AMOP 130
20. That is a matter between him and his *chi*. (49) AOG 150
21. Dead men do not come back. (54)
22. One cannot have it both ways. (61)
23. Men are blind. (73)
24. ...the outsider who wept louder than the bereaved. (78) TFA 165
25. If a man returns from a long journey and no one says *nno* to him he feels like one who has not arrived. (81)
26. ...book stands by itself and experience stands by itself. (82)
27. ...I went and poured sand into your garri. (94)
28. Na so this world be. (94) Na so dis world be. (99)
29. A kinsman cannot be bought in the market, neither is a brother bought with money. (129) ...money cannot buy a kinsman. (129) ...he who has brothers, has more than riches can buy. (129)
30. ...in a strange land one should always move near one's kinsmen. (131) Shelton 97
31. ...pregnancy could not be covered with the hand. (148)
32. ...it is from listening to old men that you learn wisdom. (159)
33. ...like a palm tree bearing fruit at the end of its leaf...(167) AOG 206

Arrow of God
34. ...it was no more than the power in the anus of the proud dog who tried to put out a furnace with his puny fart. (4)

35. If you hear me asking you about it again take my name and give it to a dog. (5)
36. People said of him (as they always did when they saw great comeliness) that he was not born for these parts among the Igbo people of the forests; that in his previous life he must have sojourned among the riverain folk whom the Igbo called Olu. (12)
37. No one eats numbers. (14)
38. ...a man does not go to his in-law with wisdom. (14)
39. A new wife should not come into an unfinished homestead. (15)
40. ...a father does not speak falsely to his son. (19) A man does not speak a lie to his son. (115) To say *My father told me* is to swear the greatest oath. (115) ...the greatest liar among men still speaks the truth to his son. (121) A man can swear before the most dreaded deity on what his father told him. (121) No man speaks a lie to his son. (233)
41. ...the lore of the land is beyond the knowledge of many fathers. (19)
42. ...an old man is there to talk. (20)
43. ...nobody eats war. (21)
44. ...what had happened might be likened to he-goat's head dropping into he-goat's bag. (30)
45. Today the world is spoilt and there is no longer head or tail in anything that is done. (32) ...the head and the tail of this matter. (206)
46. ...a man might have Ngwu and still be killed by Ojukwu. (47)
47. ...outsiders who chose to weep louder than the owner of the corpse. (60) TFA 165, NLAE 78
48. Do I look to you like someone you can put in your bag and walk away? (60) ...not the kind of person another woman could tie into her *lappa* and carry away. (265)

49. …pregnant and nursing a baby at the same time. (63) It is pregnant and nursing a baby at the same time. (228) Shelton 104

50. …the world is no longer what it was. (65)

51. …a man's debt to his father-in-law can never be fully discharged. (76) …when we marry a wife we must go on paying until we die. (76)

52. …the man who has no gift for speaking says his kinsmen have said all there is to say. (76)

53. It is not bravery for a man to beat his wife. (77) TFA 83

54. What a man does not know is greater than he. (105)

55. …a man may refuse to do what is asked of him but may not refuse to be asked. (106) …it is not our custom to refuse a call, although we may refuse to do what the caller asks. (173)

56. …he is a fool who treats his brother worse than a stranger. (117)

57. …a man always has more sense than his children. (123)

58. What do we say happens to the man who eats and then makes his mouth as if it has never seen food?…It makes his anus dry up. (137)

59. A man cannot be too busy to break the first kolanut of the day in his own house. (138)

60. We woke up one morning to find our shinbone deformed. (141)

61. …what was right was right. (142)

62. It is a story of great sorrow, but we cannot set fire to the world. (149)

63. …the matter lies between him and his *chi*. (150) NLAE 49

64. No one is born with a broom in his hand. (154)

65. A man should hold his compound together, not plant dissension among his children. (155)

66. ...a man does not talk when masked spirits speak. (160)
67. ...no man however great can win judgement against a clan. (162) ...no man ever won judgement against his clan. (287) ...no man however great was greater than his people. (287) Shelton 105
68. A man who means to buy palm wine does not hang about at home until all the wine in the market is sold. (169)
69. ...the unexpected beats even a man of valour. (176)
70. ...like rats gnawing away at the sole of a sleeper's foot, biting and then blowing air on the wound to soothe it, and lull the victim back to sleep. (179) Thomas 3:45
71. Only those who carry evil medicine on their body should fear the rain. (180)
72. ...the knowledge of herbs and *anwansi* is something inscribed in the lines of a man's palm. (182)
73. ...the language of young men is always *pull down and destroy*; but an old man speaks of conciliation. (189)
74. I tellam say O-o, one day go be one day. (191)
75. ...make them see their ears with their own eyes. (191) Thomas 3:31, 6:29
76. ...the eye is very greedy and will steal a look at something its owner has no wish to see. (196)
77. ...even a hostile clansman was a friend in a strange country. (200)
78. ...till palm fruits ripen at the tip of the frond. (206) NLAE 167
79. Hunger is better than sickness. (207)
80. ...everything was good in its season; dancing in the season of dancing. (209)
81. ...the owner of a person is also owner of whatever that person has. (213)
82. Their badness wears a hat. (228) AMOP 96
83. If my enemy speaks the truth I will not say because it is spoken by my enemy I will not listen. (232)

84. ...a god who demands the sacrifice of a chick might raise it to a goat if you went to ask a second time. (261)

85. We have planted our yams in the farm of Anaba-nti. (262)

86. ...urging your husband to put his head in a cooking pot. (265) NLAE 48, AMOP 130

87. ...it was a bad death which killed a man in the time of famine. (271)

88. ...long, long ago when lizards were in ones and twos...(274)

89. Goat has eaten palm leaves from off my hand. (284)

A Man of the People

90. Once a teacher always a teacher. (10)

91. ...a certain woman whose daughter was praised for her beauty and she said: You haven't seen her yet; wait till she's had a bath. (53)

92. Make you no min' am. (73)

93. What money will do in this land wears a hat...(96) AOG 228, Shelton 107

94. If a blind man does not know his own stick, tell me what else would he know? (96)

95. If I am not to grow bigger let me at least remain as small as I am. (100)

96. I see that you have grown too big for your coat. (115)

97. What cannot be avoided must be borne. (124)

98. ...people don't go counting their children as they do animals or yams. (125)

99. He should wait till he builds his own house then he may put his head into a pot there...(130) NLAE 48, AOG 265, Shelton 108

100. No man in Urua will give his paper to a stranger when his own son needs it...(141)

101. ...took the legendary bath of the Hornbill and donned innocence. (166)

THE FOLKTALE AS PARADIGM IN *ARROW OF GOD*

Toward the end of his third novel, *Arrow of God*, Chinua Achebe devotes five pages to the telling of a traditional Igbo folktale. On the surface this tale appears to have no bearing on the events in the novel itself. It seems merely a digression, an unnecessary detour into the folkways of a people who nearly a century ago had very little contact with the outside world. Many critics have dismissed such passages in Achebe's fiction as well intentioned but artificially unjustified attempts to embroider a story with authentic bits of aboriginal local color. Achebe, they complain, gives the impression of being primarily a sociologist,[1] for his novels are "long on native customs and idiom, and short on narrative interest."[2] *Arrow of God*, his most ambitious work, is inevitably singled out for its copious "anthropological documentation," which makes it "perhaps too elaborate, too worked out, too insistent, and a little tendentious."[3] Though an impressive imaginative achievement, this novel, it is argued, ultimately fails to satisfy the reader aesthetically because its "parts are not all, or do not appear to be, evolutionarily contingent one upon the other."[4]

The critics who make these remarks are usually European or American book reviewers who have little knowledge of traditional African modes of storytelling. They are not aware that Achebe, like many a fireside raconteur, often uses proverbs and folktales to comment indirectly on eccentricities of human behavior that have been observed or manifested recently by his audience. The lore thus serves a moral purpose, interpreting as well as reflecting contemporary social realities. In his four novels Achebe carries this technique a step further by making the folklore relate not only to the real world of his readers but also, more importantly, to the fictional world his *dramatis personae* inhabit. His proverbs and folktales are not exotic digressions but fully functional narrative progressions, not superfluous anthropological data but meaningful metaphors illuminating the special contexts in which they are set.[5] To appreciate how subtly these forms are sometimes made to operate, let us look closely at the five-page folktale in the latter part of *Arrow of God*.[6]

This prize-winning novel is concerned with Igboland in the nineteen-twenties and has as its hero a headstrong chief priest of a snake cult who falls victim to the changing times and to his own towering pride. Ezeulu, chief priest of Ulu, is professionally committed to traditional ways, but just to be on the safe side he sends one of his own sons to a mission school to "be [his] eye there" and to learn the white man's ways. This action draws criticism from some of the leaders of the clan, criticism that rapidly mounts into angry protest when the Christianized son is caught trying to kill a sacred python. Ezeulu also falls afoul of the British district officer by declining to accept an official appointment as paramount chief of his village. For this he is thrown into prison for two months. He sits there furious with the district officer and vexed with his own clansmen for failing to respond to his imprisonment with adequate strength of action or sentiment. When he returns to his village, he sees himself as an avenging arrow in the bow of his god, an instrument by which his god intends to punish his people. Ezeulu therefore refuses to perform certain seasonal rituals that must be performed before new yams can be harvested. This precipitates a crisis that results in the destruction of Ezeulu, his priesthood, and his deity. Traditional Igbo society consequently falls further apart.

Ezeulu's catastrophic mistake is to turn against his own people. While sitting in prison he formulates his wrong-headed scheme to delay the new yam harvest by denying it his blessing. However, when he returns home and receives a hero's welcome, he begins to relent and think of reconciliation. "Was it right," he asks himself, "that he should stretch his hand against all these people who had shown so much concern for him during his exile and since his return?" (231) It is in this interim period between Ezeulu's release from prison and his refusal to perform the necessary rituals, the very period during which Ezeulu is trying to decide whether or not to punish his people as he had originally intended, that the folktale we are concerned with is inserted into the narrative.

It is told by Ezeulu's youngest wife to two of her small children. Here is the entire tale:

> Once upon a time there was a man who had two wives. The senior wife had many children but the younger one had only one son. One day the man and his family went to work on their farm. This farm was at the boundary between the land of men and the land of spirits. Anyone going to work in this neigh-bourhood must hurry away at sunset because as soon as darkness came the spirits arrived to work on their own yam-fields.
>
> This man and his wives and children worked until the sun began to go down. They quickly gathered their hoes and matchets and baskets and set out for home. But on reaching home the son of the second wife discovered that he had left his flute in the farm and said he would go back for it. His mother pleaded

with him not to go but he would not listen. His father warned him it would be certain death to go but he did not listen. When they were tired of pleading with him they let him go.

He passed over seven rivers and through seven wilds before he reached the farm. When he got near he saw spirits bending over their work planting ghost-yams. They all stood up on his approach and regarded him with anger in their eyes.

"Ta! Human boy!" barked the leader of the spirits. "What do you want?" He spoke through the nose. "Have you never heard that we are abroad at this time."

"I have come to take the flute I forgot under that dead tree."

"Flute? Will you recognize it if you see it?"

The boy said yes. The leader of the spirits then produced a flute shining like yellow metal.

"Is this it?"

The boy said no. Then he produced another flute shining white like the *nut of the water of heaven*.

"Is this it?" he asked, and the boy again said no.

Finally he produced the boy's bamboo flute and asked if it was his and the boy smiled and said yes.

"Take it and blow for us."

The boy took his flute from the hand of the spirit and blew this song:

> Awful Spirit, undisputed
> Lord by night o'er this estate!
> Father warned me death awaited
> Men who ventured here so late;
> "Please, my son, please wait till morning!"
> Cried my mother. But her warning
> Wasted fell. For how was I to
> Lie awake and wait for dawn

While my flute in damp and dew
Lay forsaken and forlorn?

The spirits were delighted with the song and there was a general haw-haw-haw through their noses.

The leader of the spirits brought out two pots, one big and one small. Both pots were completely sealed.

"Take one of these," he said to the boy. He took the small one.

"When you reach home, call your mother and your father and break the pot in front of them." The boy thanked him.

"On your way home, if you hear *dum-dum* you must run into the bush; but if you hear *jam-jam* come back to the road."

On his way the boy heard *dum-dum* and ran into the bush. Then he heard *jam-jam* and came out again. He passed the seven rivers and the seven wilds and finally reached his father's compound. He called his father and his mother and broke the pot before them. Immediately the place was filled with every good thing: yellow metal, cloths and velvets, foods of all kinds, money, cows, goats and many other things of value.

The boy's mother filled a basket with gifts and sent to her husband's senior wife. But she was blind with envy and refused the gift. She did not see why she should be insulted with a meagre present when all she had to do was send her son to get the full quantity.

The next morning she called her son and said to him: "Bring your flute. We are going to the farm."

There was no work for them to do in the farm but they hung around until sunset. Then she said: "Let us go home." The boy picked up his flute but his mother hit him on the head. "Foolish boy," she said, "don't you know how to forget your flute?"

So the boy left his flute behind. They passed seven streams and seven wilds and finally reached their home.

"Now you go back for your flute!"

The boy cried and protested but his mother pushed him out and told him that the hut would not contain both of them until he had gone back to the farm and brought gifts from the spirits.

The boy passed the seven streams and seven wilds and came to the place where the spirits were bent in work.

"Mpf! mpf!" sniffed the boy in disgust. "I choke with the stench of spirits!"

The king of the spirits asked him what he came for.

"My mother sent me to get my flute. Mpf! mpf!"

"Will you recognize the flute of you see it?"

"What sort of question is that?" said the boy. "Who will not recognize his flute if he sees it? Mpf! mpf!"

The spirit then showed him a flute shining like yellow metal and the boy immediately said it was his.

"Take it and blow for us," said the spirit.

"I hope you have not been spitting into it," said the boy, wiping its mouth against his flank. Then he blew this song:

> King of Spirits he stinks
> > Mpf mpf
> Old Spirit he stinks
> > Mpf mpf
> Young Spirit he stinks
> > Mpf mpf

Mother Spirit she stinks
Mpf mpf
Father Spirit he stinks
Mph mpf

When he finished all the spirits were sullen. Then their leader brought out two pots, one big and one small. Before the word was out of his mouth the boy had pounced on the big one.

"When you reach home call your mother and father and break it before them. On your way if you hear *dum-dum*, run into the bush and if you hear *jam-jam* come out again."

Without stopping to thank the spirits the boy carried the pot and went away. He came to a certain place and heard *dum-dum*; he stayed on the road looking this way and that to see what it was. Then he heard *jam-jam* and went into the bush.

He passed the seven streams and seven wilds and reached home in the end. His mother who had been waiting for him outside their hut was happy when she saw the size of the pot.

"They said I should break it before my father and yourself," said the boy.

"What has your father got to do with it? Did he send you?"

She took the pot into her hut and shut the door. Then she filled in every crack in the wall so that nothing might escape to her husband's junior wife. When everything was ready she broke the pot. Leprosy, smallpox, yaws and worse diseases without names and every abomination filled the hut and killed the woman and all her children.

In the morning, as there was no sign of life in her hut, her husband pushed open the door, and peeped in. That peep was more than enough. He struggled with the things fighting to come out and eventually succeeded in shutting the door again. But by then a few of the diseases and abominations had escaped and spread in the world. But fortunately the worst of them—those without a name—remained in that hut. (235-39)

This story, which many will recognize as a variant of the widespread "Tale of the Kind and the Unkind Girls"[7] (#480 in the Aarne-Thompson tale type index[8]), does not appear to have much relevance to Ezeulu's tragedy until we examine its morphology and placement within in the novel. It will be recalled that the tale is introduced at the time Ezeulu is pondering whether to punish or forgive his people for failing to respond adequately to his imprisonment. After the tale is told, Ezeulu begins once again "to probe with the sensitiveness of a snail's horns the possibility of reconciliation or, if that was too much, of narrowing down the area of conflict" (240). But while he is considering the various alternatives before him, he suddenly hears the voice of his god:

> "Ta! Nwanu!" barked Ulu in his ear, as a spirit would in the ear of an impertinent human child. "Who told you that this was your own fight?"....I say who told you that this was your own fight which you could arrange to suit you? You want to save your friends who brought you palm wine he-he-he-he-he!....Beware you do not come between me and my victim or you may receive blows not meant for you!" (240-41)

After this, Ezeulu is no longer uncertain about his course of action. He views himself as "an arrow in the bow of his god" (241), a vehicle of divine retribution for the waywardness of his people. Even the most influential leaders of his clan cannot persuade him to change his mind about delaying the yam harvest. His people begin to suffer great hardships and deprivation, but he holds firm to this decision. It is only after one of his own sons dies, partly as a consequence of his vindictive obstinacy, that Ezeulu cracks under the strain and goes irretrievably mad. But by then the social and religious damage has been done. His people, to avoid starvation, have started taking offerings to the god of the Christians, who is said to have power to protect his followers from the anger of Ulu, Ezeulu's god, and thereafter most of the yams that are harvested in the village are harvested in the name of this new god. Ezeulu's perverse leadership thus results in the destruction of the very traditions that he, as chief priest, was supposed to defend and perpetuate.

The structural and thematic parallels between Ezeulu's story and our folktale may now be drawn more explicitly. In both narratives proper conduct is rewarded and improper conduct punished. The boy in the folktale who obeys the spirits of the yam-field and always tells the truth receives a pot "filled with every good thing"; his half-brother who disobeys and insults the spirits is given a pot containing horrible "diseases and abominations" that quickly kill him and his closest relatives. Similarly, Ezeulu prospers as a chief priest as long as he subordinates himself to Ulu, but he brings ruin upon himself and his kinsmen when he commits the unforgivable sin of interpreting his own will as his god's. The contrast provided by the binary repetition of opposite events in the folktale finds expression in the novel in the antithetical actions preceding and following Ezeulu's decision to upset the agricultural calendar—e.g., his performance and later nonperformance of the required rituals. It is therefore of utmost significance that the folktale is told at the precise moment that Ezeulu is trying to decide how to deal with people and that immediately after the recitation of the tale Ezeulu imagines he hears Ulu bark in his ear and tell him which course to take. The tale appears to have been deliberately inserted at this pivotal point in the novel as a commentary on previous and subsequent events, for it functions admirably as a paradigm of the entire novel, summarizing in schematic form the most relevant past action and foreshadowing the eventual downfall of the hero. Achebe could not have chosen a more appropriate tale to distil his message.

Additional proof that Achebe may have intended the tale as a gloss on Ezeulu's behavior can be found in at least two places. The action in the tale itself occurs on a farm that "was at the boundary between the land of men and the land of spirits," and it is human and spiritual interaction there that yields productive and then disastrous results. The most significant action in the novel takes place in the mind of Ezeulu, who as priest of Ulu is believed to be "half-man, half-spirit." At first his human and spiritual parts are in happy equilibrium, but later they come into conflict, ultimately tearing him apart. The analogy between the farm as demiworld and Ezeulu as demigod must have been obvious to Achebe.

There is also some evidence to suggest that Achebe, in his subtle way, may have been trying to alert the reader to make the connection between the folktale and Ezeulu's story. When Ezeulu receives the news that he is to be released from prison, he tells one of his kinsmen that he now intends to return home "to wrestle with my own people whose hand I know and who know my hand. I am going home to challenge all those who have been poking fingers into my face to come outside their gate and meet me in combat and whoever throws the other will strip him of his anklet" (221). His kinsman excitedly compares this to "the challenge of Eneke Ntulukpa to man, bird and beast" and breaks into "the taunting song with which the bird, Eneke once challenged the whole world" (221).[9] One doesn't know from reading the novel if this bird is at all related to the oft-mentioned proverbial "little bird, *nza*, who ate and drank and challenged his personal god to single combat,"[10] but even if it isn't, the image of Ezeulu as an ambitious wrestler[11] is established quite firmly in the reader's mind by Achebe's direct comparison of the old priest to Eneke Ntulukpa. The next time we hear of this world-challenging bird is just before the folktale is told. Ezeulu's children Nwafo and Obiageli are arguing over which tale their mother should tell. Obiageli suggests the tale of Onwuero, the beautiful maiden who married a fish.[12] Nwafo objects that "we have heard it too often" and is about to suggest another when Obiageli cuts in, saying, "All right. Tell us about Eneke Ntulukpa" (235). The mother, having "searched her memory for a while and found what she looked for," then proceeds to tell the tale quoted above. This is obviously not the tale of Eneke Ntulukpa, since it has nothing to do with a world-challenging bird, but rather, as demonstrated earlier, it is a paradigmatically symbolic redaction of the career of the career of Ezeulu, whose name has already been inextricably linked to that of the bird. It as if Achebe, eager for us to see the submerged parallels between the folktale and the novel, felt he had to hint, at least obliquely, that the tale had something to do with his priest-hero. This he did by making it appear that the mother was about to tell the story of Eneke Ntulukpa, a code name for Ezeulu. Indeed, the name of the bird stands almost as a title to the tale, forcing us to recognize the connection.

Achebe's sensitive handling of this tale in *Arrow of God* suggests that his art is far more subtle and sophisticated than it appears on the surface. And to this it should be added that some of his techniques appear to be more African than European. For example, his ability to utilize folktales as relevant social commentary in symbolic form is surely something he acquired at home, not abroad. Léopold Senghor once said, "The traditional African narrative is woven out of everyday events. In this it is a question neither of anecdotes nor of things 'taken from life.' All the events become images, and so acquire paradigmatic value and point beyond the moment."[13] Achebe, perhaps because he is a consummate *African* artist, transforms even seemingly trivial events in his novels into meaningful imagistic paradigms that point will beyond the moment.[14]

NOTES

1. See, e.g., the reviews of *Arrow of God* by Phoebe Adams, *Atlantic Monthly* 20 (December 1967): 150, and I.N.C. Aniebo, *Nigeria Magazine* 81 (June 1964): 150.

2. Review of *Arrow of God* by Ronald Christ, *New York Times Book Review*, December 17, 1967, 22.

3. Review by D.J. Enright, *New Statesman*, April 3, 1964, 523.

4. Robert Plant Armstrong, "The Characteristics and Comprehension of a National Literature—Nigeria," *Proceedings of a Conference on African Languages and Literatures Held at Northwestern University, April 28-30, 1966*, ed. Jack Berry et al ([Evanston, IL]: n.p., n.d.), 123.

5. For discussion of his use of proverbs in fiction, see my "The Palm-Oil with which Achebe's Words are Eaten," *African Literature Today* 1 (1968): 3-18, reprinted in this volume, and Austin J. Shelton, "The 'Palm-Oil' of Language: Proverbs in Chinua Achebe's Novels," *Modern Language Quarterly* 30, no. 1 (1969): 86-111. For discussion of his use of folktales in his novels, see Donald Weinstock and Cathy Ramadan, "Symbolic Structure in *Things Fall Apart*," *Critique* 11 (1968-69): 33-41, and John O. Jordan, "Culture Conflict and Social Change in Achebe's *Arrow of God*," *Critique* 13 (1971): 66-82.

6. All quotations are taken from Chinua Achebe's *Arrow of God* (London: Heinemann, 1964).

7. For a thorough historical-geographical study of this tale, see Warren E. Roberts, *The Tale of the Kind and the Unkind Girls Aa-Th 480 and Related Tales* (Berlin: De Gruyter, 1958).

8. Antti Aarne and Stith Thompson, *The Types of the Folktale: A Classification and Bibliography*. 2nd rev. (Helsinki: Academia Scientiarum Fennica, 1964).

9. I have not been able to find texts of this tale in published collections of Igbo folktales, but tales about a man or bird who defeats everyone in wrestling except his own *chi* (personal god) are quite common. See, e.g., Rems Nna Umeasiegbu, *The Way We Lived: Ibo Customs and Stories* (London: Heinemann Educational Books, 1969), 136-37, and Cyprian Ekwensi, *The Great Elephant Bird* (London: Nelson, 1965). Achebe himself includes such a tale in *Arrow of God*, 31-32.

Austin Shelton, in his article on Achebe's proverbs cited above, makes the following observation on Eneke Ńtùlùkpa:

The meaning here is not immediately apparent, but depends upon a juxtaposition of opposites: *énéké* is an abnoxious, inedible black spiny grasshopper, whereas *ńtūlūkpa* is a very tasty herb. Thus placing the two together creates a challenge for all people, who hate one and love the other. Nwodika's remark thus takes on an ironic tone, and can be applied to Ezeulu, who is represented as a priest of a powerful god, but widely disliked as a cantankerous person. In such a match as that proposed by Ezeulu, opponents would be happy to fight Ezeulu as a person, but would fear him as the agent of the god. (101-02)

10. This proverb is frequently used by Achebe. In *Arrow of God* it appears on page 17, in *Things Fall Apart* on page 26, and in *No Longer at Ease* on page 163.

11. For a discussion of the wrestler image in one of Achebe's earlier novels, see my essay on "The Palm-Oil with which Achebe's Words are Eaten" in this volume. Eldred Jones also mentions this image in his review of *Arrow of God* in the *Journal of Commonwealth Literature* 1 (September 1965): 176.

12. A version of this tale can be found in Ekwensi, *Great Elephant Bird*, 3-4.

13. Quoted in Janheinz Jahn, *Muntu* (London: Faber and Faber [1961]), 211.

14. I thought I had made a persuasive point in this essay about Achebe's subtle but hitherto unnoticed artistry in placing a variant of the tale of the kind and the unkind girls in a significant paradigmatic position in his narrative until I read the second edition of *Arrow of God* (London: Heinemann, 1974) and discovered that he, in revising the novel, had deleted this tale altogether. This rendered my argument moot and me mute. He had removed my sacred yam!

AN AFRICAN PARABLE

Chinua Achebe's fourth novel, *A Man of the People*, details the rise and demise of Chief the Honourable Dr. M.A. Nanga, M.P., L.L.D., a corrupt, wheeling-dealing, opportunistic semi-literate who elbows his way to a lucrative ministerial post in the Government of an unnamed African country, uses his power and newly acquired wealth to ensure his re-election, and is shaken from his lofty, befouled perch only when a group of idealistic young military officers topples the "fat-dripping, gummy eat-and-let-eat regime"[1] by launching a sudden *coup d'état*. The novel, published just nine days after the first military coup in Nigeria, has been hailed by many reviewers as a "prophetic" work,[2] one in which Achebe predicted with uncanny accuracy the end of his country's First Republic.

Certainly the accuracy of Achebe's vision cannot be disputed. It was a rather eerie experience to read the last chapter of this novel in the early months of 1966 when Achebe's descriptions of fictional events seemed to correspond so closely to newspaper accounts of what was happening in Nigeria. For example, the coup was said to have been touched off by post-election turmoil:

> What happened was simply that unruly mobs and private armies having tasted blood and power during the election had got out of hand and ruined their

masters and employers (162)....The rampaging bands of election thugs had caused so much unrest and dislocation that our young Army officers seized the opportunity to take over. (165)

The aftermath of the fictional coup corresponded with reality too.

> ...the military regime had just abolished all political parties in the country and announced they would remain abolished until the situation became stabilized once again. They had at the same time announced the impending trial of all public servants who had enriched themselves by defrauding the state. The figure was said to be in the order of fifteen million pounds.
>
> Overnight everyone began to shake their heads at the excesses of the last regime, at its graft, oppression and corrupt government: newspapers, the radio, the hitherto silent intellectuals and civil servants—everybody said what a terrible lot; and it became public opinion the next morning. (166)

It was passages such as these that made Achebe appear a seer.

Yet I would like to argue that despite these seemingly clairvoyant passages, *A Man of the People* is not and was not meant to be a prophetic novel. Indeed, given the circumstances in Nigeria during the time Achebe was writing, *A Man of the People* should be recognized as a devastating satire in which Achebe heaped scorn on independent Africa by picturing one part of it just as it was. I believe Achebe ended the novel with a military coup in order to enlarge the picture to include Nigeria's neighbors, several of which had experienced coups. By universalizing the story in this way Achebe could suggest to his countrymen that what had happened in other unstable independent African countries might easily have happened in Nigeria too. The coup was meant as an African parable, not a Nigerian prophecy.

The manuscript of *A Man of the People* was submitted to Achebe's publisher in February 1965,[3] and the book was published in London eleven months later on January 24, 1966. Achebe's third novel, *Arrow of God*, had been submitted to this publisher in February 1963[4] and had been published on March 3, 1964. Since it is unlikely that Achebe began *A Man of the People* until he had completed *Arrow of God*, it is probably safe to assume that the later novel was written some time between February 1963 and February 1965. There is evidence that he was at work on the novel early in 1964.[5] During this period he was also working as Director of External Broadcasting for the Nigerian Broadcasting Company, a job that would have kept him abreast of the latest news.

Politics dominated the news in Nigeria at this time. By February 1963 the seven-month state of emergency in the Western region had ended, and Chief Obafemi Awolowo and twenty-nine others had been arrested and charged with conspiring to overthrow the Federal Government by force. In September 1963 Awolowo and nineteen others were convicted of treasonable felony and imprisoned. On October 1, 1963 Nigeria became a Federal Republic. Then, because of the doubtful accuracy of the official results of the 1962 census, which were never publicly released, a new census was taken in November 1963. Since regional representation in the Federal Government was to be determined by the results of this census, politicians were eager that every one of their constituents be counted at least once. When the bloated preliminary results of the census were released in February 1964, they were rejected by the Eastern and Midwestern Regions and protest demonstrations were held. On March 25, 1964, an editorial in the Lagos *Daily Times* warned that "The Federal Republic of Nigeria faces the grave danger of disintegration" because of the census crisis.

Worse times were yet to come. A Federal Election was due before the year was out, and political campaigning gradually grew more and more vicious. One observer reported that "Countless acts of political violence and thuggery occurred almost daily throughout the campaign, but notably increased during the last few weeks."[6] Electioneering irregularities were so frequent and widespread that one of the major political parties, the United Progressive Grand Alliance, announced that it would boycott the elections. This precipitated another crisis, for President Nnamdi Azikiwe, judging the election invalid, refused to call upon the victorious Prime Minister Abubakar Tafewa Balewa to form a new Government. For five days the country teetered on the brink of political chaos. On January 4, 1965, Azikiwe and Balewa finally reached a compromise and Azikiwe announced to the country that Balewa would form a "broadly-based national Government." By-elections were to be held in constituencies where elections had been totally boycotted, and allegations of fraud and intimidation were to be reviewed by the courts.

It should be remembered that Achebe's publisher received the manuscript of *A Man of the People* one month after this period of crisis and compromise. Achebe must have been working on the last chapters of the novel, which dramatize the turbulence and violence of an election campaign, during the months just preceding the Nigerian election. He was obviously drawing much of his inspiration from daily news reports. The last pages of the novel, those that describe the coup, may have been written very close to the time of the five-day crisis following the election. What relevance this has to my argument I shall attempt to demonstrate in a moment.

First, however, let us look at the role of the Nigerian military before, during, and immediately after the 1964 election campaign. Before the campaign they had been used to restore order both at home and abroad. In December 1960, Nigerian troops had been sent to the newly independent Republic of the Congo (Leopoldville) to help United Nations forces keep order, and in April 1964, they had been dispatched to Tanganyika to relieve British troops who had put down a Tanganyikan Army mutiny. In Nigeria, Army troops had quelled a Tiv riot in 1960 and had maintained order in the Western region during the 1962 state of emergency. During the 1964 election campaign they were ordered to put down another Tiv riot and did so at the cost of 700 lives.[7] Throughout the campaign large squads of riot police were deployed to battle the thugs and hooligans hired by political candidates to terrorize their opposition. During the post-election crisis, troops were called out to safeguard the residences of Azikiwe and Balewa in Lagos and the cell of Awolowo in Calabar. Thus, before, during, and after the 1964 election campaign the Nigerian Army played a prominent role as a peacekeeping force in Nigeria and abroad.

During this same period armies in many other African countries had acted as a disruptive force. In 1963 there were military coups in Togo, Congo-Brazzaville, and Dahomey, and a military plot to assassinate President Tubman was uncovered in Liberia. In 1964 there were army mutinies in Tanganyika, Uganda, and Kenya, a revolution in Zanzibar, attempted coups in Gabon and Niger, and continued confusion and disorder in Congo-Leopoldville. On February 21, 1964, an editorial in the Lagos *Daily Times* deplored the use of bullets instead of ballots in French West Africa, and four days later the same paper remarked that "The constant cataclysms which have recently disrupted peace and order in Africa have produced a dangerous trend towards replacing the growing pattern of parliamentary rule with military juntas." Notice that at this time the trend toward military coups was regarded as "dangerous."

By the end of the year the mood of the country had changed considerably. The electioneering abuses, the breakdown of law and order, the numerous crises and compromises had produced a general distrust of politicians and disillusionment with democratic processes of government. In a nationwide broadcast on December 10, 1964, President Azikiwe himself predicted the end of democracy in Nigeria:

> I have one advice to give to our politicians; if they have decided to destroy our national unity, then they should summon a roundtable conference to decide how our national assets should be divided, before they seal their doom by satisfying their lust for office.... Should politicians not heed this warning, then I will venture a prediction that the experience of the Democratic Republic of the Congo (Leopoldville) will be child's play if it ever comes to our turn to play such a tragic role.[8]

After the elections Azikiwe lamented that

> People in this country now evince a mood of weariness and frustration that is a sad contrast to the elation and confidence with which we ushered in independence barely four years ago. Far from presenting a unified front, our country now shows a pattern of disintegration.[9]

The people themselves expressed their discontent with politicians in no uncertain terms. During the election crisis Lazarus Okeke wrote a letter to the *Daily Times* on January 1, 1965 asserting that

> no well-wisher of Nigeria would recommend a blow-up of the country just because certain politicians cannot have their demand [*sic*] met. The welfare of the people as a nation definitely superceeds [*sic*] in importance the various vain and sectional claims of erring politicians.

An unsigned article in the Lagos *Sunday Express* of January 1, 1965 went a step further:

> Democracy has bred corruption in our society on a scale hitherto unknown in human history.
>
> Nigeria needs a strong man with a strong hand. By this I mean, that Nigeria needs to be disciplined. Nigeria needs too to be drilled.
>
> The leadership we want is the leadership of a benevolent dictator who gets things done, not that of "democratic administrators" who drag their feet.

It is clear that a number of Nigerians would have welcomed a military coup in January 1965. Indeed, several days after Azikiwe and Balewa had worked out their compromise, one disgruntled Easterner writing in Enugu's *Nigerian Outlook* on January 16th expressed regret that the compromise had not been forestalled by military intervention:

> If civil strife had broken out on December 30, the armed forces might have gone into action as a last resort, and the President and Prime Minister might never have had an opportunity for negotiations.

If further evidence is required to prove that many Nigerians had entertained the notion of a military coup during the election crisis, one need only turn to the Lagos *Sunday Times* of February 28, 1965, and read the text of an interview with Major-General Aguiyi-Ironsi who on February 15th of that year had been appointed the first Nigerian Commander of the Nigerian Army.[10] The interviewer tried to draw out Aguiyi-Ironsi's views on the desirability of military intervention in state affairs in times of political turmoil, but the Major-General carefully sidestepped the questions.

Had you been the Officer Commanding the Nigerian Army during the constitutional crisis resulting from the Federal elections last December, what would you have done?

Ironsi: You mean, militarily, or what?

Both militarily or otherwise.

Ironsi: I think what we should get clear is that the crisis was a political crisis....It did not require military action....It was a political thing, solved in a political way.

Tell me, if there is a war, would you fight—out of conviction or would you carry out the orders of the government regardless as to which side is right or wrong?

Ironsi: ....I think it is true to say that any Army goes to war for justification....The job of the Army is to defend the country, no questions asked.

Now suppose it is an internal war...

Ironsi: ...I don't know what you are trying to get at....Whatever you have in mind, THE ARMY SUPPORTS THE GOVERNMENT THAT IS!

If you were General Mobutu, how would you effect a solution [to the Congo impasse]?

Ironsi: I'm not. I should wait until I'm confronted with such a situation.

That such questions could be asked and such cautious answers given eight weeks after the crisis suggests that the idea of a military resolution to Nigeria's political problems had occurred to many Nigerians other than Achebe and that it was still quite a live issue.

Seen in this light, Achebe's "prophecy" appears much less prophetic. He had only foreseen what many others, including President Azikiwe, had foreseen or had hoped to see. A military coup was not necessarily "inevitable" in 1964-65, but it was regarded by a number of intelligent observers[11] as one of the few options left for a nation in the brink of anarchy. In a later interview Achebe put it this way:

> ...Things had got to such a point politically that there was no other answer—no way you could resolve this impasse politically. The political machine had been so abused that whichever way you pressed it, it produced the same results; and therefore another force had to come in. Now when I was writing *A Man of the People* it wasn't clear to me that this was going to be necessarily a military intervention. It could easily have been civil war, which in fact it very nearly was in Nigeria.[12]

Achebe chose a military coup as the most appropriate ending for his story and eleven months later Nigeria happened to make the same choice to close out one of the ugliest chapters in its history.

To interpret the military coup in *A Man of the People* as a prophecy is to suggest that Achebe meant the novel to relate only to Nigeria. This, I think, is a mistake. While it is evident that the novel owes much to what Achebe had observed in his own country, many of the events described had happened and were happening in other independent African countries. By ending with a coup, an event anticipated yet unknown in Nigeria but familiar elsewhere in Africa, Achebe added a dimension of universality to his story. It was no longer merely a satire on Nigeria but a satire on the rest of independent Africa as well. If the coup had a special meaning for Nigeria in the mid-sixties, it also contained a relevant moral for other emerging African nations wracked by internal political upheavals. The ending was meant to be true to Africa and merely truthful about Nigeria. The coup was an African parable, not a Nigerian prophecy.

One of the most remarkable features of Achebe's fiction is that it never fails to transcend the local and particular and enter realms of universal significance. Achebe once said,

> After all the novelist's duty is not to beat this morning's headline in topicality, it is to explore *in depth* the human condition. In Africa he cannot perform this task unless he has a proper sense of history.[13]

The ending of *A Man of the People* reveals that Achebe has a proper sense of contemporary African history.

NOTES

1. Chinua Achebe, *A Man of the People* (London: Heinemann, 1966), 167. All quotations from the novel are taken from this edition.

2. See, e.g., Robert Green, *Nation*, April 18, 1966, 465-66; D.A.N. Jones, *New Statesman*, January 28, 1966, 132-33; *Times Literary Supplement*, February 3, 1966, 77; *Time*, August 19, 1966, 80.

3. Letter to Bernth Lindfors from W. Roger Smith of William Heinemann Ltd., London.

4. Ibid.

5. Chinua Achebe, "The Role of the Writer in a New Nation," *Nigeria Magazine* 81 (June 1964): 158. In an interview published in *Palaver: Interviews with Five African Writers in Texas*, ed. Bernth Lindfors, Ian Munro, Richard Priebe, and Reinhard Sander (Austin: African and Afro-American Research Institute, University of Texas at Austin, 1972), 11, and reprinted in this volume, Achebe stated that

the novel "was completed at least two years before January 1966. It was completed in '64." However, the fact that it was not submitted to Heinemann until February 1965 suggests that he continued to revise and polish the manuscript during the months of political unrest and crisis in Nigeria.

6. Richard Harris, "Nigeria: Crisis and Compromise," *Africa Report* 10, no. 2 (March 1965): 27.

7. Billy Dudley gives this figure in "Violence in Nigerian Politics," *Transition* 5, no. 21 (1965): 22.

8. *Nigerian Outlook*, December 11, 1964, 3.

9. *Nigerian Outlook*, January 4, 1965, 4.

10. It is perhaps significant and—considering what happened in January 1966—certainly ironic that during the election crisis Aguiyi-Ironsi led the troops that guarded Prime Minister Balewa's house.

11. See, e.g., Billy Dudley, "Violence in Nigerian Politics," 33.

12. *Cultural Events in Africa* 28 (March 1967): ii.

13. "The Role of the Writer in a New Nation," 157.

ACHEBE'S FOLLOWERS

Chinua Achebe's influence on later Nigerian novelists has been profound. He has made an especially powerful impression upon young Igbo writers who first became acquainted with his works as high school or university students. By the early 1960s many educational institutions in West Africa had adopted his first novel as a prescribed text in English courses, leading the *Times Literary Supplement* to suggest in 1965 that

> Already *Things Fall Apart* is probably as big a factor in the formation of a young West African's picture of his past, and of his relation to it, as any of the still rather distorted teachings of the pulpit and the primary school.[1]

Young Igbo readers who had grown up in villages and cities resembling those described in Achebe's novels were very excited to find their own world reflected in fiction; when they themselves turned to writing stories and novels, they naturally tried to emulate what Achebe had done. By 1968 half a dozen new Igbo novelists—Nkem Nwankwo, Elechi Amadi, Flora Nwapa, E.C.C. Uzodinma, John Munonye, Clement Agunwa—had broken into print, and it was no longer premature to generalize about a "School of Achebe" in Nigerian fiction.

The master's influence was apparent in both theme and technique. Only one of the six writers set his novel in a city. The rest dealt with traditional Igbo society, three of them describing it as it was before the coming of the white man. Three, including the urban novelist, concerned themselves with aspects of the conflict between old and new values in Igboland, Achebe's favorite subject. And all six attempted to simulate vernacular expression by incorporating into dialogue and narration many of the proverbs, idioms, and metaphors translated from their mother tongue. They were not slavish imitators. Each contributed something personal and unique to Nigerian fiction. But it is quite clear that they would not have written what they did or as they did had it not been for Achebe's example. Let us take a look at the fiction produced by these writers and by two older Igbo novelists, Onuora Nzekwu and Chukwuemeka Ike, who have also been influenced to some degree by Achebe.

THE SCHOOL OF ACHEBE

It is perhaps best to begin with the first and most original of Achebe's followers—Nkem Nwankwo, whose comic first novel *Danda*[2] was published in September 1964. A 1962 graduate of University College Ibadan, Nwankwo began as a playwright and short story writer. In 1960, when he was a first year student at the university, he won second prize in a drama competition organized by *Encounter* to mark Nigeria's independence.[3] Two years later he was awarded second prize in *Drum*'s tenth annual short story contest,[4] and in 1963 he published a collection of connected stories as a children's book, *Tales out of School*.[5] He has said that throughout his university career he was "writing voraciously,"[6] turning out not only plays and short stories but the early chapters of *Danda* as well.[7]

The novel is named after its picaresque hero, a gay, high-spirited "akalogholi" (ne'er-do-well) who, dressed in a cloak adorned with small bronze bells, jingles from one place to another in his village, dancing, singing, drinking, flirting with married and unmarried women, and entertaining crowds of people with his antics and quips. Danda's buffoonery endears him to everyone except a few stuffy elders and his father, Araba. A rich, grumpy old man who feels that he has suffered many disappointments in life, Araba wants Danda, his greatest disappointment, to bring him honor, happiness, and grandchildren in his old age. But Danda finds it difficult to change his frivolous ways and brings Araba only embarrassment and shame. The ill-tempered father's unsuccessful attempts to reform his impish, unproductive son provide most of the comic thrust in the novel.

Unfortunately, the plot is almost as directionless as its hero. Much happens but there is little pattern or sequence to the action. As episode follows episode, attention is gradually drawn away from Danda to Araba, who then dominates the last half of the book. The meandering stream of comic episodes terminates rather abruptly in Araba's death.

Reading this novel one is immediately struck by how different it is from Achebe's early works. It has neither the high moral seriousness nor the balanced artistry that one associates with *Things Fall Apart* and *No Longer at Ease*. Besides being a rather lighthearted, loose-jointed comedy, it is set in a world that Achebe only touches upon briefly in his second novel. This is the traditional village world of the mid-twentieth century. Araba and his clansmen live in a tiny village in the remote Igbo hinterland. They occasionally see automobiles (which they term "land-boats") and white missionaries, they send their children to mission schools, and they have heard travelers tell tales of life in the big cities, but they remain largely ignorant of Western civilization and culture. The little they know about the outside world has been learned from young clansmen who have returned home after working in the city. Like Obi Okonkwo's parents, indeed like Okonkwo himself, they are virtually living in another century.

So though they inhabit a different time and place and are involved in comedy rather than tragedy, Nwankwo's characters experience many of the same difficulties as the villagers in Achebe's novels. For example, there are complaints voiced about the white man ("The white man likes to throw sand in our eyes," 128), and Araba, like Okonkwo, is infuriated when missionaries convert his worthless son to Christianity. Araba has another son who works in the city, but when Araba, like Isaac in *No Longer at Ease*, tries to arrange a marriage for his Westernized son, the boy, like Obi, disappoints him by resisting the plan and later rejecting the girl. Danda's father is thus as much a victim of culture conflict as the fathers we find in Achebe's novels.

Nwankwo's greatest debt to Achebe, however, is not in subject matter but in style. Here is an example of what he does with the English language to simulate African vernacular expression:

> The scorch season was dying. The happiest time of the year, the season for feasts, when men and women laughed with all their teeth and little boys, their mouths oily oily, ran about the lanes blowing the crops of chicken to make balloons. (81)

Expressions such as "season was dying," "laughed with all their teeth," and "mouths oily oily" have been translated verbatim from Igbo.[8]

Nwankwo also puts Igbo proverbs and idiomatic expressions into dialogue. Several elders arguing about Danda's character speak as follows:

> "No man can hold on to what Danda says. What Danda says has neither head nor tail."

There was laughter.

"It does not amuse me!" roared the Ikolo man. "It is long since Danda began pouring sand into our eyes."....

"Danda springs from a big obi," said Idengeli... ."When a rich man's son breaks the golden pot his father's barn will pay. " (29-30)

Although both Nwankwo and Achebe strive to simulate Igbo expression, their styles differ in certain respects. Nwankwo cannot match Achebe's skill in weaving traditional verbal lore into the fabric of narrative. Achebe, in his first two novels, makes an attempt to explain the meaning or significance of the untranslated Igbo words he uses, but Nwankwo, who employs a larger Igbo vocabulary, does not pause to interpret words for the reader. Sometimes the reader is left to decipher passages such as the following:

The izaga dance is a perilous one, perilous for the dancer. For there are always among the spectators some malevolent dibias who would want to try out the power of a new ogwu by pulling the izaga down. To counter the nsi the izaga needed to be as strong as dried wood. (22)

"I used to think it was agwu but I don't think so now....It is my misfortune....I have a weak Ikenga, I think..."

Okelekwu thought: "Has he a weak Ikenga?... And there is his large barn and he is an ozo and has ten women. Has he a weak Ikenga?" But aloud he said: "One's chi brings one so many troubles..."

"Why should my chi bring an akalogholi into my compound? Have I committed an alu?" (33)

To help the reader Nwankwo adds a glossary at the end of the book. This glossary helps Nwankwo too for it frees him from the responsibility of providing anthropological information in the narrative, information that would slow down the pace of the novel. *Danda*, a comic novel, requires a brisk pace and Nwankwo's vernacular style helps to furnish it. Achebe's vernacular style yields a slower pace, a space more appropriate for his stately, gradually overwhelming tragedies. Nevertheless, it is clear that Nwankwo learned a great deal from Achebe's pioneering efforts to Africanize English prose.[9]

Nwankwo's originality lies in his wit, zany imagination, and deft characterization. He has a keen sense of the ridiculous that greatly enlivens his depiction of individuals and events. Danda and Araba are brilliant comic creations, and lesser figures are etched in swift, sure caricature. Here, for instance, are two capsule character sketches:

> He was a burly figure cushioned with fat and carrying a barrel of a belly like a distinguished burden. Below belly a small but rich cloth draped his extensive waist. (29)
>
> He was a little gnome of a man with small, sharp eyes and a dry, parched face. His neck was thin, leathery and bent permanently sideways so that he walked like a crab. (119)

Writing like this makes *Danda* lively reading. Although the structure of the novel remains loose at the seams, the narrative has enough vitality to compensate for lack of sure direction. Nwankwo's agile sense of humor makes him one of the most original and amusing pupils in the School of Achebe.

Elechi Amadi's talents are of a different order. A sober, serious-minded author, he writes with a calm detachment and warm human sympathy that are very reminiscent of Achebe. His fiction is not completely solemn, but the quiet dignity of his humor contrasts sharply with Nwankwo's boisterous laughter in *Danda*. He focuses on the past, describing in lavish detail the character of traditional Igbo village life before the coming of the white man. He is not interested in culture conflict but rather in personal conflicts, social tensions, and fateful events that disrupt the routine of everyday life in a well-ordered pre-colonial African society. He is essentially a historian reconstructing a way of life that has now all but disappeared.

His novel *The Concubine*[10] tells the story of Ihuoma, an extraordinarily beautiful young woman plagued by bad luck. She is only twenty-one years old when her husband dies of "lock-chest" after suffering serious injuries in a wrestling bout with an unfriendly neighbor, Madume. She is left with three small children. Madume, who wants to marry her, continually pesters her with his attentions until he is blinded by a spitting cobra. Later, in despair, he hangs himself. An attractive young bachelor named Ekwueme then falls in love with her and proposes marriage. Although she is strongly attracted to him, she refuses, recognizing she would shame herself in the eyes of the clan by taking as her second husband an unmarried man who, as a child, had been betrothed to another woman. Ekwueme, realizing he cannot change her mind, reluctantly marries his "fiancée," but their marriage is not a happy one. To win his affections from Ihuoma, Ekwueme's wife dopes him with a love potion that unfortunately turns him into a lunatic. Only Ihuoma's presence and the ministrations of a local witchdoctor can restore him to sanity. When he recovers, he divorces his wife and persuades Ihuoma to consent to marriage. The witchdoctor, however, advises them not to marry for he has divined that Ihuoma is an incarnated sea goddess and the favorite wife of the Sea-King, who will destroy any mortal to makes love to her. Ikwueme, still intent on marrying her, tries to propitiate the Sea-King and is killed in a freak accident.

It is not until the closing chapters of the novel that we learn Ihuoma is a *femme fatale*, and by then we have been so convinced by Amadi's skilful evocation of Igbo traditional life that we can easily suspend our disbelief in the Sea-King's supernatural intervention into human affairs. Amadi is describing a world governed by its own immutable cosmological laws, a world in which the man who struggles against his fate and wrestles with his gods will inevitably be crushed. One is reminded of Ezeulu in *Arrow of God*, but as Margaret Laurence has perceptively remarked,

> Amadi goes even further than Chinua Achebe in portraying traditional religious concepts, for the Ibo society about which Achebe is writing was already affected and altered by life-views dissimilar to its own. Amadi's Ibo villages in *The Concubine* represent a society which has not yet fallen prey to self-doubts. Its gods could be cruel, but they were real, and they affected the lives of mortals in real and inexplicable ways.[11]

It is true that Amadi goes a step deeper into the Igbo past than Achebe, but it is unlikely that he would have gone so far without the inspiration and guidance he found in Achebe's first three novels. There are many similarities in substance and style between *The Concubine* and Achebe's early writings that point to the impact of the latter on the former. As a woman contracted to a god, Ihuoma is not unlike Clara, Obi's *osu* fiancée in *No Longer at Ease*. Madume, the short-tempered wrestler who hangs himself in despair, bears some resemblance to Okonkwo, and Ekwueme in his madness and passionate pride is at moments very like Ezeulu. Moreover, Amadi's leisurely descriptions of marriage and funeral customs, religious rituals, even mundane domestic arts such as soup making, appear to owe a great deal to Achebe's almost nostalgic recreations of Igbo village life. Also, the central religious question posed by the novel—how obedient must a man be to his gods?—is answered in a very similar fashion in *Arrow of God*. These are not small details, and taken together they give clear evidence of Achebe's enormous influence on Amadi.

This influence is even more apparent in Amadi's style. Amadi is neither as flamboyant as Nwankwo nor as consistent as Achebe in Africanizing his style, but he does employ many of the techniques that Achebe first popularized. Take, for example, his use of proverbs in narration and dialogue:

> The normal period of negotiations was a year, but Wigwe had rushed things. Each time Wagbara pointed out that a hen cannot lay eggs and hatch them on the same day, Wigwe countered by saying that the slow-footed always fail in battle. (168)
>
> "Listen, my son, you must not be like the caterpillar that holds fast to tree branches when small but loses its grip and falls to its death when much older. So far you have showed all signs of growing into a sensible young man. If at this critical stage you turn into a fool, it will be most unfortunate. I do not say there is anything wrong with Ihuoma. She is a good young woman, but nevertheless a wrong choice for you. She has three children. She is looking after her late husband's compound. Her allegiance to you would take second place. Remember that a hen cannot scratch for food with her two legs simultaneously." (139)

Like Achebe in *Things Fall Apart*, Amadi is sometimes quite self-conscious about using proverbs. He deliberately calls attention to them, making sure the reader understands they are proverbs.

> "The old men say that death is a bad reaper; it is not always after the ripe fruit." (28)
> "There is a saying that every mother thinks her child is a leopard for strength." (29)

> "As I think the parable says, a diseased village is a
> good village to a medicine man." (108)
> "As the saying goes, one cannot learn to be left-
> handed in old age." (126)

He also labors to explain unfamiliar Igbo words:

> She could hear the sound of oduma (a dance employ-
> ing a xylophone) coming from Omigwe, the next
> village. (16)
> "Ihuoma, are your yams dry enough to be tied into
> ekwes?" (An ekwe is a vertical column with yams
> dexterously tied along it.) (102)
> It was a loose surrounding fence made from climbers,
> but anyone could tell it was impregnated with
> "ogbara"—a charm whose peculiar quality was to
> cause persistent rashes on the skins of trespass-
> ers. (211)

These asides to the reader are distracting, just as they were
in Achebe's early fiction. However, Amadi quickly learned
to avoid them, as Achebe did, in his later works. His second
novel *The Great Ponds* (London: Heinemann, 1969) shows
greater finesse in conveying information about traditional
Igbo society.[12]

Competent as Amadi's fiction is, it does not have the
profundity or resonance of Achebe's. *The Concubine* is a story
very well told, but it is little more than that. It lacks the
symbolic dimension of Achebe's works. Nevertheless, next
to *Danda*, it ranks as one of the finest Igbo novels and marks
Amadi as one of the most gifted of Achebe's followers.

Flora Nwapa's first novel *Efuru*[13] is a far less accomplished
work. Like *The Concubine*, it concerns a heroine who is bound
to a deity—this time a lake goddess—but it does not have
the drama and technical assurance of Amadi's narrative.
Efuru, like Ihuoma, is a beautiful young woman in distress.

Her troubles begin when she marries a worthless man who deserts her for another woman. Then her only child dies. She remarries but never conceives another child, so her new husband, fearing she is barren, begins to court other women. After six years Efuru's second marriage breaks up and she returns to her father's home. Her goddess, we discover, is also beautiful but barren.

Nwapa tells this melancholy story in a lifeless monotone that robs it of all life and color. For example, she introduces Efuru as follows:

> Efuru was her name. She was a remarkable woman. It was not only that she came from a distinguished family. She was distinguished herself. Her husband was not known and people wondered why she married him. (1)

A more skillful writer would have been careful to avoid such a succession of short, flat statements and so many repetitions of "was." The story is also made boring by Nwapa's tendency to state too much and dramatize too little. She tells readers what to think of her characters instead of letting readers form their own impressions by observing the characters in action. When her characters do act, they say and do things of little importance. Every chapter is littered with trivia, the detritus of an inexperienced novelist.

The few critics who admire *Efuru* point out that it takes the reader into an African woman's world.[14] Certainly this is true. Nwapa has us witness a female circumcision, two childbirths, native medical practices, beauty treatments, and various homely domestic activities. The dialogue seldom rises above the level of women's gossip. Perhaps a male writer would not have been able to describe an Igbo woman's world so faithfully,[15] but Nwapa's problem is that she cannot move beyond sheer documentation of her society into meaningful interpretation of it. Her story seems pointless and inconsequential, merely a long, rambling succession of insignificant events.

Although Nwapa is not a very skilful imitator, she still shows unmistakable signs of having been influenced by Achebe's novels. She sets her story in a traditional Igbo village that has had little contact with the white man but has nevertheless begun to feel some of the effects of Westernization. Mission schools are commonplace and Christianity is already disrupting village life. One character complains:

> The world is bad. In my youth, there was no stealing. If you stole you were sold as a slave. If your property was stolen, you simply went to one of the idols and prayed him to visit the thief. Before two or three days, you recovered your property. But these Church-goers have spoilt everything. They tell us our gods have no power, so our people continue to steal. (223)

Nwapa, however, does not sustain her attacks on Western institutions. Indeed, she welcomes some of the changes brought by the white man, such as modern medicine. Characters who are healed by a London-trained physician say, "these white people are great" (126). Moreover, Nwapa does not blame white men or their institutions for her heroine's unhappiness. Efuru is not a victim of culture conflict, as are most of Achebe's heroes. But she does reside in much the same world as Okonkwo and Ezeulu. Nwapa's evocation of this world no doubt owes a great deal to Achebe.

The debt is most obvious in her style. Though she employs fewer proverbs than Achebe, she frequently translates colorful Igbo idiomatic expressions into English:

> "I nagged and nagged and when it was too much and I did not want any quarrel, I put my mouth in a bag and sewed it up. I don't want to be accused of being a 'male woman.'" (129)

"You wanted to be called a good wife, good wife
when you were eating sand, good wife when you were
eating nails." (96-97)
"You know what, I was nearly robbed of all my money
in Onicha market. The god of my fathers is awake."
(139)
"You are only a child of yesterday." (104)

Thus, like Nwankwo and Amadi, Nwapa creates an African
vernacular style similar to Achebe's. She is not the master's
most talented pupil, but she nonetheless belongs in his
school.

Perhaps the least talented of Achebe's followers is E.C.C.
Uzodinma, whose first novel *Our Dead Speak*[16] was published
in 1967. The novel, probably intended for use in secondary schools,[17] begins as a story about a feud between two
Igbo villages untouched by Western civilization, but when a
leading warrior in one of the villages dies mysteriously, the
focus abruptly shifts from the feud to the hunt for his killer,
and the novel degenerates into a murder mystery. It ends, of
course, with the feud resolved and the mystery solved, but
all along the way Uzodinma has trouble bringing the separate strands of his story together and tying off loose ends of
irrelevant local lore. As a consequence, the novel takes too
many needless turns and loses direction. Uzodinma's inept
craftsmanship is not at all suggestive of Achebe's coherent,
purposeful artistry.

In content, however, there are many points of similar-
ity between *Our Dead Speak* and Achebe's novels set in
traditional society. Dike, Uzodinma's warrior hero, bears a
striking resemblance to both Okonkwo and Akukalia, the
excessively headstrong warrior in *Arrow of God*. The scenes in
which Dike is appointed by his clan to carry a threat of war
to a neighboring village and in which he is received as a mes-
senger by leaders of the enemy village appear to be modeled
on similar scenes in *Things Fall Apart* and *Arrow of God*.

Moreover, when war breaks out between the two villages, the battles are very brief and minimally bloody, just as they were in the days of Okonkwo and Ezeulu. Many other important events in the novel—the arrival of locusts, the masquerade, the native court trial, the consultation of the "oracle of the hills"—have close parallels in Achebe's two novels set in rural communities.

Uzodinma also makes frequent use of Igbo proverbs, but he does not handle them as skillfully as Achebe. Often they seem superfluous instead of functional. One example will suffice:

> Chigbo was lucky to escape, and he did not try to hide the fact that he was afraid of something. And if he felt such anxiety then he must be guilty of a yet undiscovered offence. For the toad never runs in broad daylight for nothing. On the other hand, Ogbuefi Ebie might have noticed that his visitors were suspicious of Chigbo, but Chigbo himself might not have done so, for the dancer never sees his own back.
>
> "I feel Chigbo knows a little bit more than he cares to tell," Odia said.
>
> "That is the point. And I feel something ought to be done, because if you leave the mouth alone it will seal up," Ilechi argued. (108-09)

Uzodinma appears to use Igbo proverbs merely to add local color to his narrative. He has not learned to employ them with Achebe's precision and subtlety.

One element of *Our Dead Speak* that owes nothing to Achebe is the murder mystery. This may have been inspired by Uzodinma's reading of popular fiction, school readers, or the novels of Cyprian Ekwensi. Whatever the source of inspiration, Uzodinma's originality lies in adapting the whodunit formula to a completely traditional African setting. To accomplish this, he unfortunately has to sacrifice his most promising character, Dike, early in the story. After Dike's death Uzodinma's plot begins to meander erratically, because there is no other character large enough to dominate the action and unify all the various narrative threads. One wishes Uzodinma had learned from Achebe how to build a novel around a strong, well-defined hero.

John Munonye is another Igbo novelist who has been greatly influenced by Achebe's fictional matter but has not been able to match his polished fictional manner. Munonye's first novel *The Only Son*[18] tells of changes in the relationship between a widow, Chiako, and her only son, Nnanna. During Nnanna's boyhood, mother and son are quite close, but as he grows older he begins to pull away from her. The rift widens when he enrages her by sneaking off to attend a mission school. In the end Chiaku remarries and Nnanna goes off to another village to work for an Irish priest.

In dramatizing the tensions between Chiaku and Nnanna, Munonye sometimes fails to provide sufficient information about the different forces playing upon mother and son. Years pass rapidly, attitudes change abruptly, and important events are not described in adequate detail. As a consequence, it is not always easy to understand why characters behave as they do or to predict how they will behave in a later chapter. Nor is it easy to decide whether the story is to be taken as a tragedy about a mother who is separated from her son by Christianity and Western education or a comedy about an only son who is slowly weaned away from his domineering mother. Perhaps it was meant as neither, perhaps as both. Munonye's intention is not entirely clear.

Munonye's description of the infiltration of Igboland by Christian missionaries corresponds very closely to Achebe's account of the same era in *Things Fall Apart*. The first church builders are not taken seriously; it is assumed that traditional gods and witchdoctors will soon dispose of them. Later, when missionaries and their converts aggressively attack local customs and violate some of the clan's religious taboos, they are either killed or driven away. The forces of Christianity begin to make much greater progress when led by a cautious, circumspect missionary who sets up a school on the mission compound. Soon young schoolboys like Nnanna are turning their backs on traditional beliefs and abandoning the ways of their parents and ancestors. Things start to fall apart in Igbo society.

Munonye's depiction of the missionaries is as objective as Achebe's. He shows that the men who served the white man's god were neither saints nor monsters but ordinary human beings whose sincere dedication to their work often made them ruthlessly intolerant of pagan beliefs and customs. They usually made no attempt to understand African ways. Munonye pictures Catholic missionaries en route to Africa being exhorted to concentrate on making converts and not to waste time studying native culture:

> "In this our early phase," the Superior expatiated in his slow and solemn voice, as of a prayer, "with so many Christian denominations literally pouring into that pagan world, our first emphasis must be on statistical successes....We want on our side the vast numbers who in Africa of the future will sustain the church with their numerical strength....In pursuit of that objective, I'm afraid we've got to be impatient with the culture of the people. There just isn't the time to sort out first and label their customs as acceptable and unacceptable." (193)

In their haste to make converts, well-intentioned missionaries thus bring moral confusion to a traditional African society, setting children against their parents. As in Achebe's novels, two different worlds collide and the weaker one gives way.

To evoke the cultural milieu his characters inhabit, Munonye, like Achebe's other followers, studs dialogue and narration with Igbo proverbs and idioms, sometimes employing them very self-consciously:

> "Odu, my friend and age-grade, what a man cannot eat he must keep for himself. That is a proverb as well as a statement of fact." (90)
> "Many are the days between acceptance of coconut and marriage-outing." That was not only a common saying of the land. It was a statement of fact. (91)

He also carefully defines untranslated Igbo words and labors to explain the literal meaning of Igbo names. At one point he even goes so far as to parenthetically apologize for not disclosing the real names of secret cult objects: "(The Nigerian Society for the Preservation of African Culture forbids that the names be revealed.)" (153). Munonye's earnestly didactic style may be based on Achebe's techniques of annotation in *Things Fall Apart*, but it is a far cry from the uncompromising and fully functional exoticism one finds in Achebe's later writers.

Clement Agunwa, another in Achebe's school, tries to avoid awkward translations and explanations of Igbo usage by prefacing his first novel *More Than Once*[19] with the following note to the reader:

> It should be understood that although the book is in English, the characters speak (except where otherwise stated) in Igbo, and in perfect, idiomatic Igbo. An effort has thus been made to render dialogue in acceptable English, but there are occasional intentional departures, especially where this best echoes the Nigerian idiom or figurative usage.

Agunwa is thus free to introduce stylistic innovations that Munonye does not dare to attempt. He is not as adventurous as Nwankwo in Africanizing his language but he does achieve some colorful, highly original effects. Besides employing Igbo proverbs and idioms in abundance, he occasionally writes dialogue in pidgin or transcribes African mispronunciations of English. Characters say "Gidifinsa" for "Good evening, sir," "Dafunu sa" for "Good afternoon, sir," and "Mishishi" for "Mrs." Agunwa also reproduces the English writing style of semiliterate villagers. Here is a typical letter:

> My dear son,
>   This leta is to ask about your plesent condishon of helt. I wanti to tel you dat yuer fader is veri veri sick. He is nearly daing. Please riton at once. I am craing.
> I am,
>   Your moder. (176)

Achebe had used techniques like these in *No Longer at Ease.*

Achebe's earliest urban novel appears to have had considerable influence on *More Than Once.* Both novels deal with the financial problems of a young man in the city. Agunwa's hero is Nweke Nwakor, an ambitious, uneducated village boy who enters the sack trade in Onitsha and rises from rags to riches in six years. Both in the city and in his home village, where he makes an ostentatious display of his new wealth, he gains a reputation as a man of substance. To preserve this reputation he foolishly fritters away his capital reserves, and a sudden business reversal ruins him. Worse yet, people find out he is illiterate. Humiliated and dejected, Nwakor attempts suicide. He is rescued but remains morose until given a psychological boost by a young university graduate who reassures him that opportunity knocks more than once. Nwakor resolves that his newborn son will never lack the means to go to school.

Education and social change are discussed at length in the novel. Nwakor regrets that he was not compelled to attend school as a boy and blames his financial fall on his lack of education. The young university graduate who returns from England with an M.Sc. in Economics points out that Nwakor was "properly educated for the old society but not necessarily for the new" (205) and that the solution to his problems lies in "steady readjustment to the changing times" (207). Nwakor had lost his capital by trying to impress clansmen back home with the wealth he had earned in the city. He had taken expensive titles, built a huge home on his father's compound, and provided an elaborate feast for everyone in the village. He had, in short, done everything a man in traditional society had to do in order to win a reputation as a man of distinction in the clan. But while seeking a prominent place in the old world, he had lost his position in the new, Westernized, commercial world of the city. Like Obi Okonkwo, he had been caught in the crossfire of conflicting cultures. He must indeed learn to adjust to changing times.

The young university graduate, whose name—perhaps not by coincidence—happens to be H. Obi, bears a striking resemblance to Obi Okonkwo. His education abroad has been financed by a "scholarship" in the form of a loan from the Ndigwe Patriotic Union, an organization of his clansmen in the city. When addressing members of this Union at a reception held to celebrate his return from overseas—a reception apparently modeled on that held for Obi Okonkwo by the Umuofia Progressive Union—he promises to repay the scholarship. A very idealistic young man, he occasionally complains about the high standard of living his kinsmen now expect him to maintain. Unlike Obi, however, he does not yield to temptation. *More Than Once* is the story of Nwakor's fall, not H. Obi's.

The structure of Agunwa's novel also may owe something to *No Longer at Ease*, for Agunwa makes frequent use of flashbacks. He does not, however, handle them as adroitly as Achebe. Indeed, at times he digresses, flashing back to events that do not advance the story. As a consequence, *More Than Once*, unlike Achebe's fiction, gradually deteriorates into a patchwork of entertaining scenes lacking a coherent overall design. The novel is too loosely strung together and too heavily knotted with messages at the end to make an effective statement. Agunwa, like the other young Igbo novelists whose works we have examined, lags far behind Achebe in artistry.

The "school of Achebe" in Nigerian fiction must be considered a school of apprentice writers, not masters, who have imitated Achebe's style and subject matter but have not managed to equal his achievement as a literary craftsman. Nevertheless, they remain a significant presence in Nigerian literature. In the mid-sixties, less than a decade after the publication of *Things Fall Apart*, they produced six novels, accounting for nearly one-fifth of Nigeria's total output of full-length fiction in English. No other Nigerian novelist, dramatist, or poet had attracted so many followers.

ONUORA NZEKWU

Onuora Nzekwu began his writing career as a special kind of journalist. Between 1956 and 1966, while working first as an editorial assistant and later an editor of *Nigeria Magazine*, "a quarterly publication for everyone interested in the country and its peoples,"[20] he wrote numerous feature articles on aspects of traditional and modern life in Nigeria. He was particularly interested in describing the customs, rituals, and annual festivals of his own people, the Onitsha Igbo of Eastern Nigeria, but he also delved into the traditions of several other Nigerian ethnic groups. By inclination he was an amateur cultural anthropologist.

By professional training, however, he was an elementary schoolteacher. Unlike Achebe and several other Igbo novelists who attended universities in Nigeria and England, Nzekwu received no more than the equivalent of a secondary school education at a Nigerian "Higher Elementary Teacher Training College" in the mid-1940s.[21]

These biographical facts help to explain Nzekwu's failures as a novelist. His earliest works, *Wand of Noble Wood* (1961) and *Blade Among the Boys* (1962), have been justly condemned by nearly every reviewer and critic as being too didactic, too explanatory, too anthropological. Martin Banham was quick to point out that "Nzekwu is too consciously writing for a foreign audience, perhaps because of his training on the *Nigeria* magazine, and this rather irritating habit gives [*Wand of Noble Wood*] too much of a feeling of being a sociological thesis."[22] Margaret Laurence has voiced a similar complaint, suggesting that this particular novel fails because "Nzekwu is frequently distracted from real contact with his characters by his tendency to explain Igbo rituals and social forms in a stilted and textbook manner."[23] It has even been reported that *Wand of Noble Wood* was "actually conceived as a piece of anthropology" and later transformed into a novel.[24] Nzekwu's second novel, *Blade Among the Boys*, may have been conceived as fiction, but it too suffers from an overly pedantic style. In both works Nzekwu seems more interested in illustrating various features of Igbo life than in dramatizing the intense personal struggle of his hero.

Evidence that Nzekwu's early fiction was greatly influenced by his writings for *Nigeria Magazine* is not difficult to find. Here is a passage from an article he wrote on the kola nut:

The role kola nut plays in some Nigerian communities leaves it without a substitute. An Ibo host, no matter how hospitable he may prove, offers an apology on informal occasions if he does not present his guest with a kola nut. For a while the guest may enjoy, on more formal occasions, any act of hospitality and thank his host profusely for the honour done him, when the day of reckoning comes he denounces, in no uncertain terms, the inability of his host to present him with a kola nut—very cheap, very common yet most significant and therefore most important.[25]

Now here is an excerpt from the two pages Nzekwu devotes in *Wand of Noble Wood* to the function of the kola nut in Igbo society:

> While it is true that the role it played left it without a substitute, kola-nut is nowadays sometimes replaced by cigarettes and drinks socially. On informal occasions a host apologizes for not presenting his guest with kola-nut. On more formal occasions he may entertain his guest lavishly. The guest may enjoy immensely his host's hospitality and thank him profusely for it. But, because he has not presented him with a kola-nut, when the day of reckoning came the guest denounced in no uncertain terms his host's inability to present him with a kola-nut—very cheap, very common, yet most significant, and, therefore most important.[26]

It was glossy magazine journalism like this that made Nzekwu's early novels read like textbooks of anthropology.

After the publication of *Blade Among the Boys* in 1962, Nzekwu's prose style and his fictional technique underwent a remarkable transformation. His third novel *Highlife for Lizards*, published in 1965, gave evidence of the change. Gone were the lengthy explanations of tribal customs and beliefs, the distracting enactments of ritual and ceremony that did nothing to advance the plot, and the stilted Oxbridge English in which the earlier novels were written. *Highlife for Lizards* was a coherent, efficient, well-structured story told in an idiom that suited the society portrayed. Nzekwu had learned to write in an African vernacular style. He, like the other Igbo writers who produced novels in the mid-sixties, had come under the influence of Chinua Achebe. To document this dramatic change in his fiction, it is necessary to examine *Wand of Noble Wood* and *Blade Among the Boys* in some detail before turning to *Highlife for Lizards*.

Wand of Noble Wood tells the story of Peter Obiesie, a young magazine journalist who is in need of a wife. He does not want to marry his pregnant mistress in Lagos because she comes from an ethnic group different from his own. And he does not want to follow Igbo tradition completely by asking his parents and relatives to arrange a marriage for him back home in the village. He agrees to let his family search for suitable prospective brides for him but insists that the final choice must be his own and that his choice will be determined more by love than by family considerations. The story is thus built around a major theme in Nigerian fiction: the conflict between old and new values. Detribalized by his education and urban experience, Peter tries to assert himself as an individual free from the domination of family and clan. However, he finds he has to make several concessions to tradition in order to marry the woman he loves. Yet even after making these concessions, he loses her to mysterious forces that control life in the village. Through suffering he learns to respect the ancient customs and beliefs to which he can no longer subscribe. The old ways triumph, leaving the Westernized hero crushed and confused.

Nzekwu's method of telling this story is almost as artificial as the story itself. His hero is sometimes merely an automaton mouthing ethnographic data. In the early chapters of the novel there are several unreal conversations in which two of Peter's Lagos friends question him closely about Igbo customs. Their questions enable Nzekwu to mount the schoolmaster's platform and lecture.

"You mentioned the *ofo*-staff a little while ago," Nora said. Does it mean anything more than the symbol of priesthood?"

"Yes," I said. "It is a means whereby the priest comes in contact with ancestral spirits and communes with them. Whoever takes charge of the *ofo* is regarded as the abode of ancestral spirits."

"What does it look like?"

"It is a short piece of stick…cut from the *ofo* plant (*Detarium Senegalense*) which, when consecrated, is a symbol of authority and a guarantee of truth. Freshly obtained, it is consecrated and becomes dynamized. There are different kinds of *ofo*—the family *ofo*, which is the one we are now discussing; the personal *ofo*; the *ofo* used by medicine men; the cult of *ofo* and so on. The family *ofo* are of two types: that of the men and that of the women. Both are used in invoking relative ancestral spirits, in the administration of oaths, in effecting curses on people who have offended grievously and in warding off evil. The staff is regarded with awe and is believed to be more powerful than poison or black magic." (45)

This longwinded discussion serves no useful purpose in the novel; it is merely an irrelevant scrap of Igbo anthropology.

When Peter's remarks to his friends do have relevance, they sometimes have too much. He is made to state things that should be left to the perception of the reader. Here is the way he summarizes his predicament early in the novel:

"Of the desirability of having a wife I am well aware. Mine is not a question of whether I shall marry or not. It is a problem of time. It is the problem of overcoming the dilemma created by the conflict between tradition and Westernism, a problem arising out of our attempts to blend present relative social practices with worthy concepts which tradition has established. That, in short, is the crux of the matter." (65-66)

A subtler novelist would have allowed his readers to come to this conclusion by themselves.

Nzekwu's diction also leaves much to be desired. His village characters who purportedly express themselves in Igbo speak in an idiom no different from those employed by urban characters speaking in English. When they use traditional Igbo proverbs, they usually preface them with self-conscious introductions:

> "Our people have a saying…" (63)
> "Remember the saying…" (81)
> "It is now I realize the truth of the saying…" (120)
> "As our people say…" (160)
> "It was our fathers who said…" (190)

The English-speaking characters quote at unconvincing length from Shakespeare, Southey, and Scott and occasionally resort to British slang terms such as "blighter" and "bugger." Worse still, the narrative sometimes lapses into banal sentimentality: "We kissed and it was heavenly. She lay on my lap and we drank in the new beauty which our love had infused into every object around us" (126). Nzekwu never succeeds in finding an appropriate language for the novel.

Many of Nzekwu's blunders in *Wand of Noble Wood* were repeated in *Blade Among the Boys*, published twelve months later.[27] This is not surprising, since most or all of the second novel must have been written before the first appeared in print. Nzekwu simply did not have an adequate opportunity to profit from some of the adverse reactions of reviewers and critics to *Wand of Noble Wood*.

The hero of *Blade Among the Boys*, like Peter Obiesie, is a young man caught between two worlds. Patrick Ikenga is brought up a Roman Catholic so he will be eligible to attend the local mission school, but he is also encouraged by his family to participate in traditional religious rituals. While at boarding school, Patrick is won over by Christianity and announces his determination to become a priest. His mother and uncle try to dissuade him, pointing out that he has been designated the next *okpala* ("spiritual head") of his patrilineage, an office that demands allegiance to tribal traditions. It would be shameful if an *okpala* refused to marry and produce children. Patrick is not swayed by these arguments until he is unjustly expelled from school by Catholic fathers.

The novel dramatizes the cruel dilemma confronting a young African who steps outside his own culture to obtain Western education from European missionaries. At first Patrick is quite comfortable living in two worlds and moves with ease from one to the other. But as he matures, he feels he must stop vacillating and make a deliberate choice between the old ways and the new. If he chooses the new, he cuts himself off from his family; if he chooses the old, he turns his back on everything he has learned at church and school.

Nzekwu introduces several complicating factors that make Patrick's dilemma even more difficult to resolve. Patrick has observed the narrow-mindedness and racial prejudice of Catholic missionaries. He has also seen the almost chauvinistic conservatism of village elders. He recognized that no matter what choice he makes between Christianity and traditionalism, he will have to ally himself with people and agencies he does not entirely respect. Like Achebe's Obi Okonkwo, Patrick Ikenga is a cultural hybrid no longer at ease in the old dispensation yet not entirely comfortable in the new. Being a perceptive young man, he recognizes the presence of good and evil in both worlds.

What spoils the novel is Nzekwu's inept craftsmanship. Instead of dramatizing the conflict between old and new, he has his characters talk about it. The book is filled with lengthy discussions about the impact of Christianity on traditional life, the loyalty of a young African to his family and clan, and the advantages and disadvantages of mission education. As in *Wand of Noble Wood*, debate substitutes for action and the story never comes alive.

Nzekwu also continues to write in an annoyingly pedantic style. Elaborate descriptions of traditional rites, customs, and beliefs and unnecessary translations of irrelevant Igbo terms are commonplace. When Nzekwu ventures to depart from the stiff formality of textbook prose, he sometimes slips into an equally inappropriate cliché-ridden slang.

> When he felt like giving his sexual passion a free rein he "imported" just the right girl, a "ripe" baby, one who had the right vital statistics and a practical knowledge of sex technique, to spend a week as his guest. He was very generous with his money and she liberal with the goods. He never invited any girl twice, for he believed strongly that variety was the spice of life. (126)

Nzekwu obviously still had much to learn about the use of appropriate diction.

Fortunately, after *Blade Among the Boys* he learned rapidly. His third novel, published three years later, was written in an entirely different idiom. Compare the passage just quoted with a scene from *Highlife for Lizards* in which a man reflects on his wife's infertility:

> "It's a pity she had no child. Yes, she's never even been pregnant, much less suffered a miscarriage. After all, what is needed in a seed yam is its crown. No one snaps his fingers without using a thumb. What shall I tell my ancestors when I go to them? That while the dance lasted all I did was make preparations to join in it?"[28]

By writing in this manner Nzekwu succeeded as never before in capturing the color and flavor of African vernacular expression. In addition to employing proverbs and metaphorical expressions that were completely rooted in African experience, he sprinkled his narrative with occasional folktales and untranslated Igbo words. It was apparent that Nzekwu had finally learned from Achebe how to Africanize his style.

In *Highlife for Lizards* he changed his subject too. Instead of dealing once again with the effects of culture conflict on a young unmarried man, he described the problems of a married woman in traditional Igbo society. Agom, an Igbo woman of Onitsha, is childless and fearful of sterility eight years after her wedding to Udezue. Her relationship with her husband has deteriorated into quarreling, nagging, bickering. An unhappy but proud woman, Agom seeks fulfillment outside her home by becoming a trader, but when she goes to another town for several months to help a sick relative, Udezue, without her knowledge or consent, takes a second wife, Nwadi. By the time Agom returns home, Nwadi is pregnant. Agom, very bitter and jealous, berates Udezue for his underhanded action, but she accepts Nwadi and rejoices with Udezue when Nwadi gives him his first child, a daughter. Agom's fortunes begin to change when she herself conceives and gives birth to Udezue's first son. She thus wins the highest place in her husband's affections, a position strengthened when Nwadi is caught in adultery and sent away by Udezue. Agom, a much happier woman now, goes on the live a long and rewarding life, becoming a successful trader and leader in her community. In the end, she has everything a woman could desire—a happy home, children, wealth, prestige.

What is most exciting about this novel is that it gives us, better than any anthropological text could, an inside view of what it is to be a married woman in a polygynous African society. Nzekwu's portrait of Agom is rich, consistent, and very well drawn, portraying her in many different moods and situations. As we watch her change from a bitter, disappointed, shrewish wife into a happy, contented, completely fulfilled mother, we learn a great deal not only about Agom but also about the culture in which she lives.

It is Nzekwu's rich evocation of Igbo culture that reminds us of Achebe. Although *Highlife for Lizards* and Achebe's rural novels differ in theme, they are quite similar in style and setting. Each gives us an in-depth view of life in a traditional Igbo society. Each tells us a thoroughly African story in thoroughly African terms. Achebe remains the better craftsman, but Nzekwu, by adopting his techniques, succeeds in narrowing the artistic gap between them considerably. If *Highlife for Lizards* is still too rigid in structure and too deafening in message to be regarded as a mature work of literary art, it nevertheless provides us with a very full portrayal of married life and one of the finest portraits of a heroine that Nigerian fiction has given us. However great his debt to Achebe, Nzekwu in this novel proves he is the kind of workman who accomplishes much with borrowed tools.

CHUKWUEMEKA IKE

In an informal interview in 1966 Chukwuemeka Ike stated that he began writing full-length fiction because so many of his friends were doing it.[29] He had always taken an interest in creative writing and had published several short stories in Nigerian magazines,[30] but he probably wouldn't have attempted a novel had he not been inspired by the early works of pioneering writers such as Chinua Achebe, Cyprian Ekwensi, and Onuora Nzekwu. He had attended secondary school and University College Ibadan with Achebe and had later made the acquaintance of both Ekwensi and Nzekwu, at that time the only other published Igbo novelists. Though favorably impressed with their works, he felt he could do as well, so he began *Toads for Supper* in the early nineteen-sixties while working as Registrar at the new University of Nigeria at Nsukka.

Ike set his novel in a Nigerian university environment and built his story around Amobi, an undergraduate with one foot in the old world and one in the new. Amobi's major problems are amatory rather than academic. His family has arranged a marriage for him with a pretty hometown girl, but at the university he falls in love with a classmate who, unfortunately, comes from a different part of the country; she is Yoruba, he is Igbo. The situation is further complicated when a prostitute from Lagos claims she is pregnant by him, and the university authorities rusticate him for refusing to marry her. Because of this extracurricular affair, Amobi finds himself rejected both by his family and by the girl he loves. He finally agrees to marry the whore in order to regain admittance to the university, but when she gives birth to a mulatto, obviously the child of another man, Amobi severs his connection with her and immediately begins to make plans to marry his Yoruba sweetheart. Unfortunately, his father suddenly falls ill and on his deathbed insists that Amobi promise to wed the hometown girl to whom he was betrothed as a child. After his father dies, Amobi feels he cannot break this promise, even though it was made under duress. When he tells his Yoruba fiancée about it, she goes mad.

This is light comedy that ends in disaster. Ike is at his best when describing the hilarious adventures and minor tribulations of a Nigerian university undergraduate. His gently satirical thrusts at university professors and administrators are well and wittily aimed. He also wrings good humor out of Amobi's love entanglements, revealing quite clearly how an inexperienced young man trying to steer a true course between his allegiance to the past and his ambitions for the future may lose sight of both and go astray in the crosscurrents of the present. Ike's error is to give so light a story a heavy ending. The sudden, unexpected weight throws the whole structure badly out of balance, and what began as good comedy collapses into mediocre melodrama.

Ike's debts to previous Igbo writers are quite conspicuous throughout the novel. Several incidents and motifs appear to have been borrowed wholesale from earlier works by Achebe, Nzekwu, or Ekwensi and adapted to fit Amobi's story. An educated young man's troublesome engagement to a village girl, for example, can be found in *No Longer at Ease*, *Wand of Noble Wood*, *Blade Among the Boys*, and Ekwensi's *People of the City*. Amobi's liaison with a Lagos whore is very reminiscent of similar sexual relationships in *Wand of Noble Wood* and Ekwensi's *Jagua Nana*, and her seduction of him may have been inspired as much by the dormitory room seduction of Patrick Ikenga in *Blade Among the Boys* as by Jagua Nana's frequent amours. Furthermore, in both *No Longer at Ease* and *Wand of Noble Wood* one finds a lovesick hero whose engagement to an educated woman of unusual ancestry horrifies his parents and results in tragedy. The tragedy, paralleling that in *No Longer at Ease*, is precipitated by a promise made to a dying relative. Obviously Ike was drawing heavily upon the novels written by his friends. Unlike other young Igbo writers, he was influenced as much by Ekwensi and Nzekwu as by Achebe.

His style, however, certainly owes more to Achebe than to anybody else. Proverbs are employed in abundance both in the speech of village characters and in the speech of university students who hail from rural areas of the country. Ike sometimes uses the very same proverb Achebe had used to achieve similar effects. For instance, the title of Ike's novel *Toads for Supper* is derived from the proverb Achebe had quoted to comment on Obi Okonkwo's shameful behavior: "If you want to eat a toad you should look for a fat and juicy one."[31] In Ike's novel this becomes "Not only had he eaten a toad, but he had chosen to eat a scraggy one!"[32] Ike was apparently trying to create a character much like Obi Okonkwo, so he used the same toad-eating proverb at least three times as an agent of characterization.[33] It may be well to give one more example of this and other proverbs to show how deftly he created a vernacular style similar to Achebe's. In the following passage Amobi is being scolded by his father for chasing after a Lagos prostitute:

> "Amobi. My words are few. You have painted my face and your mother's face with charcoal. I have always pulled your ears with my hand and warned you to beware of these township girls. I have begged you to put your sword in its sheath because one day you will be tired of lying down with a woman. I and your mother were anxious that you should marry quickly because we feared that young men of today find it difficult to control themselves. Nwakaego is waiting for you, just as the water in the broken pot waits for the dog to drink it. But I knew your mind was not on Nwakaego. You wanted someone who had gone to England to study, somebody who could speak English to you. Now that you have eaten the thing that has kept you awake let me watch you sleep! Now that you have fallen into the hands of those township girls who help the gods to kill, you will understand why I have been warning you to avoid women as you would avoid lepers. When a child eats a toad, it kills his appetite for meat." (120)

Since Nwankwo's *Danda* and Nzekwu's *Highlife for Lizards* were not published until after Ike had finished the manuscript of *Toads for Supper*,[34] Ike could not have learned to write in this manner from anyone but Chinua Achebe.

Of the sixteen Nigerians who wrote novels in English between 1952 and 1968, eight, as we have seen in this survey, were profoundly influenced by the writings of Chinua Achebe. All eight were Igbo, and all but one had been educated in Nigerian universities. Nzekwu, the only veteran novelist among them, was a late convert to the "School of Achebe" but he, like the others, proved himself a faithful follower in the mid-sixties.

The fact that these writers learned more from Achebe than from any other author, African or non-African, sets them apart as a group, for earlier Nigerian writers had received their inspiration from other sources. Amos Tutuola's accomplishment had been to translate traditional oral art into literary art by emulating Yoruba novelist D.O. Fagunwa's method of weaving short Yoruba tales into a single long narrative. Cyprian Ekwensi, a prolific popular writer, had produced mostly third-rate novels and novelettes that were transparent imitations of English and American juvenile adventure stories, westerns, whodunits, and paperback potboilers about urban crime, politics, and sex. Even Achebe himself, though undoubtedly the first Nigerian to write original fiction of unquestioned merit in English, had worked well within the conventions of the realistic novel as shaped by such classic authors as Hardy, Conrad, Lawrence, and Forster. His major contribution to the Great Tradition of the English language novel had been to develop a new prose style that expressed the flavor of African experience more accurately and artistically than it had ever been rendered before. To achieve this, Achebe did not move outside the Great Tradition but rather added a new dimension to it by extending the boundaries of English literature to accommodate yet another world view. Like any great writer, he bent language to suit his own particular purposes without destroying its viability as a medium of universal communication. He was as much an English writer as an African one, for he clearly owed a substantial debt to English fiction as well as to traditional African verbal art.

The Nigerian writers of the sixties, particularly the Igbo novelists, were far more African than English because they followed the lead of their immediate predecessors, looking primarily to Achebe and occasionally to Ekwensi for guidance. They were a new generation adopting the methods and techniques that the most successful writers of the previous generation had proven effective. So this "school" of locally trained novelists dominated the Nigerian literary scene, and a distinctive national literature began to emerge. Nigerian fiction, by building on itself, was rapidly creating traditions of its own.

NOTES

1. "Finding Their Voices," *Times Literary Supplement*, September 16, 1965, 791.
2. *Danda* (London: Deutsch, 1964). All quotations are taken from this edition.
3. Reported in *West Africa*, October 8, 1960, 1154.
4. *Drum*, Nigerian edition, February 1962, 35.
5. *Tales out of School* (Lagos: African Universities Press, 1963).
6. Reported on the book jacket of *Danda*.
7. His early short stories include "The Optimist," *Ibadan* 15 (March 1963): 14-16; "The Gambler," *Black Orpheus* 9 (1961): 49-54; "His Mother," *Nigeria Magazine* 80 (1964): 58-60; "The Man Who Lost," *Nigeria Magazine* 84 (1965): 68-72. A mimeographed copy of his play *Eroya*, which was performed at University College Ibadan in 1963, can be found in the African Studies Collection of the Northwestern University Library.
8. I wish to thank Ben Akpati, a former graduate student in the Geography Department at the University of California at Los Angeles, for this information.
9. He may have learned form J.P. Clark and Wole Soyinka as well. See, e.g., his review of a performance of their plays in *Nigeria Magazine* 72 (March 1962): 80.
10. *The Concubine* (London: Heinemann, 1966). All quotations are taken from this edition.
11. Margaret Laurence, *Long Drums and Cannons: Nigerian Dramatists and Novelists 1952-1966* (London: Macmillan, 1968), 182.
12. For a discussion of this novel and others by Igbo writers that were published during or after the Nigerian-Biafran war, see my "New Trends in West and East African Fiction," *Review of National Literatures* 2, no. 2 (1971): 15-37.

13. *Efuru* (London: Heinemann, 1966). All quotations are taken from this edition. Nwapa's later works *Idu* (London: Heinemann, 1970) and *This is Lagos and Other Stories* (Enugu: Nwankwo-Ifejika, 1971) show little improvement over *Efuru*. Both may have been written before the outbreak of the Nigerian civil war but they are not discussed here.

14. Laurence, *Long Drums and Cannons*, 190; John Povey, "African Literature in English," *Books Abroad* 41 (Autumn 1967): 419.

15. However, Onuora Nzekwu, as we shall see, is very successful in presenting a woman's world in *Highlife for Lizards* (London: Hutchinson, 1965).

16. *Our Dead Speak* (London: Longmans, 1967). All quotations are taken from this edition.

17. It was published only in a paperback edition that appears to have been designed for use in schools.

18. *The Only Son* (London: Heinemann, 1966). All quotations are taken from this edition.

19. *More Than Once* (London: Longmans, 1967). All quotations are taken from this edition.

20. This statement was carried on the cover of *Nigeria Magazine* while Nzekwu was its editor.

21. Biographical information on Nzekwu can be found in *West Africa*, February 3, 1962, 147, and on the book jacket of his *Highlife for Lizards* (London: Hutchinson, 1965).

22. Martin Banham, "The Beginnings of a Nigerian Literature in English," *Review of English Literature* 3 (April 1962): 95.

23. Laurence, *Long Drums and Cannons*, 191.

24. John Povey, "Canons of Criticism for Neo-African Literature," *Proceedings of a Conference on African Languages and Literatures held at Northwestern University, April 28-30, 1966*, ed. Jack Berry, et al ([Evanston, IL]: n.p., n.d.), 79. Povey has also written at greater length on "The Novels of Onuora Nzekwu," *Literatures East and West* 12, no. 1 (1968): 68-84. For another view of his fiction, see G.D. Killam, "The Novels of Onuora Nzekwu," *African Literature Today* 5 (1971): 21-40.

25. Onuora Nzekwu, "Kola Nut," *Nigeria Magazine* 71 (December 1961): 299.

26. Onuora Nzekwu, *Wand of Noble Wood* (London: Hutchinson, 1961), 68. All quotations are taken from this edition.

27. *Blade Among the Boys* (London: Hutchinson, 1962). All quotations are taken from this edition, which was published on July 23, 1962. *Wand of Noble Wood* had been published on July 17, 1961.

28. *Highlife for Lizards* (London: Hutchinson, 1965), 54.

29. Interview conducted at the University of California at Los Angeles on May 13, 1966.

30. I have not been able to trace any of these stories. In her bibliography, *Black African Literature in English Since 1952: Works and Criticism* (New York: Johnson Reprint Corp., 1967), Barbara Abrash lists the following story: "Waiting for His Programme," *African Writer* 1, no. 1 (August 1962): 13-15.

31. Chinua Achebe, *No Longer at Ease* (London: Heinemann, 1960), 6.

32. Chukwuemeka Ike, *Toads for Supper* (London: Harvill, 1965), 144. All quotations are taken from this edition.

33. Ibid., 120, 144, 161.

34. In the interview at the University of California at Los Angeles on May 13, 1966, Ike stated that he had submitted the manuscript of his novel to several American publishers before sending it to Harvill Press. Thus, it must have been finished before 1964, the year *Danda* was published.

TOWARDS AN ICONOGRAPHY

Chinua Achebe has become a conspicuous global literary figure, and photographs of him now regularly appear in the international press and in books and articles about his writings. However, not many photos taken during his formative years as a writer are in general circulation, and few of the drawings of him that have appeared in Nigerian newspapers in more recent years have been seen outside Nigeria. To give readers an impression of how he looked as a young man and how he was pictured in the Nigerian press later in his career, here are samples of some of the indigenous visual images available. A caricature by one of America's finest cartoonists is also included.

Achebe attended Government College Umuahia, reputed to be one of the best secondary schools in West Africa, before entering University College Ibadan in 1948. Umuahia had many strong traditions, one of which was an Old Boys' Reunion held in July each year. The earliest photos we have of Achebe as a university student are three taken at his school's Old Boys' Reunion and published in successive annual issues of *The Umuahian*. In 1951 (fig. 1) he is seated at the left end of the front row attired in a white suit. In 1952 (fig. 2) and 1953 (fig. 3) he is standing in the center of the second row wearing perhaps the same white suit. (In the 1951 photo his schoolmate Christopher Okigbo, who became one of Nigeria's finest poets, is standing third from the right in the middle row; in the 1952 photo he is at the right end of the middle row wearing a hat at a rakish angle.) Achebe evidently was a loyal Old Boy who never missed a reunion and, obedient to tradition and/or economy, always dressed the same.

We have two other photos from Achebe's university days. In the first (fig. 4) he is standing between Christopher Okigbo (left) and Alex Ajayi (right). In the other (fig. 5) he is pictured with members of the 1952-53 Editorial Board of the *University Herald;* Achebe, Editor-in-Chief, is seated at the left end beside Vincent Chukwuemeka Ike, who also later rose to prominence as a novelist. Both Achebe and Ike wrote regularly for the *University Herald,* publishing their first short stories and essays there.

The next photo (fig. 6), taken in 1964, shows Achebe working in Lagos as Director of the Voice of Nigeria. By this time his first three novels—*Things Fall Apart* (1958), *No Longer at Ease* (1960), and *Arrow of God* (1964)—would have been published.

These photos give us a sense of how young Achebe was when he started his writing career. In 1951, when the first Old Boys' Reunion shot was taken, he would have been 20 years old. In 1964, with three major works behind him, he would have been only 33.

The rest of the images are caricatures, all but one of which appeared in the Nigerian press in the 1980s and 1990s. Four of them were drawn for Nigeria's leading literary newspaper, *The Guardian,* by cartoonists Cliff Ogiugo (fig. 7), Tony Olise (fig. 8), Ake Didi Onu (fig. 9), and Obe Ess (fig. 10). Achebe and other prominent local literary personalities (especially Nobel Prize winner Wole Soyinka) are frequently caricatured in the Nigerian press.

The final image (fig. 11) may provide irrefutable evidence of Achebe's literary canonization in the West. It was drawn by David Levine, the cartoonist for the *New York Review of*

Books, to accompany a review (published on March 3, 1988) of Achebe's novel *Anthills of the Savannah.* To be drawn by Levine, even in an unflattering manner, is considered a rare honor. He has sketched many of the leading personalities of contemporary times as well as a good number of the literary, political, sports, and entertainment giants of the past—everyone from Winston Churchill to Walt Disney, Charles de Gaulle to Princess Di, Leonardo da Vinci to Muhammad Ali, Sigmund Freud to Woody Allen. Among the literary "immortals" who have been cut down to size by his witty strokes are Brecht, Conrad, T.S. Eliot, F. Scott Fitzgerald, Gogol, Hemingway, Henry James, Joyce, Kipling, Milton, Pope, Pound, Sartre, Shakespeare, Stendahl, Voltaire, Wilde, Wordsworth, and Zola. Needless to say, this places Achebe in very distinguished company indeed. But in one respect he is ahead of all the rest. Achebe is the only author in the entire group shown seated before a computer!

A copy of the Levine caricature, matted and framed (17" x 21"), may be purchased for $150, plus handling and shipping, from the *New York Review of Books,* 435 Hudson St., 3rd Floor, New York, NY 10014.

*F*igure 1: Old Boys's Reunion, 1951 (Achebe seated at far left; Christopher Okigbo in middle row, third from far right). Photo: Government College, Umuahia Magazine.

*F*igure 2: Old Boys' Reunion, 1952 (Achebe standing, seventh from right). Photo: Government College, Umuahia Magazine.

Figure 3: Achebe (centre, rear) at Old Boys' Reunion, Government College Umuahia, 1953. Photo: Government College, Umuahia Magazine.

Figure 4: Christopher Okigbo, Chinua Achebe and Alex Ajayi as students at University College, Ibadan. Photo: Chinua Achebe.

Figure 5: *Editorial Board*, University Herald, *Ibadan, 1952–53*
(Achebe at far left). Photo: Chinua Achebe.

Figure 6: *Director of the* Voice of Nigeria, *Lagos, 1964.*
Photo: Chinua Achebe.

*F*igure 7: *Chinua Achebe.*
Caricature by Cliff Ogiugo of the Guardian *(Lagos).*

*F*igure 8: *Chinua Achebe.*
Caricature by Tony Olise of the Guardian *(Lagos).*

*F*igure 9: Chinua Achebe.
Caricature by Ake Didi Onu of the Guardian (Lagos).

*F*igure 10: Chinua Achebe.
Caricature by Obe Ess of the Guardian (Lagos).

Figure 11: Chinua Achebe. Caricature by David Levine,
New York Review of Books, 3 March 1988.

ACHEBE AT HOME
AND ABROAD

According to one recent estimate, *Things Fall Apart* has been translated into fifty-five languages, and more than eight million copies of the original English-language version have been sold worldwide. Such impressive numbers, which probably exceed those of any other text circulating in Africa except perhaps the Bible and the Koran, attest to the classic status of this influential novel. It is being read everywhere year after year after year. As early as 1965 the *Times Literary Supplement* could report that "Already *Things Fall Apart* is probably as big a factor in the formation of a young West African's picture of his past, and of his relation to it, as any of the still rather distorted teachings of the pulpit and the primary school."[1] Today that claim could be expanded to embrace much of the intelligent international reading public, for the book has made a major impact on the way Africa's historic encounter with the wider world has been interpreted and understood by outsiders as well as insiders. The tale told offered a new reading of the consequences of colonialism, a reading made persuasive by a skillful blending of art and argument, notion and narration, explication and implication, fact and metaphor. *Things Fall Apart* brought all these things together into a coherent whole, crafting them into a compelling story with resonant undertones.

The novel's high international standing can be measured by reference not only to sales figures and translations but also to data extrapolated from empirical studies of teaching and critical practices in various parts of the world. Let me offer a few examples from projects I have undertaken in India as well as in anglophone areas of Africa.

From September through December of 1989 I conducted research in India on the teaching of non-British literatures in English Departments at Indian universities. I was curious to know to what extent the so-called "new literatures in English" were being taught and studied—not just Third World anglophone literatures from Africa, the Caribbean, and South Asia (most notably from India itself) but also the not-so-new First World literatures from Canada, Australia, New Zealand, and even the United States of America. To put it another way, I wanted to find out how far university English studies in India, a former British colony, had been decolonized after independence. How much of the rest of the English-speaking world was now visible in the literature curriculum? Which authors and which texts from outside the traditional English canon were being read? And how seriously were they being studied? Did the courses in which they were included make up part of the program of work required of all undergraduates and post-graduate students, or were such courses relegated to the status of exotic options available to whoever might wish to venture a bit beyond the mainstream syllabus? Did non-British literatures command as much respect in Indian universities as British literature did?

I had done a similar survey of curricular change in anglophone Africa three years earlier, examining the degree to which African literature had been accommodated in English programs at forty universities in fourteen independent nations. The results of that study[2] showed that African literature was being taught on nearly all the campuses surveyed (the University of Mauritius being the only exception), and that in a few places it had achieved paramountcy, figuring in fifty percent or more of the courses required for a literature degree. In most undergraduate programs, however, British literature still got the lion's share of attention. North American literature, especially its African American and Afro-Caribbean offshoots, had made striking gains here and there, but the literary output of the remainder of the English-speaking world (India, Canada, Australia, New Zealand, Singapore, and the South Pacific islands) had been granted almost no recognition at all, being virtually ignored in even the most innovative programs. The tendency was for African and other black literatures to drive out some of the British literature but never to rout it completely. Many English Departments claimed to be aiming at a balanced curriculum, one that exposed students to the classic British authors (Shakespeare, Dickens, and the rest) as well as to the best contemporary African writers, but there was little agreement on what constituted the ideal mix. One program's balance was another program's disequilibrium. The winds of curricular change were still blowing across the African continent, so the dust hadn't quite settled yet.

In India, on the other hand, the opening up of the English curriculum to non-British subject matter had been a slower and more orderly process. It had proceeded in three distinct phases, with American literature, aided by a postwar infusion of Fulbright funds for teaching and research, infiltrating the syllabus in a significant way in the 1950s, then Indian literature in English gaining a secure foothold about a decade later, and finally "Commonwealth Literature" (by which was meant the literatures of the rest of the English-speaking world) earning a small niche for itself only as recently as the 1970s and 1980s. But not all English programs in the nation were affected by these changes in the same way. Today there are still some English Departments at Indian universities that teach only British literature, others that teach mainly British literature with a small admixture of American and Indian literatures, and yet others that offer courses in

American, Indian, and Commonwealth literatures only at a postgraduate level. In fact, the great majority of English programs at Indian universities remain steadfastly anglocentric, elevating British literature above all others and tolerating little substantive deviation from the type of curriculum that existed during colonial times. Some of these fossilized programs appear to have resisted or effectively deflected the winds of change. Unlike their counterparts in anglophone Africa, most university English Departments in India have not undergone a major curricular revolution. Britannia still rules the waves.

But in those institutions where there has been change, African literature has made some headway, especially wherever the new anglophone literatures have gained a place in the curriculum. Out of 66 Indian university English Departments that responded to a questionnaire sent to 110 institutions eliciting information about current teaching practices, only three reported offering a separate course on African literature, and in one of these the coverage of Africa was combined with the coverage of literature in the West Indies. A few Departments taught representative African texts in courses on "Postcolonial Literature," "the New Literatures in English," and "Modern Fiction," but the large majority (25 of the 33 that fielded such new courses) subsumed African literature under the umbrella of "Commonwealth Literature." One practical consequence of this absorption was that only a few African works were being read in these courses—usually two or three at most but sometimes merely a single text. Judging from the sample of responses received, one could conclude that half (i.e., 33 of the 66 respondents) of these university English Departments in India offered at least one course on the new literatures in English but that the African component of such courses was quite small, though perhaps no smaller than any other area of the Commonwealth.

What does an Indian teacher of a course on Commonwealth literature do when confronted with the problem of selecting one or two texts to represent the literary output of the entire African continent? From the evidence now in hand the answer is clear: teach Achebe. If there is extra time, teach Soyinka too and then perhaps Ngugi and a few poets, but start with the most important writer and the most significant single text. Start with Achebe. Start with *Things Fall Apart*. Achebe's works were taught in 37 courses at 32 of the 33 institutions in India that reported offering courses in the new literatures in English. *Things Fall Apart* was the text selected in 24 of these courses, *Arrow of God* and *No Longer at Ease* were chosen in 3 courses each, *A Man of the People* was used in 2 courses, and selections from Achebe's poetry and short stories were assigned in 3 courses.

In comparison, Soyinka's works were required reading in 28 courses at 25 institutions, but there was no consensus on which of his works was most important. *The Road* was used in 11 courses, *A Dance of the Forests* in 6, *The Lion and the Jewel* in 3, and *The Interpreters*, *Kongi's Harvest*, and *Death and the King's Horseman* in 2 each. Ngugi's works were assigned in only 10 courses at 9 institutions: *Homecoming* and *A Grain of Wheat* in 2 courses each, and *The River Between*, *Weep Not, Child*, *Devil on the Cross*, and *Decolonizing the Mind* in one course each. Other authors occasionally read in Indian university English courses included Okigbo and Okara in 3 courses each, Armah and Clark in 2 each, and Awoonor, Brutus, Coetzee, Gordimer, La Guma, Paton, Peters and Rubadiri in one each. These statistics prove very clearly that Achebe is the African author most frequently taught and that *Things Fall Apart* is the African text most widely read at these institutions. Most Indian students are introduced to African literature through Achebe, and for some of them African literature begins and ends with *Things Fall Apart*.

The same pattern holds in Indian scholarship on African literature. Although there have been occasional essays covering such writers as Abrahams, Amadi, Brutus, Clark, Egbuna, Mphahlele, Mwangi, Nwankwo, Nwapa, Okara, Okigbo,

Okot, Rubadiri, Ruganda, and Tutuola, most attention has focused on the big three: Achebe, Soyinka, and, to a far lesser extent, Ngugi. Moreover, the interest in Soyinka and Ngugi is relatively recent, but discussion of Achebe's work goes back a full quarter of a century. Again, the bulk of the commentary has dealt with *Things Fall Apart*, the book Indian teachers and students know best.

How do these pedagogical and critical patterns compare with those in anglophone African universities. Let's start in South Africa, where university English curricula have been slower to change than in tropical Africa. In 1992 I was able to analyze 139 course descriptions collected from English Departments at 22 South African universities.[3] At that time South Africa was in the middle of what Nadine Gordimer, following Gramsci, had called an interregnum—a transitional phase—in this case, two years after the release of Nelson Mandela from prolonged detention and the concomitant unbanning of the African National Congress and two years before the country's first truly democratic election. Some white universities had already started admitting black students in significant numbers a few years earlier, and there had been a great deal of public discussion about the need for curricular reform in a changing educational environment. Even before the interregnum several reforms had taken place. For instance, South African literature had gradually earned a niche for itself in an otherwise heavily British literature curriculum, but this had been due more to nationalistic pedagogical pioneering than to dramatic changes in the political climate in South Africa. Modifications of the old Curricula Britannica had already been introduced at every level of English teaching before the walls of apartheid had finally started crumbling, so that by 1992 there was no South African English program that did not offer some instruction in African literature.

That was the good news. The bad news was that the reforms had not gone far enough, that African literature on most campuses was still a marginalized stepdaughter of traditional EngLit, which remained the queen mother of all its undernourished anglophone offspring. Moreover, in South Africa the battle for official recognition of indigenous literary legitimacy had only been half won, for native sons and daughters had crowded out most of the interesting foreigners from parts further north, the result being a kind of geographical partition in which Africa above the Limpopo was underrepresented in the pantheon of African letters. South African university students were now introduced to a sample of their own national literary heritage, but they were taught very little about Nigerian, Ghanaian, Kenyan, Zimbabwean, or any other anglophone African national literatures.

Indeed, only three authors from other parts of anglophone Africa (Achebe, Ngugi, Soyinka) were regularly taught, with only two texts each by Achebe and Ngugi, and one each by Armah and Dangarembga appearing relatively frequently on the preferred list of readings. Of these half-dozen putative canonical texts from abroad *Things Fall Apart* was the clear favorite, followed at some distance by Ngugi's *A Grain of Wheat*.

A similar set of preferences can be seen in a survey of American teaching practices conducted by Zinta Konrad back in 1976, when novels by Achebe and Ngugi were cited most frequently as assigned texts in African literature courses, with *Things Fall Apart* topping the list by a considerable margin.[4]

A somewhat different pattern of teaching preferences can be discerned in data collected from tropical African universities in the mid-1980s.[5] A survey of reading lists for 194 literature courses taught at 30 universities in 14 nations revealed that the favorite assigned text was Achebe's *Arrow God*, followed closely by Ngugi's *A Grain of Wheat* and *Petals of Blood*. Achebe's *A Man of the People* scored fourth, and other texts by Ngugi, Armah, Soyinka, and Okigbo rounded out the top ten. *Things Fall Apart* did not rank higher than twelfth on the list, but this anomaly can probably be explained by the fact that it is so widely taught as a set book in secondary schools throughout tropical Africa that university teachers may prefer to assign one of his later works rather than a text that their students already know quite well. Today one may safely assume that *Things Fall Apart* has been read by more African secondary school students than any other African or non-African novel. Throughout the African continent it has become a staple of the high school literature curriculum.

A final study comparing African and non-African production of scholarship on the three most important anglophone African writers (the Achebe, Ngugi, Soyinka triumvirate) revealed some interesting critical patterns.[6] For instance, more study guides have been produced on Achebe's works, most often on *Things Fall Apart*, than on all the works of Soyinka and Ngugi combined. In addition, more doctoral dissertations and book chapters have been written on Achebe than on either Ngugi or Soyinka. Up to 1976, non-African critics produced about 63% of the scholarship on Achebe, but by 1995 their portion of the total critical output on his works had dropped to only 46%, showing that African scholars were beginning to reclaim him for Africa. Moreover, whereas 92% of the non-African scholars who have ever written on Achebe have published their works outside Africa, 70% of the Nigerians who have ever written on him have published their works at home. This lack of critical reciprocity, especially on the part of Western scholars, is to some extent a degree worrisome, but it may also signal the extent to which Achebe has become an internationally recognized literary figure. Non-African scholars apparently have experienced no difficulty in placing their scholarship on him in Western academic media. This might not have been the case had he been unknown outside Africa. The book that initially made him famous in the wider world and continues to spread his reputation to the very ends of the earth is *Things Fall Apart*.

The evidence from these pedagogical and critical surveys thus confirms that *Things Fall Apart*, both in Africa and elsewhere, remains the most widely read and durable of African literary masterworks, a truly international classic. One may expect it to remain so for it has proven itself to be constructed sturdily enough to withstand the ravages of time in many different parts of the globe. *Things Fall Apart* is the kind of ageless book that will never fall apart, never be forgotten, never disappear.

NOTES

1. *Times Literary Supplement*, September 16, 1965, 791.
2. "The Teaching of African Literature in Anglophone African Universities: An Instructive Canon," *Wasafiri* 11 (1990): 13-16.
3. "African Literature Teaching in South African University English Departments," *Alternation* 3, no. 1 (1996): 4-14.
4. Zinta Konrad, "African Literature in the American University Curriculum," *Research in African Literatures* 9 (1978): 259-81.
5. "The Teaching of African Literature in Anglophone African Universities: An Instructive Canon," 15.
6. "Counting Caliban's Curses: A Statistical Inventory," *Ariel* 31, nos. 1-2 (2000): 153-64, 170-77, and reprinted in the next chapter.

COUNTING CALIBAN'S CURSES: A STATISTICAL ANALYSIS

Once upon a time, during a stormy season in human history, a band of seafarers found themselves shipwrecked on the coast of a tropical island inhabited by several peoples they had never before encountered. Accustomed to misadventures in foreign lands, the mariners quickly set up camp, made themselves at home, and sent out small parties to explore the island and establish commerce with the natives. Thus was communication initiated between heterogenous language communities, one globally expansive, the others relatively fixed and stationary. As in other parts of the world, the mobile language community penetrated, occupied, and colonized the immobile language communities, extending communicative hegemony over numerous widely scattered peoples by implanting its own tongue in the mouths of all it met. English, already an international lingua franca, proved an expeditious vehicle for this ambitious networking enterprise. The British—for so these seadogs were called—soon were in control of much of the import-export trade, for their voices carried farther than anyone else's. They came, they communicated, and they conquered, forging linguistic links not only directly between themselves and their many hosts but also laterally between all those hosts with whom they had established productive parasitic intercourse. Their empire was a vast, worldwide internet connected by a single operational code. Anglophonia ruled the waves.

This alien code did not always work to the disadvantage of those who adopted it or adapted to it. At first a disgruntled, inarticulate Caliban might complain to Prospero and Miranda that "You taught me language, and my profit on't/ Is, I know how to curse," but once he had achieved a fuller fluency and learned how to read and write, Caliban discovered himself in command of an expressive power that went well beyond impotent imprecations. English became for him an instrument of self-assertion, a tool of liberation, a means to desirable counterhegemonic ends. He could now talk back to those who had stolen his island and could make his grievances known to an international tribunal. He was hooked up and plugged into a global information superhighway, a brave new world of intelligible interactive discourse.

But to gain access to this larger universe he had to pay a heavy price. Taking the leap from the past to the future required years of schooling, including faithful adherence to a grueling gymnastic regimen that bent him out of his original shape. By the time he mastered all the necessary moves, he had become a different person—acculturated, assimilated, melded, hybridized. He was now a man of two worlds, no longer at ease in the old dispensation yet not entirely at home in the new. And he was far more conspicuous, far more vulnerable, than before, for whatever he wrote could be read and evaluated not only by others like himself but also by countless strangers abroad who operated in the same metropolitan register. His international idiom had made him an islander no more.

This tempestuous little allegory may serve as a useful cautionary tale for those of us considering problems of scholarly authority and intellectual production in African literature studies today, for it may alert us to some of the lingering geographical, political, racial, and linguistic tensions that have produced peculiar distortions in postcolonial literary studies throughout the Third World. The complaint everywhere seems to be that there are still too many Prosperos and Mirandas calling the critical shots, that the little islanders are being crowded out of their own domain by uncouth continentals, that careerist Northerners with easier access to money, machines, and magazines are monopolizing discussion of literary works by Southerners, that First Worlders and Third Worlders are not engaged in any sort of dialogue but are speaking only to their own kind, the first Worlders through electronically amplified megaphones, the Third Worlders through baffles and mufflers. Furthermore, in the West the language of literary criticism has itself changed, moving toward higher and higher levels of abstraction and self-reflexivity, leaving many non-Western-ers speaking in a quaint, old-fashioned hermeneutic dialect, if they are allowed to speak at all. In short, Africa, a silent partner in its own intellectual marginalization, may be losing control of its own anglophone literature.

To test these explosive charges, it may be helpful to examine a few statistical charts that reveal in plain, stark numbers where the greatest imbalances in African and non-African production of literary scholarship have existed and continue to exist today. The following data have been gleaned from four consecutive volumes of *Black African Literature in English*, a bibliography listing more than twenty thousand books and articles on anglophone black African literature published between 1936 and 1991. The first of these volumes, covering forty-one years of scholarly activity, ran to 3305 items; the third five-year update, covering only 1987 to 1991, contains 8772 entries, almost a threefold increase over the original compilation. This sharp upsurge in scholarly productivity reveals that literary criticism has been a major growth industry in African studies in recent years.

To reduce these charts to manageable proportions I have listed the relevant figures for only the top three writers in anglophone Africa: Wole Soyinka, Chinua Achebe, and Ngugi wa Thiong'o. More has been written about these authors than about any others, so together they provide a sufficiently large sample for statistical analysis. But I have narrowed the data base a bit by concentrating exclusively on literary criticism and eliminating from the count all other forms of scholarship—e.g., bibliographies, biographical books and articles, and published interviews. I have also excluded all works that deal with more than a single author, for they would have complicated the scoring system considerably. So the numbers on these tables represent only those scholarly studies that are devoted to one of the big three: Soyinka, Achebe, or Ngugi. And I have subdivided the data into six categories—books, study guides, book chapters, articles, doctoral dissertations, master's theses—each of which may tell us something different about the authors and critics concerned.

In order to get a sense of how the chart works, let us start with the smallest category: books published on a single author (chart 1). BALE is an acronym for *Black African Literature in English*, each volume of which is represented by a roman numeral. To bring the record further up to date, a fifth column covering book production in 1992-95 has been added. NI stands for Nigerian, OA for Other African, NA for Non-African, KE (under Ngugi) for Kenyan, IN (under Grand Totals) for Indigene, T for Total, SGT for Super Grand Total, and GTSGT for Grand Total of Super Grand Totals. The horizontal plane represents the place of publication, and the vertical plane indicates the nationality of the scholar. If, for example, we look at the first combinations of figures listed in column I, we see that between 1936 (actually 1965) and 1976 there were a total of four books published on Soyinka, three on Achebe, and none on Ngugi. One of the books on Soyinka was by a Nigerian and was published in Nigeria, one was by a scholar from another part of Africa and was published outside Africa, and two were by non-African scholars and were published outside Africa. Similarly, all three of the books on Achebe were published outside Africa, one by a scholar from another part of Africa, the other two by non-Africans. So from this slice of the chart we may draw the conclusion that most of the earliest book-length scholarship on these two authors was published outside Africa (as it happens, in London, Paris, and New York), and nearly all of it was produced by non-Nigerian critics. As can be seen from the figures listed in columns II and III, this pattern in scholarly production continued through the next decade, but began to change between 1987 and 1995, when Nigerian scholars started to assert themselves more vigorously and turn to writing and publishing books at home on Soyinka and Achebe. But if one examines the Grand Totals for each author as well as the Super Grand Total that combines the numbers for all three authors, one cannot fail to notice that the majority of the seventy books on Soyinka, Achebe and Ngugi have been produced by non-Africans and that an even greater majority, including some books by Nigerians and other Africans, have been published outside Africa.

One may refine these generalizations still further by taking into account the nationalities of the scholars who produced the books, noting the languages in which they wrote. Achebe-philes have the widest geographical distribution, hailing from five African countries (Nigeria - 7, Cameroon - 1, Ghana - 1, Kenya - 1, Zaïre - 1) and eleven non-African countries (U.S.A. - 3.5, U.K. - 2.5, Canada - 1, Germany - 1, France - 1, Sweden - 1, Italy - 1, Russia - 1, India - 1, Australia - .5, and Denmark - .5). Most of them wrote in English, but two published books in French, one in Italian, and one in Russian. The Soyinka-philes have a similar broad distribution, coming from four African nations (Nigeria - 12, Sierra Leone - 1, Ivory Coast - 1, Swaziland - 1) and eight non-African nations (France - 4, U.K. - 3.5, India - 3, Sweden - 2, U.S.A. - 1.5, Germany - 1, Russia - 1, Australia - 1). Most wrote in English, except for five who chose to publish in French, one in German, and one in Russian. Ngugiphiles are from three African countries (Nigeria - 1.5, Kenya - 1, Senegal - 1) and seven non-African counties (Canada - 2, Germany - 2, U.K.- 1.5, France - 1,

Sweden - 1, Italy - 1, India - 1). Ten of them expressed themselves in English, one in German, one in French, and one in Swedish. Significantly, no book has been written on Soyinka, Achebe or Ngugi in an African language. All three authors are well known abroad, even in non-English-speaking parts of the world, but they have not yet been introduced to other language communities in their own countries.

Study guides (chart 2)—booklets prepared as aids to students—reveal which of these authors are being read most regularly in high schools. As might be expected, Achebe is the clear leader in this category, especially in Nigeria, where his books often have been prescribed for School Certificate examinations. But he also scores well in other parts of Africa and overseas. Ngugi is a distant runner-up, yet he too is studied with some frequency in other parts of Africa (particularly Nigeria), and his books were educational staples in Kenya until he fell afoul of the Kenyatta and Moi regimes, at which point they were removed from the high school syllabus. No study guide on any of Ngugi's works has been published in Kenya since 1985. Many of Soyinka's books are considered too difficult for high school students to deal with, so they seldom are assigned at the secondary level. This may explain why there are so few study guides published in Africa on his work; those published in Europe appear to be aimed at university students.

Book chapters (chart 3) tell a different story. Here the overwhelming majority of studies have been written by non-African scholars for books published outside Africa. This may reflect a significant difference in indigenous and foreign publishing practice: African presses seldom bring out edited collections of essays on literary topics, but Western presses are not reluctant to do so. The sudden increase after 1987 in indigenous collections in which essays on Soyinka and Achebe appeared may be attributed to two extraordinary events, both of them significant milestones: Soyinka's winning of the Nobel Prize in December of 1986, and Achebe's sixtieth birthday celebration in February of 1990. Nearly all the fourscore and more essays recorded in Achebe's Nigerian column were abstracts of papers delivered at an academic Symposium held as part of the birthday commemoration festivities, most of which were published in 1996. Discounting these volumes that were brought out in Nigeria to celebrate the achievements of its two greatest writers, the statistics present us with a striking instance of imbalance in scholarly production. Since 1975 (the date of the first contribution of this kind) Nigerians have produced only 14 book chapters on Wole Soyinka, 10 of them for edited volumes published outside Africa. Since 1968 Nigerians have produced only 22 book chapters on Achebe, 14 of them for edited volumes published outside Africa. Since 1973 Kenyans have produced only 6 book chapters on Ngugi, 4 of them for edited volumes published outside Africa. Non-African critics in the meantime have produced 112 book chapters on Soyinka, 97 book chapters on Achebe, and 68 book chapters on Ngugi, publishing all but a handful of them outside Africa. They have produced only two chapters—one on Soyinka and one on Achebe—for books published in Nigeria, and only one chapter on Ngugi for a book published in Kenya. And they have produced only two chapters—one on Soyinka and one on Ngugi—for books published elsewhere in Africa. So in this form of scholarship we have very clear evidence not only of underproduction in Africa and overproduction in the West but also of a disturbing lack of intellectual reciprocity between African and non-African critics. At this level there is hardly any contact, much less exchange, between the two groups, and there is no evidence that the situation has been improving over time. Since books published in the West are too expensive for most scholars based in Africa to buy, and since their financially strapped university libraries may not be able to afford to acquire many of them either, communication via such vehicles has been moving almost entirely in one direction. Westerners have been talking to Westerners, and a few Africans have been talking to Westerners, but hardly anyone has been talking to Africans.

A similar pattern can be discerned in the statistics on articles that have appeared in serial publications (chart 4), but here there is one noteworthy difference. Non-African critics continue to write largely for non-African media; 88% of their essays on Soyinka, 92% of their essays on Achebe, and 87% of their essays on Ngugi have appeared in journals and magazines published outside Africa. African critics, on the other hand, have shown a marked preference for writing for their own media, especially in recent years. This tendency has been most pronounced in Nigeria, but it also prevails in all other parts of Africa except Kenya, where there has actually been a marked decline in interest in Ngugi since 1987. This of course may be connected with his status during this time as persona non grata in his motherland. Elsewhere in Africa, with the understandable exception of Nigeria, Ngugi is a more popular subject among literary critics than Soyinka and Achebe are.

The recent spurt in Nigerian interest in its two favorite literary sons may be attributed in part to the historic events mentioned earlier—the Nobel Prize and the birthday party—but it may also be seen as a natural consequence of the proliferation of indigenous media—particularly newspapers—that carry literary criticism. The cultural columns in the Nigerian press have literally democratized literary debate in that country, moving it from university ivory towers directly to the streets. Nowhere else in Africa has this happened on the same scale. Unfortunately, however, the energy expended in these palavers does not resonate far abroad, for the papers that have promoted such dialogue—mainly the *Guardian, National Concord, Daily Times* and *Vanguard*, the first two of which have on occasion been banned for political reasons—do not circulate widely outside Nigeria. So Nigerians may be talking productively to one another but what they are saying cannot easily be heard beyond their national borders. Their arguments are internal domestic affairs, not international media events.

If we turn now to doctoral dissertations (chart 5), a similar tendency toward indigenization can be detected, but at this point it is only an incipient tendency. Before 1987 Nigerians and other Africans who wrote doctoral dissertations on Soyinka or Achebe did so at institutions outside Africa, but in recent years about fifty percent of the Nigerians have been writing such dissertations at their own national institutions. Most other Africans, notably those from Francophone territories, have continued to do their Ph.D.s on these Anglophone writers at non-African universities, but since 1987 at least two Algerians and two Nigerians chose to write dissertations on Ngugi at institutions at home rather than abroad. The non-African doctoral students working on African literature on the other hand have overwhelmingly elected to earn their degrees at non-African universities, the sole exception to date being an Indian woman who completed her doctorate on Soyinka in 1985 at the University of Ife (now called Obafemi Awolowo University) where Soyinka himself was then teaching. What is perhaps most encouraging about the figures on this chart is that they show that more African scholars have written doctoral dissertations on Soyinka, Achebe, and Ngugi than non-African scholars have. A majority of the real experts on these writers, in other words, are African-born, though not necessarily African-trained. But this fact contrasts sharply with the data we have already seen on scholarly production of books, book chapters and articles. Western-trained non-Africans, many of whom have not studied Soyinka, Achebe, or Ngugi as deeply as the African dissertation writers, are nonetheless producing the bulk of the scholarship on them. Is this a case of opportunistic foreigners rushing in where abler Africans fear to tread, or is it an infrastructural problem that gives a real edge and incentive to energetic interlopers who are under disciplinary pressure to publish or perish and who possess the means and media to do so? Why should so much of the discourse be dominated by the untrained and self-taught, many of whom have never set foot in Africa?

The incipient tendency toward indigenization perceptible in the doctoral dissertations chart becomes more pronounced on the chart devoted to master's theses (chart 6). Here we can see a real move on the part of young Nigerian academics to claim Soyinka and Achebe as their own intellectual property. Whereas initially they tended to write their theses abroad, most of them writing on these authors since 1982 have been doing their work at home. They have also claimed Ngugi as one of their own. The great majority of theses done on Ngugi by African students at universities outside Kenya have been produced by Nigerians, mostly at Nigerian institutions. Non-Africans, unsurprisingly, have written most of their master's theses on African literature at non-African universities, although lately a few have ventured as far afield as Nigeria and Kenya to write on Soyinka, and Tanzania to write on Ngugi. Again, the exceptions tend to prove the rule: Africans are now increasingly being educated in Africa, while non-Africans, as before, are being educated almost exclusively outside Africa. Perhaps this is nothing to worry about; indeed, it may be what we should expect to happen at the lower postgraduate level. The Nigerian hijacking of Ngugi may also be normal and natural, given the number of Nigerian universities that are now offering graduate degrees.

If we look now at the final set of figures—the Grand Totals and the Super Grand Totals (chart 7)—some interesting patterns emerge. First, up to 1976, non-Africans had produced approximately 60% of the scholarship on Soyinka, Achebe and Ngugi. Nowadays their share of the total output has dropped to about 51%, so it is clear that African critics, particularly Nigerians, have been making gradual gains in the last twenty years. Non-African critics used to produce 59% of the commentary on Soyinka, but now they account for no more than 54% of the total. They also used to produce

63% of the scholarship on Achebe, but today their portion of the total critical corpus has dropped to only 46%. With Ngugi the picture is a little different, with non-Africans, formerly producers of 50% of the criticism, now weighing in slightly higher, at 53%. Yet the drift toward Africanization of the critical industry is unmistakable. Far from losing control of their own anglophone literature, African critics are slowly taking it back. If this trend continues, they may be able to claim more than 50% of the critical enterprise before the end of twentieth century. This is real progress.

Yet if one examines the bottom line—the places of publication—one finds that a majority of the studies of Soyinka, Achebe, and Ngugi are still being published outside Africa. In 1976 the figure stood at roughly 61%; today it stands at almost 63%. But even here the news is not all bad, for 66% of all the Nigerians who have written on Soyinka, 70% of all the Nigerians who have written on Achebe, and 67% of all the Kenyans who have written about Ngugi have published their works at home. But offsetting this promising homeward-looking orientation among the Africans is a far more chauvinistic attitude among the Westerners. 90% of the non-African scholars who have written about Soyinka or Ngugi and 92% of the non-African scholars who have written about Achebe have published their works outside Africa. This is where the greatest inequity (not to mention iniquity) lies. Non-African scholars appear to have little desire to exchange ideas with African scholars. They are eager to publish on African literature but not in African media. They are interested in African writers but not in African readers. These modern-day Prosperos and Mirandas would rather sit in armchairs at home making majesterial theoretical pronouncements in antiseptic isolation than risk getting their feet a little muddy on Caliban's island.

Unfortunately, they are not the only ones with this kind of phobia. A good number of African critics betray some of the same pathological symptoms. These reluctant travelers might be prepared to publish occasionally in Prospero and Miranda's distant kingdom, but they do not appear to be keen to address their own neighbors next door. Of the 321 books, study guides, essays, dissertations and theses that Nigerians have written about Soyinka, only 21 (6.5%) have seen print in other African nations. Of the 339 contributions Nigerians have made to the critical literature on Achebe, only 15 (4.4%) have been placed in non-Nigerian African media. Of the 55 scholarly works Kenyans have published on Ngugi, not one (0%) has been published elsewhere in Africa. And when scholars from other parts of Africa write about Soyinka, only 4.5% of what they write reaches print in Nigeria. When they write about Achebe, fewer than 1% of their books, booklets, articles, dissertations and theses get placed in Nigeria. And when they write about Ngugi, less than 1.8% of their scholarship sees the light of day in Kenya. So the absence of transnational, crosscultural communication is a striking phenomenon within Africa too. Nigerians may talk to Nigerians, Kenyans may talk to Kenyans, and both Nigerians and Kenyans do talk to Westerners with some regularity, but there is hardly any intramural transcontinental dialogue going on among anglophone Africans. The little islanders don't mind mixing and mingling with big islanders far away, but they prefer to avoid having close contact with nearby little islanders like themselves. They appear to be suffering from an interiority complex.

The statistics on these charts suggest that scholars of anglophone African literature, wherever in the world they happen to be placed, need to broaden their cultural horizons by exposing themselves to more give and take with their African colleagues. They need to find ways to communicate more effectively with critics, teachers and readers all over the African continent, reaching out to make contact even with those in remote hinterlands who have been routinely cut off from the stimulation of literary debates. Only by thereby Africanizing their own intellectual production will they be able to achieve any measure of true scholarly authority. For if they continue to sail on, oblivious of indigenous conditions and deaf to local alarms, they will surely be blown off course, experience more calamitous shipwrecks, and suffer greater insularity. And for ignorantly visiting such avoidable catastrophes upon themselves and others, they will certainly deserve all of Caliban's curses.

SOURCES

Lindfors, Bernth. *Black African Literature in English: A Guide to Information Sources.* Detroit: Gale Research Co., 1979.

_____. *Black African Literature in English: 1977-1981 Supplement.* New York: Africana Publishing Co., 1986.

_____. *Black African Literature in English, 1982-1986.* London: Hans Zell Publishers, 1989.

_____. *Black African Literature in English, 1987-1991.* Oxford: Hans Zell Publishers, 1995.

Chart 1: **BOOKS**

SOYINKA

	BALE I (1936-76)				BALE II (1977-81)				BALE III (1982-86)				BALE IV (1987-91)				(1992-1995)				GRAND TOTALS			
	NI	OA	NA	T	NI	OA	NA	T	NI	OA	NA	T	NI	OA	NA	T	NI	OA	NA	T	NI	OA	NA	T
NI	1			1									5			5	4			4	10			10
OA			1	1										1		1						1	1	2
NA			2	2			3	3	1		4	5			6	6	1	1	2	4	2	1	17	20
T	1		3	4			3	3	1		4	5	5	1	6	12	5	1	2	8	12	2	18	32

ACHEBE

	BALE I (1936-76)				BALE II (1977-81)				BALE III (1982-86)				BALE IV (1987-91)				(1992-1995)				GRAND TOTALS			
	NI	OA	NA	T	NI	OA	NA	T	NI	OA	NA	T	NI	OA	NA	T	NI	OA	NA	T	NI	OA	NA	T
NI					1			1	1			1	2		1	3	2			2	3		4	7
OA			1	1									1		1	2					1		3	4
NA			2	2			2	2			1	1			7	7			2	2			14	14
T			3	3	1		2	3			2	2	3		9	12			5	5	4		21	25

NGUGI

	BALE I (1936-76)				BALE II (1977-81)				BALE III (1982-86)				BALE IV (1987-91)				(1992-1995)				GRAND TOTALS			
	KE	OA	NA	T	KE	OA	NA	T	KE	OA	NA	T	KE	OA	NA	T	KE	OA	NA	T	KE	OA	NA	T
KE									1			1									1			1
OA																		1		1		1		1
NA							3	3		.5	1.5	2	1		4	5	1			1		1.5	9.5	11
T							3	3	1	.5	1.5	3	1		4	5	1	1		2	1	2.5	9.5	13

GRAND TOTALS

	BALE I (1936-76)				BALE II (1977-81)				BALE III (1982-86)				BALE IV (1987-91)				(1992-1995)				SGT			
	IN	OA	NA	T	IN	OA	NA	T	IN	OA	NA	T	IN	OA	NA	T	IN	OA	NA	T	IN	OA	NA	T
IN	1			1	1			1	1		1	2	7		1	8	4		2	6	14		4	18
OA			2	2									1	1	1	3		1	1	2	1	2	4	7
NA			4	4			8	8	1	.5	6.5	8		1	17	18	1	1	5	7	2	2.5	40.5	45
SGT	1		6	7	1		8	9	2	.5	7.5	10	8	2	19	29	5	2	8	15	17	4.5	48.5	70

Chart 2: STUDY GUIDES

SOYINKA

	BALE I (1936-76)				BALE II (1977-81)				BALE III (1982-86)				BALE IV (1987-91)				GRAND TOTALS			
	NI	OA	NA	T	NI	OA	NA	T	NI	OA	NA	T	NI	OA	NA	T	NI	OA	NA	T
NI	2			2					2			2	2			2	6			6
OA		1	1	2						1		1		2		2		4	1	5
NA		1		1			3	3			3	3	1		1	2	1		8	9
T	2	1	2	5			3	3	2	1	3	6	3	2	1	6	7	4	9	20

ACHEBE

	BALE I (1936-76)				BALE II (1977-81)				BALE III (1982-86)				BALE IV (1987-91)				GRAND TOTALS			
	NI	OA	NA	T	NI	OA	NA	T	NI	OA	NA	T	NI	OA	NA	T	NI	OA	NA	T
NI	3			3	5			5	7		1	8	8			8	23		1	24
OA		1	1	2		3	1	4		2		2		5		5		11	2	13
NA			5	5			4	4			4	4			1	1			14	14
T	3	1	6	10	5	3	5	13	7	2	5	14	8	5	1	14	23	11	17	51

NGUGI

	BALE I (1936-76)				BALE II (1977-81)				BALE III (1982-86)				BALE IV (1987-91)				GRAND TOTALS			
	KE	OA	NA	T	KE	OA	NA	T	KE	OA	NA	T	KE	OA	NA	T	KE	OA	NA	T
KE	1			1	2			2	1			1	1			1	4			4
OA		3		3		1		1		9		9		1		1		14		14
NA		1		1			1	1			1	1			1	1			4	4
T	1	3	1	5	2	1	1	4	1	9	1	11	1	1		2	4	14	4	22

GRAND TOTALS

	BALE I (1936-76)				BALE II (1977-81)				BALE III (1982-86)				BALE IV (1987-91)				SGT			
	IN	OA	NA	T	IN	OA	NA	T	IN	OA	NA	T	IN	OA	NA	T	IN	OA	NA	T
IN	6			6	7			7	10		1	11	10			10	33		1	34
OA		5	2	7		4	1	5		12		12		8		8		19	3	32
NA			7	7			8	8			8	8	1		3	4	1		26	27
SGT	6	5	9	20	7	4	9	20	10	12	9	31	11	8	3	22	34	19	30	93

Chart 3: BOOK CHAPTERS

SOYINKA

	BALE I (1936-76)				BALE II (1977-81)				BALE III (1982-86)				BALE IV (1987-91)				GRAND TOTALS			
	NI	OA	NA	T	NI	OA	NA	T	NI	OA	NA	T	NI	OA	NA	T	NI	OA	NA	T
NI	1		1	2	2		3	5	1		2	3	18		4	22	22		10	32
OA	1	2	4	7		1	1	2		1		1		1	3	4	2	4	8	14
NA			11	11	1		16	17			21	21	3	1	62	66	4	1	110	115
T	2	2	16	20	3	1	20	24	1	1	23	25	22	1	69	92	28	5	128	161

ACHEBE

	BALE I (1936-76)				BALE II (1977-81)				BALE III (1982-86)				BALE IV (1987-91)				GRAND TOTALS			
	NI	OA	NA	T	NI	OA	NA	T	NI	OA	NA	T	NI	OA	NA	T	NI	OA	NA	T
NI	2		1	3	1		1	2	5		1	6	76	1	10	87	84	1	13	98
OA		4	1	5	1	1		2		1		1		3		3		9	2	11
NA	1		17	18			16	16			19	19	10		44	54	11		96	107
T	3	4	19	26	1	1	18	20	5	1	20	26	86	4	54	144	95	10	111	216

NGUGI

	BALE I (1936-76)				BALE II (1977-81)				BALE III (1982-86)				BALE IV (1987-91)				GRAND TOTALS			
	KE	OA	NA	T	KE	OA	NA	T	KE	OA	NA	T	KE	OA	NA	T	KE	OA	NA	T
KE	1			1	1			1			2	2			1	1	2		4	6
OA	1	1		2						1	3	4		2	1	3	1	4	4	9
NA			5	5	1		7	8		1	17	18			37	37	1	1	66	68
T	2	1	5	8	2		8	10	2		22	24	2		39	41	4	5	74	83

GRAND TOTALS

	BALE I (1936-76)				BALE II (1977-81)				BALE III (1982-86)				BALE IV (1987-91)				SGT			
	IN	OA	NA	T	IN	OA	NA	T	IN	OA	NA	T	IN	OA	NA	T	IN	OA	NA	T
IN	4		2	6	4		5	9	6		5	11	94	1	15	110	108	1	27	136
OA	2	7	5	14		2	2	4		3	3	6	1	5	4	10	3	17	14	34
NA	1		33	34	2		39	41		1	57	58	13	1	143	157	16	2	272	290
SGT	7	7	40	54	6	2	46	54	6	4	65	75	108	7	162	277	127	20	313	460

Counting Caliban's Curses: A Statistical Analysis

Chart 4: ARTICLES

SOYINKA

	BALE I (1936-76)				BALE II (1977-81)				BALE III (1982-86)				BALE IV (1987-91)				GRAND TOTALS			
	NI	OA	NA	T	NI	OA	NA	T	NI	OA	NA	T	NI	OA	NA	T	NI	OA	NA	T
NI	17	4	2	23	14	3	10	27	41	5	21	67	72	9	25	106	144	21	58	223
OA	2	10	4	16		4	6	10		15	8	23	1	17	8	26	3	46	26	75
NA	6	13	42	61	5	3	32	40	2	2	71	75	1	6	145	152	14	24	290	328
T	25	27	48	100	19	10	48	77	43	22	100	165	74	32	178	284	161	91	374	626

ACHEBE

	BALE I (1936-76)				BALE II (1977-81)				BALE III (1982-86)				BALE IV (1987-91)				GRAND TOTALS			
	NI	OA	NA	T	NI	OA	NA	T	NI	OA	NA	T	NI	OA	NA	T	NI	OA	NA	T
NI	11	6	11	28	9	1	24	34	29	4	7	40	64	2	21	87	113	13	63	189
OA		10	4	14		7	12	19		10	6	16		10	7	17		37	29	66
NA	5	7	57	69	4		56	60	2		37	39	1		66	67	12	7	216	235
T	16	23	72	111	13	8	92	113	31	14	50	95	65	12	94	171	125	57	308	490

NGUGI

	BALE I (1936-76)				BALE II (1977-81)				BALE III (1982-86)				BALE IV (1987-91)				GRAND TOTALS			
	KE	OA	NA	T	KE	OA	NA	T	KE	OA	NA	T	KE	OA	NA	T	KE	OA	NA	T
KE	3			3	8		2	10	13		2	15	2		6	8	26		10	36
OA	1	7	1	9		9	8	17		16	17	33	1	19	17	37	2	51	43	96
NA	2	2	8	12	1	4	15	20	1	5	34	40		4	70	74	4	15	127	146
T	6	9	9	24	9	13	25	47	14	21	53	88	3	23	93	119	32	66	180	278

GRAND TOTALS

	BALE I (1936-76)				BALE II (1977-81)				BALE III (1982-86)				BALE IV (1987-91)				SGT			
	IN	OA	NA	T	IN	OA	NA	T	IN	OA	NA	T	IN	OA	NA	T	IN	OA	NA	T
IN	31	10	13	54	31	4	36	71	83	9	30	122	138	11	52	201	283	34	131	448
OA	3	27	9	39		20	26	46		41	31	72	2	46	32	80	5	134	98	237
NA	13	22	107	142	10	7	103	120	5	7	142	154	2	10	281	293	30	46	633	709
SGT	47	59	129	235	41	31	165	237	88	57	203	348	142	67	365	574	318	214	862	1394

Chart 5: DOCTORAL DISSERTATIONS

SOYINKA

	BALE I (1936-76)				BALE II (1977-81)				BALE III (1982-86)				BALE IV (1987-91)				GRAND TOTALS			
	NI	OA	NA	T	NI	OA	NA	T	NI	OA	NA	T	NI	OA	NA	T	NI	OA	NA	T
NI							3	3			7	7	4		3	7	4		13	17
OA											3	3			4	4			7	7
NA							3	3	1		7	8			9	9	1		19	20
T							6	6	1		17	18	4		16	20	5		39	44

ACHEBE

	BALE I (1936-76)				BALE II (1977-81)				BALE III (1982-86)				BALE IV (1987-91)				GRAND TOTALS			
	NI	OA	NA	T	NI	OA	NA	T	NI	OA	NA	T	NI	OA	NA	T	NI	OA	NA	T
NI							1	1			3	3	2		2	4	2		6	8
OA			2	2			5	5			7	7			8	8			22	22
NA			3	3			2	2			5	5			8	8			18	18
T			5	5			8	8			15	15	2		18	20	2		46	48

NGUGI

	BALE I (1936-76)				BALE II (1977-81)				BALE III (1982-86)				BALE IV (1987-91)				GRAND TOTALS			
	KE	OA	NA	T	KE	OA	NA	T	KE	OA	NA	T	KE	OA	NA	T	KE	OA	NA	T
KE															3	3			3	3
OA						1		1			4	4	1	4	9	14	1	5	13	19
NA											1	1		1	3	4		1	4	5
T						1		1			5	5	1	5	15	21	1	6	20	27

GRAND TOTALS

	BALE I (1936-76)				BALE II (1977-81)				BALE III (1982-86)				BALE IV (1987-91)				SGT			
	IN	OA	NA	T	IN	OA	NA	T	IN	OA	NA	T	IN	OA	NA	T	IN	OA	NA	T
IN							4	4			10	10	6		8	14	6		22	28
OA			2	2		1	5	6			14	14	1	4	21	26	1	5	42	48
NA			3	3			5	5	1		13	14		1	20	21	1	1	41	43
SGT			5	5		1	14	15	1		37	38	7	5	49	61	8	6	105	119

Chart 6: M.A. THESES

SOYINKA

	BALE I (1936-76)				BALE II (1977-81)				BALE III (1982-86)				BALE IV (1987-91)				GRAND TOTALS			
	NI	OA	NA	T	NI	OA	NA	T	NI	OA	NA	T	NI	OA	NA	T	NI	OA	NA	T
NI			2	2			1	1	10		1	11	17		2	19	27		6	33
OA		1	2	3			2	2		2		2		1		1		4	4	8
NA			9	9			4	4			2	2	1	1	4	6	1	1	19	21
T		1	13	14			7	7	10	2	3	15	18	2	6	26	28	5	29	62

ACHEBE

	BALE I (1936-76)				BALE II (1977-81)				BALE III (1982-86)				BALE IV (1987-91)				GRAND TOTALS			
	NI	OA	NA	T	NI	OA	NA	T	NI	OA	NA	T	NI	OA	NA	T	NI	OA	NA	T
NI	1		1	2					7			7	4			4	11	1	1	13
OA						1		1		1	1	2		1		1		3	1	4
NA			4	4							4	4			2	2			10	10
T	1		5	6		1		1	7	1	5	13	4	1	2	7	11	4	12	27

NGUGI

	BALE I (1936-76)				BALE II (1977-81)				BALE III (1982-86)				BALE IV (1987-91)				GRAND TOTALS			
	KE	OA	NA	T	KE	OA	NA	T	KE	OA	NA	T	KE	OA	NA	T	KE	OA	NA	T
KE									1			1	2		1	3	3		1	4
OA										7	2	9		13	7	20		20	9	29
NA			1	1			2	2						1	8	9		1	11	12
T			1	1			2	2	1	7	2	10	2	14	16	32	3	21	21	45

GRAND TOTALS

	BALE I (1936-76)				BALE II (1977-81)				BALE III (1982-86)				BALE IV (1987-91)				SGT			
	IN	OA	NA	T	IN	OA	NA	T	IN	OA	NA	T	IN	OA	NA	T	IN	OA	NA	T
IN	1		3	4			1	1	18		1	19	23		3	26	41	1	8	50
OA	1		2	3	1		2	3		10	3	13		15	7	22		27	14	41
NA			14	14			6	6			6	6	1	2	14	17	1	2	40	43
SGT	2		19	21	1		9	10	18	10	10	38	24	17	24	65	42	30	62	134

Chart 7: GRAND TOTALS

SOYINKA

	BALE I (1936-76)				BALE II (1977-81)				BALE III (1982-86)				BALE IV (1987-91)				(1992-1995)				SGT			
	NI	OA	NA	T	NI	OA	NA	T	NI	OA	NA	T	NI	OA	NA	T	NI	OA	NA	T	NI	OA	NA	T
NI	21	4	5	30	16	3	17	36	54	5	31	90	118	9	34	161	4			4	213	21	87	321
OA	3	14	12	29		5	9	14		19	11	30	2	21	15	38					5	59	46	110
NA	6	13	65	84	6	3	61	70	4	2	108	114	6	8	227	241	1	1	2	4	23	28	463	514
SGT	30	31	82	143	22	11	87	120	58	26	150	234	126	38	276	440	5	1	2	8	241	108	596	945

ACHEBE

	BALE I (1936-76)				BALE II (1977-81)				BALE III (1982-86)				BALE IV (1987-91)				(1992-1995)				SGT			
	NI	OA	NA	T	NI	OA	NA	T	NI	OA	NA	T	NI	OA	NA	T	NI	OA	NA	T	NI	OA	NA	T
NI	16	7	13	36	16	1	26	43	48	4	13	65	156	3	34	193			2	2	236	15	88	339
OA		15	9	24		12	19	31		14	14	28	1	19	16	36			1	1	1	60	59	120
NA	6	7	88	101	4		80	84	2		70	72	11		128	139			2	2	23	7	368	398
SGT	22	29	110	161	20	13	125	158	50	18	97	165	168	22	178	368			5	5	260	82	515	857

NGUGI

	BALE I (1936-76)				BALE II (1977-81)				BALE III (1982-86)				BALE IV (1987-91)				(1992-1995)				SGT			
	KE	OA	NA	T	KE	OA	NA	T	KE	OA	NA	T	KE	OA	NA	T	KE	OA	NA	T	KE	OA	NA	T
KE	5			5	11		3	14	16		4	20	5		11	16					37		18	55
OA	2	11	1	14		11	8	19		33	26	59	1	39	34	74		1		1	3	95	69	167
NA	2	2	15	19	2	4	28	34	1	6.5	54.5	62		7	123	130			1	1	5	19.5	221.5	245
SGT	9	13	16	38	13	15	39	67	17	39.5	84.5	141	6	46	168	220		1	1	2	45	114.5	308.5	468

SUPER GRAND TOTALS

	BALE I (1936-76)				BALE II (1977-81)				BALE III (1982-86)				BALE IV (1987-91)				(1992-1995)				GTSGT			
	IN	OA	NA	T	IN	OA	NA	T	IN	OA	NA	T	IN	OA	NA	T	IN	OA	NA	T	IN	OA	NA	T
IN	41	11	18	71	43	4	46	93	118	9	48	175	279	12	79	370	4		2	6	486	36	193	715
OA	5	40	22	67		28	36	64		66	51	117	4	79	65	148		1	1	2	9	214	174	397
NA	14	22	168	204	12	7	169	188	7	8.5	232.5	248	17	15	478	510	1	1	5	7	51	54.5	1052.5	1158
GTSGT	61	73	208	342	55	39	251	345	125	83.5	331.5	540	300	106	622	1028	5	2	8	15	546	304.5	1419.5	2270

TEACHING
THINGS FALL APART
IN TEXAS

About twenty years ago the Modern Language Association invited me to edit a collection of essays on *Approaches
to Teaching Achebe's Things Fall Apart* for their Approaches to
Teaching World Literature series.[1] This I was happy to agree
to do, for I was curious to know how others handled this
novel in the classroom. My job was to solicit contributions
from members of the Modern Language Association as well
as from teachers who did not belong to that organization but
who might have something interesting to say about how they
chose to present this text to students. The purpose of the collection was to bring together an array of diverse pedagogical
strategies that might prove helpful to anyone faced with the
challenge of teaching *Things Fall Apart* for the first or the
fortieth time. It was meant to be a handbook created by many
different hands—new hands as well as old hands—so I cast
my net far and wide, encouraging colleagues in a variety of
educational settings and circumstances to describe practices
that they had found effective in dealing with this particular
African masterwork.

The response was gratifying. In fact, so much material
arrived that I was forced to make a judicious selection from
the heap, picking only those essays that stood out from the

rest because they were strikingly original in orientation or methodology. The book was divided into three parts, first five essays on background to the novel featuring biographical and historical approaches, then ten contributions foregrounding a range of critical and theoretical concerns, and finally a brief survey of the deployment of the text in special contexts—for instance, in a humanities core course or a criticism course. The middle section was by far the largest with mythologists, structuralists, deconstructionists, postcolonialists, feminists, Marxists, comparatists, and other interested specialists weighing in with suggestions on how to assist students to look at the novel by squinting at it through a distinctive interpretive lens.

I did not take part in this festival of pragmatic pedagogical hermeneutics. I wrote an introduction to the volume and prepared a bibliography of relevant source material, but I felt I should not usurp any of the remaining space by inserting an essay of my own, even though my approach to teaching *Things Fall Apart* differed from all the others described in the book. Today I feel less reticent about sharing with you how I taught this novel during the thirty-three years I was employed at The University of Texas at Austin, for I regard it as a way of paying back in small measure the large debt I owe to an influential work of art that created an entirely new field of study in which I could teach and write. I believe I owe my career to this book.

But before telling you how I taught it, I should say something about students at The University of Texas. The undergraduates I met there, like those at most other American universities, knew very little about Africa, and much of the little that they did know was wrong. Few had had any experience on the ground anywhere in Africa, so their notions of that continent and the peoples who inhabited it were shaped to a large degree by media images, too many of which were extremely negative, even latently, if not positively, racist.

The graduate students were better, far better. The doctoral dissertations I directed were written by mature individuals from Nigeria, Ghana, Cameroon, South Africa, Germany, Canada, Gibraltar, and various parts of the United States. They at least knew where in the world Africa was and what had been happening there since its encounter with Europe.

Most of the younger undergraduates I taught were taking their first course on anything African, so in sophomore-level classes on African literature I began with a slide show that was meant to introduce them to Africa's diversity—a collage of contrasting landscapes, living conditions, religions, cultural practices, artistic traditions, clothing styles, etc. I then brought out a large map of Africa, but before unrolling it and hanging it on a wall, I handed out copies of a blank political map of Africa and asked the students to fill in as many country names as they could. This exercise usually took no more than a minute because most of them were stumped after identifying only Egypt and South Africa. But at least they were made painfully aware of their limited knowledge of the terrain we were about to explore.

At the next class meeting I followed this up with a brief survey of the geography and history of Africa, covering in 75 minutes the major physical features of the continent and the five hundred or more years of African experience since the Portuguese navigations. I also went over the reading list of the ten or twelve texts we would be studying during the semester, placing them where and when the events recounted in each were represented as having taken place. The readings were organized in a chronological sequence in line with the historical sketch I had just given them. First we would look at Africa before the coming of Europe, then at early and late stages of the colonial period, next at the rise of nationalism and the struggle for independence, and finally at the postcolonial era.

The book selected to give a sense of pre-colonial African experience was Thomas Mofolo's *Chaka*, always a favorite among students for the intriguing ambiguity of its portrait of an ambitious African leader. Was Chaka exercising free will when making decisions, or was he being manipulated by a clever medicine man to choose a course that ultimately would destroy him? Was he responsible for his own fate? A whole class period would be devoted to debating this issue. It was the icebreaker that got the students talking.

From there we would go on to Amos Tutuola's *The Palm-Wine Drinkard*, which is also set in an entirely African universe but in a nonhistorical imaginative realm that is described in a language quite unlike anything the students had ever read before in a literature class. This unusual narrative served as a way of illustrating the influence of oral tales on written literature and the emergence of English-language fiction in West Africa.

The third text in this sequence was invariably *Things Fall Apart*, which was meant to move us to the colonial era. But how does one explain a period in history to students who have had no direct experience of it? The method I chose was to expose them to ideas about Africa that were in circulation in the West in the nineteenth century, ideas founded on a bedrock assumption of racial inequality. This was quite clear in the scientific writings of the day. An excellent example was the crude taxonomy of races formulated by France's leading naturalist, Baron Georges Cuvier, in the first volume of his comprehensive study of *The Animal Kingdom* (1817):

> The Caucasian, to which we ourselves belong, is chiefly distinguished by the beautiful form of the head, which approximates to a perfect oval. It is also remarkable for variations in the shade of the complexion, and colour of the hair. From this variety have sprung the most civilized nations, and such as have most generally exercised dominion over the rest of mankind.

The Mongolian variety is recognized by prominent cheek-bones, flat visage, narrow and oblique
eyes, hair straight and black, scanty beard, and olive
complexion. This race has formed mighty empires
in China and Japan, and occasionally extended its
conquests on this side of the Great Desert, but its
civilization has long appeared stationary.

The negro race is confined to the south of Mount
Atlas. Its characters are, black complexion, woolly
hair, compressed cranium, and flattish nose. In the
prominence of the lower part of the face, and the
thickness of the lips, it manifestly approaches to the
monkey tribe. The hordes of which this variety is
composed have always remained in a state of complete barbarism.[2]

This kind of racial chauvinism could also be found in Sir
William Lawrence's *Lectures on the Physiology, Zoology and
the Natural History of Man* (1819) in which the intellectual
and ethical characteristics of whites and blacks were con-
trasted with devastating clarity:

The distinction of colour between the white and
black races is not more striking than the pre-emi-
nence of the former in moral feelings and in mental
endowments. The latter, it is true, exhibit generally a
great acuteness of the external senses, which in some
instances is heightened by exercise to a degree nearly
incredible. Yet they indulge, almost universally, in dis-
gusting debauchery and sensuality, and display gross
selfishness, indifference to the pains and pleasures
of others, insensibility to beauty of form, order, and
harmony, and an almost entire want of what we comprehend altogether under the expression of elevated
sentiments, manly virtues, and moral feelings.[3]

My favorite examples of this kind of wholesale racial reductionism, however, came from a book published as late as 1912 by a liberal white Southern scholar—a Texan, in fact—named on the cover as W.D. Weatherford, Ph.D. Seeking to demonstrate how far African-Americans had advanced by the beginning of the twentieth century, he called his book *Present Forces in Negro Progress* and filled it with upbeat chapters on "Race Leadership and the Growth of Race Pride," "The New Type of Negro Farmer," "Improvement in the Rural Schools," "What the White Churches are Now Doing for the Negro," "What the Associations are Doing," etc. This was a patently pro-black book, but in an effort to be frank and fair, Weatherford prefaced it with a chapter on "Traits of Negro Character" in which he presented "a brief inventory of [the Negro's] weaknesses and his strength."[4] What is striking about this catalogue of inborn characteristics is how many of the defects of Negro character are traced back to Africa. For instance,

> Perhaps the characteristic in which the Negro differs most radically from the white man is in lack of self-control….the Negro, as a race, has not so far developed what psychologists call the power of inhibition. He cannot forego the pleasure of present gratification in order that he may reap an increased, but a far-off, reward….Some reasons for this lack of self-control are not far to seek, when one looks into tropical environment. One of its commonest manifestations is what we, in common parlance, call laziness. The future reward is not vivid enough to induce a man to lay aside his present ease that he may attain a larger good in the future. This habit of self-indulgence would be greatly accentuated in a tropical climate, where the abundant hand of nature supplies most of the actual necessities of food and clothing. Furthermore, in such a climate hard labor frequently is

punished by death. Those who are over-industrious
are eliminated and there is bred by natural selection
a race of listless people. (16-17)

This was a neat perversion of Darwinian theory, an argument that in the African tropics harsh environmental circumstances led to survival of the least fit.

But that was not all:

> Furthermore, the abundance of food at one season and
> its paucity at another...foster a disposition to gorge
> during the time of plenty in order not to suffer in the
> leaner days. But here again is a form of indulgence
> which breaks down the power of self-control. (18)

Weatherford also believed that this propensity to overindulge explained the Negro's exaggerated sexual appetite and antisocial behavior. Here he cited the scholarship of a Professor Dowd, an authority on "Negroes of the Banana Zone":

> Their wills are inundated and paralyzed by the
> surging of every passion and impulse towards immediate gratification. The riotous clamor of their passions explains their ungovernable temper, propensity
> to murder, steal, lie, deceive, or to overindulge their
> sexual appetite, their love for liquor, tobacco or anything that may momentarily strike their fancy. (19)

Weatherford then went on to note that Negroes were not only passionate but also profoundly superstitious:

> It is unnecessary here more than to refer to the dark
> superstition of practically all of the African tribes.
> They live in constant fear of angry spirits, of the
> power of the fetich, of the witchdoctor and what not.

Much of this has become so deeply ingrained in the nature of the Negro that the slaves and their descendants have never been able to shake themselves free from its terrible hold. (20-21)

Next on the list was Negro cruelty:

Undoubtedly this cruelty is a survival of the old savagery, where the hand of every man was set against his neighbor. (22)

In this xenophobic nightmare scenario Africans were pictured as having no system of law and order, no social cohesion; they were too busy pummeling their neighbors next door.

The rest of the Negro's deeply ingrained faults were largely matters of style. They were said to be "naturally vain, conceited, verbose, pompous, [and] lacking in the power of initiative" (24). Weatherford concluded his list of negative racial traits with the hope that "white and colored alike may see the weaknesses of the Negro and unite in an effort to save him from himself" (25).

The positive side of Weatherford's ledger was equally racist and tinged with an unconscious master/servant mindset. Negroes were said to exhibit fidelity, gratitude, generosity, kindliness, and good humor. Moreover, they were essentially religious and wonderfully musical. Weatherford summed up these characteristics in a stirring peroration:

What a catalogue of splendid qualities is this: Fidelity amid trying circumstances; gratitude where blessings have been bestowed; forgiving in spirit even when grossly wronged; patient in the face of sore trial; generous in spite of bitter poverty; always seeing the humor of a situation, thus saving many a tragic scene; deeply and intensely religious, even though their

religion is often perverted; with souls responsive to
the truest of musical rhythm; and, one might truly
add, cheerful in the midst of privations; sympathetic
to the point of suffering; intensely curious and eager
to know. What if the race is not the most brilliantly
intellectual? What if they are lacking in self-mastery?
What if there is often a lack of industry and thrift?—
here is a catalogue of race traits enough to make any
race happy, virtuous, useful, and even great. (31)

Such remarks remind us that if you have friends like W.D.
Weatherford, Ph.D., you don't really need enemies. Friends
like this do more damage than good by repeating and thereby
perpetuating age-old racial stereotypes.

My lecture on pseudo-scientific theories of racial difference did not end there. I also focused on contributions made
to the denigration of Africa by former colonial officers, by
missionaries, and by serious novelists like Conrad and Joyce
Cary as well as by influential purveyors of popular culture such
as P.T. Barnum and Edgar Rice Burroughs. Even relatively
recent films like *King Solomon's Mines, The African Queen, The
Endless Summer, Out of Africa,* and *Zulu* were brought in to
emphasize the point that Africa and Africans continue to be
portrayed in a negative light.

Through all of this I said not a word about *Things Fall
Apart.* I concentrated entirely on what the scientists, officials,
and creative artists had expressed about Africa. It was such
thinking that defined the West's attitude toward Africa and
rationalized its intervention there. Faulty racial theorizing
served as a justification for European colonialism. It was
assumed that Africans needed to be saved from themselves.

Students came to understand this through their reading
of *Things Fall Apart.* We spent the next class period discussing differences between Western stereotypes of Africans and
the people they saw in Achebe's novel. How did Igbo society
and Igbo individuals differ from those imagined by Cuvier,

Lawrence, Weatherford, and a host of other foreign image makers? The students were quick to recognize that Igbo society was well-organized, hierarchically structured, yet democratically administered, egalitarian, and peaceful. There was a strict system of law and order and a profound respect for religious authority, both of which placed firm constraints on what even the richest and most powerful members of the community could do. If someone violated an established code of conduct, he was punished, regardless of the position he had attained in society. Clearly this was not the heart of darkness. There wasn't a savage anywhere in sight.

The Igbo also worked very hard. Laziness was considered disgraceful, but the industrious son of a lazy man could win respect for what he was able to accomplish on his own. This was an upwardly mobile society, one in which prestige was earned, not inherited. But the social set up had some unappealing features, too. The killing of twins seemed brutal, the unequal position of women in village life appeared unenlightened, and among some men there was an unhealthy emphasis on proving one's manliness. So this was not a perfect society by any means. It had its blemishes, its weaknesses.

Ironically, one of these weaknesses, the one that led to its eventual collapse, derived from its own strong sense of morality. In this peace-loving society one could not raise one's hand against a kinsman, so it proved impossible to chase away those villagers who converted to Christianity or collaborated with white authority. Things fell apart because the bonds of kinship were too tight to be completely severed. Traditional Igbo society was too humane, too pacific, to survive intact.

The importance of such insights was that they were coming not from me or from *CliffsNotes on Things Fall Apart* but from the students themselves. These undergraduates were articulating what they had discovered about African village life by reading the novel and contrasting what they saw represented there with what Western commentators had said about Africans. They had gained a more accurate conception of African society and could now appreciate that Africans had a distinctive civilization and culture of their own before the intrusion of Europeans into their midst.

I would call this an inductive method of teaching. Provide the relevant data and let the students draw their own conclusions from it. Give them a basis for comparison and let them work out the significance of the differences they discover. Don't preach. Let them learn the truth independently. Get out of the way, and let *Things Fall Apart* be their teacher.

NOTES

1. *Approaches to Teaching Achebe's Things Fall Apart* (New York: Modern Language Association of America, 1991).
2. Quoted in Philip D. Curtin's *The Image of Africa: British Ideas and Action, 1780-1850* (Madison: University of Wisconsin Press, 1964), 231.
3. Quoted in ibid., 232.
4. W.D. Weatherford, *Present Forces in Negro Progress* (New York and London: Association Press, 1912), 16. All quotations are from this edition. I may be doing Weatherford a disservice by quoting his remarks out of their wider context. In his time and place he was a pioneer in promoting better race relations and improving the lot of the less advantaged, particularly African-Americans but also poor whites in the Appalachians. For a more balanced appraisal of his life and works see the biography by Wilma Dykeman, *Prophet of Plenty: The First Ninety Years of W.D. Weatherford* (Knoxville: University of Tennessee Press, 1966).

Achebe speaking at The University of Texas at Austin, November 1969

THE WRITER AND THE AFRICAN REVOLUTION

CHINUA ACHEBE

Through glass windowpane
Up a modern office block
I saw, two floors below, on wide-jutting
concrete canopy a mango seedling newly sprouted
Purple, two-leafed, standing on its burst
Black yolk. It waved brightly to sun and wind
Between rains—daily regaling itself
On seed yams, prodigally.
For how long?
How long the happy waving
From precipice of rainswept sarcophagus?
How long the feast on remnant flour
At pot bottom?
  Perhaps like the widow
Of infinite faith it stood in wait
For the holy man of the forest, shaggy-haired
Powered for eternal replenishment.
Or else it hoped for Old Tortoise's miraculous feast
On one ever recurring dot of cocoyam
Set in a large bowl of green vegetables—
This day beyond fable, beyond faith?
  Then I saw it

Poised in courageous impartiality
Between the primordial quarrel of Earth
And Sky striving bravely to sink roots
Into objectivity, midair in stone.

I thought the rain, prime mover
To this enterprise, someday would rise in power
And deliver its ward in delirious waterfall
Toward earth below. But every rainy day
Little playful floods assembled on the slab.
Danced, parted round its feet,
United again, and passed.
It went from purple to sickly green
Before it died.
  Today I see it still—
Dry, wire-thin in sun and dust of the dry months—
Headstone on tiny debris of passionate courage.

Aba, 1968
("Mango Seedling")[1]

Ithought I should begin with that poem because it says
something on the subject that I have chosen to speak about
tonight. That poem was written to a friend of mine, a fellow
writer who was killed last year, in 1967, in the Nigeria-Biafra
war. He was a poet, one of the finest in Africa, who felt a
sense of commitment, commitment to what his people were
fighting and dying for. So, I think it is important to begin
with it, because people often wonder what a writer should be
doing in a situation like what we have in Biafra today.

In fact, whenever I have traveled out in the last two years,
my own friends have always asked one question, that is, "Are
you writing anything now?" And when I have said, "No, I'm
too busy fighting," they've replied, "Oh, yes, that's very sad.
We hope that all that sad business will soon be over so that
you can return to your writing." Therefore, it seems to me

that there is something that needs to be said about the place of the writer in this kind of situation. Another reason why I thought I should begin with a poem is that I have noticed in some of the places I have visited of late, a certain reluctance to talk politics, a certain reluctance to listen to a writer talking politics. It is felt that a writer should talk about writing. And to avoid any criticism, therefore, I thought I should begin with a poem; and having started on the right foot, I hope that if I talk about politics, if I talk about life, in the main body of my speech, you will not be too upset.

Two weeks ago (or four weeks ago) just before I left home, I received a letter of invitation from the Norwegian Students Association—a letter from their secretary. In this letter, he said that they had been following with sadness and sorrow the continuing tragedy in Biafra. These were his words. He said that they had learned and gained a lot of insight into what was happening from a televised interview which I had given a Norwegian journalist and which they had seen. And he ended by inviting me to visit Norway to talk to Norwegian students—of course, all expenses would be paid—and he chose the topic of the lecture for me, and it is this: "Tribalism, the Black Man's Burden" [audience laughs]. Well, I didn't find it funny at all. I was in fact in despair. I was really in despair when I read that portion, because in my mood at that time, and I think at the present moment, it seemed to me that in that letter Europe had framed yet another charge against Africa, and I was being called to come forward and begin my defense all over again. Well, I say "all over again," because I have argued endlessly in the past. To the slave traders, I had entered the plea that I was human, that I was not a commodity. To those apostles of Europe's civilizing mission to Africa, I had said that my own civilization was perfectly adequate to my needs. I had told that gangster Cecil Rhodes and his band of adventurers—who said they were carrying the white man's burden for my benefit—I had told them that what they were carrying was a bag of diamonds stolen from my people.

Of late, I have been telling Europe, and Europe here embraces America, that independence for African nations cannot mean the limited independence, the limited freedom to follow like a tame animal wherever Europe or America cared to lead. So, you see, over the centuries, I have done nothing but argue. Were it possible for me to be blue in the face (I don't know whether you have that expression here; they have it in England), were it possible for me to be blue in the face, I would have become blue arguing, pleading, defending. I have indeed carried an intolerable and irksome burden, but it is not the burden of tribalism, as my Norwegian friends thought. It was the burden of having to stand at the bar of the white world to explain and justify myself endlessly. I often ask myself, "Why is it necessary to go through this long, this interminable trial? Is it because the white world is genuinely concerned with justice for me?" I think not. I think the white world is concerned with its own image, its own estimation. It's concerned; it has what you might call a legal-istic conscience. It doesn't do anything without first framing a charge, going through a trial, and passing judgment.

Once upon a time, a hungry lion met a lamb, and decided to eat her. But he was a legalistic-minded lion. He was a lion that was concerned about his image, a lion that wouldn't do anything without framing a charge, without putting it into its proper legal form. So, he said to the lamb: "Three years ago, at this very spot, you said all kinds of nasty things about me. Why did you do it?" The lamb said, "I'm sorry, sir, but I didn't do anything like that. In fact, I wasn't even born three years ago." To which the lion said, "Well, it must have been your mother or father, or somebody else in your family," and he ate the lamb.

What you may say is that I am overreacting; you may say that I'm reading too much into a simple letter of invita-tion from simple students in Norway who, in all probability, only want to be informed, only want enlightenment. I do not suggest, for one moment, that these students are wicked. I do not suggest that they are consciously participating in a conspiracy against me. But what I say is that whether or not they know it, whether or not they are aware of it, they have spoken for white men. It's like a little child can sometimes quite innocently divulge to a neighbor what his parents said privately, to everyone's embarrassment.

Now, why did the Norwegian students think that the burden of the black man today is tribalism, and why did they ask me to come and talk about it? Well, I suppose as a writer I'm supposed to have all kinds of insight. And as a Biafran I'm assumed to be participating, at this moment, in one of the most vicious displays of tribalism in Africa, which is the way they see what is going on.

You see, Africa, in the mind of the West, in the mind of Europe, is a strange, mysterious place. It is the dark continent. It is inhabited by that peculiar breed which Rudyard Kipling—you know that famous imperial poet—called "half devil, half child" in Africa. In Africa—this is the mind of Europe I'm reporting—there are no nations, only tribes. In Africa there is no logic or reason, only that irrational passion. In short, Africa is a world of its own, and this world is the very antithesis of Europe. The British Broadcasting Corporation, which is very knowledgeable in these things, has a special daily program which it calls "News of the African World." You see, it sounds right, doesn't it? "News of the Australian World" sounds strange, but "News of the African World" is right, because Africa is a world apart. This world is the world of tribes, the world of irrational passions, the dark world.

I often play with irreverent ideas sometimes. One that occurred to me lately was: supposing the late President Kennedy had been an African President, how would the news of his death have been carried by the world press? I suggest it might have run something like this: President Kennedy, a member of the tribe of New England, was today shot and killed by a tribesman believed to be from the big hostile tribe of Texas [audience laughs].

When the Russians invaded Czechoslovakia, the world was outraged, quite rightly, because the Czechs were understood as a nation; they were entitled to freedom and self-determination. When the Russians, the British, the Nigerians invade and devastate Biafra, they do so to prevent Africa from relapsing back into tribalism—you know, that fatal disease which it is the mission of Europe to cure in Africa. It is the white man's mission in Africa to create stable modern nations out of the turbulent bedlam of tribes; and they have already done it. If you know anything about the history of the last century, you will know how this was done. I'll sketch it in very briefly.

Towards the end of the last century European missionaries, European traders, European soldiers were fighting one another in Africa, tearing one another's throats in their bid to civilize Africa. The squabbling became rather unseemly. So, in 1884, Bismarck called a conference in Berlin. He called all the parties concerned to Berlin to sort out this matter. The diplomats assembled had a map in front of them. It was a map of Africa, a map without nations, without people, without boundaries. It was a huge, mango-shaped land mass of chaos and darkness. Over this impenetrable darkness, the spirit of the diplomats brooded for a while. Then they took up their pencils and began to make lines, they began to draw lines to fill in the vacuum. When they were through, you had modern Africa: the Africa of the British, the French, the Italians, the Portuguese, the Spaniards, the Germans, the Belgians, etc. In short, an Africa created by Europe in her own image. It was a good Africa, a redeemed Africa.

Naturally, there were some minor inconveniences for the natives, as indeed there are bound to be in all acts of redemption [audience laughs]. For instance, one of the natives may have gone to a neighboring village to visit his old friends when the line was made. Well, in that case, he had to stay where he was. It is true he had lost his hut, had lost his wife and children, and things like that, but he had gained a nation [audience laughs]. So Europe, like God on creation morning, looked down on the work he had done and saw that it was good [audience laughs]. A few natives would lose their huts, and their wives and children, and things like that; some may even lose their lives, but they have gained modern African nations. They have gained Nigeria, for instance. How could anyone be so wrong-headed, be so blind as not to appreciate this fact? Somebody like myself [audience laughs].

They said they lost their houses, their wives and children, and things like that, in Nigeria—it's very sad, very sad. It shows, by the way, that the work of redemption is not complete. But surely, they must admit that in certain circumstances it is better to dissolve the people than the state. Of course, you don't speak such scandal in Europe about European people. As we have seen, Africa is different. It is the duty of Europe to save Africa from itself.

Fanon, Frantz Fanon, describing the role of Europe in Africa, compared it to that of a mother who unceasingly restrains her fundamentally perverse offspring from managing to commit suicide and from giving free reign to his evil instincts. And we all know that the worst of these instincts is the compulsive way of the native to resort to the tribe—rather like Prester John in the novel who shook off his civilization, his religion, his veneer of Europe, and went back to the tribe.

This myth of the tribe is the greatest block to an understanding of Africa by the white world. It makes it impossible for the white world to know and understand what is going on in Africa. As long as you can say it is tribalism, you don't have to worry anymore, you won't have to think. Tribalism…

Somebody said to me in Holland: "But you have always run after one another with spears; this is what the tribes have always done." This myth of the tribe was actually invented by Europeans. It was invented by Europeans to distinguish between themselves and their African victims of colonial exploitation. It was necessary, it was absolutely necessary to invent it, because if you didn't, you would have to concede that Africans were people, and were nations. Then you would face a crisis of conscience. You would have to answer such questions as "What are you doing there?" So you needed a pejorative word—and words are very potent—you needed a word to set them apart, to dehumanize them, to turn them into brutes. Thereafter you could say with that incredible character in Joseph Conrad's *Heart of Darkness* "Exterminate all the brutes!" Unfortunately, at that point that character himself, Kurtz, is completely dehumanized. He has become a brute, powerful because he has a gun, but a brute. My people have a saying, they say that you can't pull another man down in the mud without being there yourself. What this means in Queen's English is that humanity is indivisible. It is either all of us or none of us.

So to my friends in Norway and elsewhere, I would say let us get rid of shibboleths, let us get rid of non-speech that blocks understanding. The truth is really quite simple, it is simpler than the myth. And the truth is that Africa is people. The truth is that Biafra is people, that Biafra is a nation.

What then is a nation, you may say, in the context of Africa, in the context of anywhere, for that matter? A nation is a people with common cultural consciousness. Where this consciousness exists, you have a nation; it may be small, it may be big. Where it doesn't exist, you may have a formal state but you haven't got a nation. This is bad news for many people. African nations were scrambled and moulded together into formal states at the end of the last century, in the manner I have described, by Europe. Today, some of these states are striving, are struggling to become nations. Some of them will succeed when they have created a common cultural and spiritual consciousness through the will of their people, the revolutionary will of their people, to be a nation.

I have talked about cultural consciousness (we talk about that a lot; we talk about culture). What do we mean by culture, especially when we are talking about Africa?

When people talk about culture in terms of Africa, they quite often mean an assortment of old customs and oddities. The reason for this is quite clear. When Europe came to Africa and said, "You have no culture, you have no civilization, you have no religion, you have no history," Africa was bound sooner or later to reply by displaying her own accomplishments. To do this, her spokesmen—her writers and intellectuals—stepped back into the past, into what you might call the "era of purity" before the coming of Europe. What they uncovered there they put into their books, into their poems, and this became known as their culture, their answer to Europe's arrogance. They spoke of civilizations that were satisfying to those who were born into them; they spoke of their gods with whom they were at ease; they wept over the death of these gods, over the destruction of these civilizations, like in this poem where the sacred python weeps for the death of the river god:

> I was there when lizards
> were ones and twos, child
> Of ancient river god Idemili. Painful
> Teardrops of Sky's first weeping
> Drew my spots. Sky-born
> I walked the earth with royal gait
> And crowds of human mourners
> Filing down funereal paths
> Across lengthening shadows
> Of the dead acknowledged my face
> In broken dirges of fear.
>
> But of late
> A wandering god pursued,
> It seems, by hideous things

He did at home has come to us
And pitched his tent here
Beneath the people's holy tree
And hoisted from its pinnacle
A charlatan bell that calls
Unknown monotones of revolts,
Scandals, and false immunities.
And I that none before could meet except
In fear though I brought no terrors
From creation's day of gifts I must now
Turn on my track
In dishonorable flight
Where children stop their play
To shriek in my ringing ears:
   Look out, python! Look out, python!
   Christians relish python flesh!

And mighty god Idemili
That once upheld from earth foundations
Cloud banks of sky's endless waters
Is betrayed in his shrine by empty men
Suborned with the stranger's tawdry gifts
And taken trussed up to the alter-shrine turned
Slaughterhouse for the gory advent
Feast of an errant cannibal god
Tooth-filed to eat his fellows.

And the sky recedes in
Disgust; the orphan snake
Abandoned weeps in the shadows.

("Lament of the Sacred Python")[2]

That is the grief of the African intellectual or the African poet writing about the death of his civilization, the death of his gods. And as I said, this became known as his culture.

But culture is more than books; culture is more than poems. The culture of a people is their cooperative effort, it is their cooperative will to make a clearing in the jungle and build on it a place of human habitation. If this place is disturbed or destroyed, as long as these people are alive, they will move to another spot, they will make a new clearing, and they will begin to build on it another home. So, while the African intellectual was busy displaying the past culture of his people, the past culture of Africa, the peoples of Africa themselves, people caught in new emergencies, in new predicaments, were already creating new revolutionary cultures—cultures which take into account their present condition, because, as long as the people are alive, their culture is alive; as long as the people are changing, their culture will be changing. The only place where culture is static, where culture exists independently of people, is the museum, and this is not an African institution. Even there it is doubtful whether culture exists, in museums. It is already dead, to my mind. Of course, it you have a good curator, a good museum official, he will display the artifacts so skillfully as to give the impression of completeness, or even life. But it is no more than the complete skin which a snake has discarded and gone its way.

This has been the problem of the African intellectual, the African artist: that he has been left far behind by the people who make culture, and he must hurry, he must now hurry and catch up with the people, catch up with them in that zone—to borrow the beautiful expression of Fanon—that zone of occult instability where people dwell. It is there, at that zone, that customs die and cultures are born. It is there that the regenerative powers of the people are most potent. These powers are manifest today in the African revolution, a revolution that aims towards true independence, as opposed to phony independence, formal independence; a revolution that moves toward the creation of modern states in place of the neocolonial enclaves we have today, a revolution that is informed with African ideologies.

What is the place of the writer in this movement? I suggest that his place is right in the middle of it, in the thick of it—if possible, at the head of it. Some of my friends say, "No, it isn't, it is too rough there. A writer has no business being where it is so rough. He should be at the sidelines with his note-paper and pencil, where he can observe with objectivity." I say that a writer in the African revolution who steps aside on the sidewalk can only write footnotes, he can only write a glossary when the event is over. He will become like the intellectual of today in many other places, the intellectual of futility asking many questions like: "Who am I? What's the meaning of my existence? Does this place belong to me or to somebody else? Does my life belong to me or to some other person?"—questions that no one can answer, questions like "Why am I lonely?"

I have a poem which asks such questions. The intellectual here even poses questions to particles of dust:

> Angled sunbeam lowered
> like Jacob's ladder through
> sky's peephole pierced in the roof
> to my silent floor and bared feet.
> Are these your creatures
> these crowding specks
> stomping your lighted corridor
> to a remote sun, like doped
> acrobatic angels gyrating
> at needlepoint to divert a high
> unamused god? Or am I
> sole stranger in a twilight room
> I called my own overrun
> and possessed long ago by myriads more
> as yet invisible in all
> this surrounding penumbra?

("Question")

242

That is the question that no one can answer, the question of futility. The answer must come from within, and the answer is in action.

> I broke at last
> the terror-fringed fascination
> that bound my ancient gaze
> to those crowding faces
> of plunder and seized my
> remnant life in a miracle
> of decision between white-
> collar hands and shook it
> like a cheap watch in
> my ear and threw it down
> beside me on the earth floor
> and rose to my feet. I
> made of their shoulders
> and heads bobbing up and down
> a new ladder and leaned
> it on their seating flanks
> and ascended till midair
> my hands so new to harshness
> could grapple the roughness of a prickly
> day and quench the source
> that fed turbulence to their
> feet. I made a dramatic
> descent that day landing
> backways into crouching shadows
> into potsherds of broken trance. I
> flung open long-disused windows
> and doors and saw my hut
> new-swept by rainbow brooms
> of sunlight become my home again
> on whose trysting floor waited
> my proud vibrant life.

("Answer")

NOTES

1. LINE 14: *the widow of infinite faith* refers to the story of the widow of Sarephath in the First Book of Kings, chapter 17.

    LINE 18: *Old Tortoise's miraculous feast*: Once upon a time Tortoise went to work for an old woman, and at the end of his labors she set before him a bowl containing a lone cocoyam sitting on a mound of cooked green leaves. Naturally, Tortoise protested vehemently and refused to touch such a meager meal. In the end, however, he was persuaded, still protesting, to give it a try. Then he discovered to his amazement (and nearly his undoing) that another cocoyam always appeared in the bowl as soon as he ate the previous one.

    LINE 24: *the primordial quarrel of Earth and Sky*: This was a dispute over who was sovereign. It led finally to Sky's withholding of rain for seven whole years, until the ground became hard as iron and the dead could not be buried. Only then did Earth sue for peace, sending high-flying Vulture as emissary.

2. LINE 10:*acknowledged my face in broken dirges*: One of the songs that accompany the dead to the burial place at nightfall has these lines:

    Look a python! Look a python!

    Python lies across the way!

    LINE 24: *creation's day of gifts*: We all choose our gifts, our character, our fate from the Creator just before we make our journey into the world. The sacred python did not choose (like some other snakes) the terror of the fang and venom, and yet it received a presence more overpowering than theirs.

[This text of this lecture was transcribed by Christian Njimma. Footnotes to the poems have been added from Achebe's *Collected Poems* (New York: Anchor Books; Manchester, UK: Carcanet Press Limited, 2005.)]

A GROUP INTERVIEW WITH ACHEBE IN 1969

When Chinua Achebe spoke at The University of Texas at Austin, he was asked many questions in discussions afterward. Some of these questions were informed and penetrating, others quite inane, but he fielded them all with impressive candor, intelligence, and wit. What follows is a transcript of a selection of his remarks on literary matters.

What are you doing in the United States?
I'm here on a program arranged by the Committee for Biafran Writers and Artists. This is an American committee which is trying to bring over Biafran artists and writers to show that Biafra is all kinds of people and not only starving children, though that is a part of it. The Committee is also trying to send American writers into Biafra to see things for themselves.

What is your position in Biafra?
It's difficult to say. If things were normal, I would be at the University of Biafra, but the university is not functioning.

As a professor?
Well, as some kind of writer in residence.

Are you doing any writing now?
Yes, but not novels. I do articles and some poetry, but I can't do more than that. I started a novel just before the war which seemed to me at the time terribly important—I already had the idea for it as far back as '66—but I finally gave it up because it later seemed to me completely unimportant. Poetry—something short and intense—seems more relevant now and suits my mood better.

Is there much writing going on in Biafra today?
Oh yes, a tremendous amount—mostly poetry and drama. In the last two months I have seen two really good plays, one a kind of opera with a war theme. In fact, the title of the opera is the name of one of the devastating weapons which Biafran scientists developed in the course of this war. The play is very good—very ambitious and very well done.

Are most of the writers in Biafra today young writers?
Yes. I'm supposed to be a sort of "elder statesman."

Do you foresee a time when you will go back to writing novels?
Oh yes, it's always possible, if one survives. There's always time. But these are not normal times, not for me. These are not normal times at all.

Can we talk a bit about your past writing? In the four novels you have written do you try to bring out one message, one theme, or do you give each book a different theme?
I like to make each book I write different; otherwise, to my mind, there wouldn't be any point in writing another.

Do you believe literature should carry a social or political message?
Yes, I believe it is impossible to write anything in Africa without some kind of commitment, some kind of message,

some kind of protest. Even those early novels that look like very gentle recreations of the past—what they were saying, in effect, was that we had a past. That was protest because there were people who thought we didn't have a past. What we were doing was to say politely that we *did*—here it is. So commitment is nothing new. Commitment runs right through our work. In fact, I should say all our writers, whether they're aware of it or not, are committed writers. The whole pattern of life demanded that you should protest, that you should put in a word for your history, your traditions, your religion, and so on.

Some literary critics, however, don't regard you as a protest writer because you write with such restraint.
Well, according to my own definition of protest, I *am* a protest writer. Restraint—well, that's my style, you see.

Do you write mostly for the story or for the message?
There is no distinction. I mean you can't really draw this line. I think a good story immediately carries a huge message. Any good story. And in the form of the novel—given the kind of society in which I operate, a society that has been under great pressure from the white world—the story is bound to be pregnant with message. One big message of the many that I try to put across, is that Africa was not a vacuum before the coming of Europe, that culture was not unknown in Africa, that culture was not brought to Africa by the white world. You would have thought it was obvious that everybody had a past, but there were people who came to Africa and said, "You have no history, you have no civilization, you have no culture, you have no civilization, you have no religion. You are lucky we are here. Now you are hearing about these things from us for the first time." Well, you know, we didn't just drop from the sky. We too had our own history, traditions, cultures, civilizations. It is not possible for one culture

to come to another and say, "I am the way, the truth, and the life; there is nothing else but me." If you say this, you are guilty of irreverence or arrogance. You are also stupid. And this is really my concern.

But you don't picture the Europeans who came to Igboland as black-hearted villains.
No, I don't think that is necessary. I think they were very ignorant. And that's very bad, you know, when you are trying to civilize other people. But you don't really need to be black-hearted to do all kinds of wrong things. Those who have the best intentions sometimes commit the worst crimes. I think it's not my business to present villains without any redeeming features. This would be untrue. I think what's more likely to be true is somebody coming with the best of intentions, really believing that there is nothing here, and that he is bringing civilization. He's wrong, of course. He's completely wrong and misguided. But that's the man that interests me because he has the potentialities for doing great harm.

Would you say that the focus of your protest has changed considerably over the years?
Well, my role has been changing. And I think this is true of all the other writers in one way or another. We started off—and this was necessary—showing that there was something here—a civilization, a religion, a history. Then we had to move on to the era of independence. Having fought with the nationalist movements and been on the side of the politicians, I realized after independence that they and I were now on different sides, because they were not doing what we had agreed they should do. So I had to become a critic. I found myself on the side of the people against their leaders—leaders this time being black people. I was still doing my job as a writer, but one aspect of the job had changed. I think what you do as a writer depends on the state of your society.

And do you see the role of the African writer being partly that of teaching African people about their own culture, their own traditions, and so forth?

Yes. In fact, I wrote an essay on this subject some years back called "The Novelist as Teacher." I'll tell you something I discovered. I have a daughter who was five at the time that I began to buy literature for her. We were living in Lagos then. All I did was go into the big store and pick up these glossy children's books and give them to her. I never read those things myself, so I never knew what was inside. But before very long I discovered that this girl was developing strange ideas about color. So it occurred to me to take some interest in the literature she'd been reading. And what I discovered was that all the good characters in her books are white, except the villain who's called a golliwog. A golliwog is always black. Now this is dangerous—very, very dangerous in Africa. And there's a lot of this going on, a lot of stuff we're not aware of going on quietly, in the name of education. And it's our business to do something about it. I was in fact involved in setting up with a friend of mine—one of our finest poets [Chistopher Okigbo] who unfortunately was killed during this war—a publishing house in Biafra for children's books.

Do you think it would be possible in a modern African nation to have communities of the simplicity of that one you describe in Things Fall Apart—*not only economic but intellectual simplicity—and still have the nation competing or holding its own against the sophisticated nations outside of Africa or even within it?*

Well, I won't quarrel with the words "sophisticated" and so on because we'd get bogged down. I think that society you talk about was highly sophisticated. If you get the impression of naïveté, then it's my fault as a portrayer of the society or your fault for missing some of the points. That society was very complex. But the point you make is valid: is it possible to recapture that kind of society's ideas and so on and make use of them for modernization? I don't know. It's too late anyway. The best we can do is to catch what we can; we can't recapture that life in its entirety. It was a society with a highly integrated worldview: man in society, men and their gods, men and nature—all were one. Every man had his place, society had its place, even the gods had their parts to play, and if a god failed to play his part, he was punished. I know examples where a god that was supposed to protect the lives of the people failed to do his job and the people carried him outside the village and set fire on him. Well, that kind of society you cannot transplant, even if it hadn't been disturbed so badly today. But there are aspects of it that can be made use of—the extended family, for instance. My family at home doesn't mean myself, my wife, and one child; our idea of family is much more extended. We can make use of that and still modernize.

Ezeulu, the hero of your third novel Arrow of God, *is a chief priest who tries to manipulate another religion—Christianity—for political reasons. What do you think of his behavior?*
Well, he was a man I have a lot of respect for, a great intellectual. He saw what was happening; he saw that change was inevitable—unlike the intellectual today who perhaps doesn't see that the change has in fact happened. He saw this and he asked himself, "How do I use this new force, while still retaining my position, and make it my own?" That was good. He failed, unfortunately, but he saw clearly what was happening, unlike my character in *Things Fall Apart* who was not an intellectual and did not see what was going on. Okonkwo just saw his duty to protect his own and stand against the assault. So he failed. Ezeulu said, "Right, I've seen this thing; these people are powerful but that doesn't mean they are superior to me. I'll make use of them." But he failed too, and that's a pity.

So Ezeulu didn't really believe that Christianity was better because it was more powerful?
No, he didn't believe it was right. He didn't accept it. He was concerned with tactics, with basic realities, and he recognized the need to make temporary alliances. He said, "This thing is coming. I'll send someone to go and make an alliance with them, but the assumption is that I will remain in power—that the religion, the civilization, the tradition I embody will still remain in power. Let us absorb this thing that is coming; let's arrest it before it ruin or break us."

But Ezeulu's opponent Nwaka charged that he was trying to become more than a chief priest, that he wanted to become king as well. Do you think this was true?
What that man was saying in reality was that Ezeulu was getting too powerful. You see, the idea of kings really was not accepted among the Igbos. We did not go in for kings. So the word "king" was used here to describe someone who was trying to become too powerful. And this runs against the Igbo belief in the complete integration of life, which I was talking about earlier, because you can also see it in terms of an individual versus society. I think people were reacting as they normally do whenever they see the possibility of someone becoming too strong in the society.

Do you think Ezeulu might have had a tendency to try and assume too much power?
I think he had enough priestly arrogance to attempt it. This shows from time to time, like when he's confusing his thinking with the thinking of the god. These are natural feelings for a man who is a priest. Every priest, I think, can fall into that danger.

Our class has just finished reading A Man of the People, *and we wondered what your outlook on Odili was. Did you picture him as being naïve and idealistic or did you intend him as an object of satire, even burlesque?*

My picture of him is there. What you are asking me is what your picture of him should be, which is not really fair. Well, I like that young man. He was idealistic, he was naïve, he was this and he was that, but I think he was also basically honest, which makes a difference. He was very, very honest. He knew his own shortcomings; he even knew when his motives were not very pure, and he admitted that these motives were not pure. This puts him in a class worthy of attention, as far as I'm concerned. And I think he probably would return to do a better job next time. He suffered in this kind of society because it was very cruel, very ruthless. But he was learning very fast, and at the end I think he had improved his chances of being of service, of doing the things he thought should be done. He'd improved those chances.

What is the significance of the sex in A Man of the People?
What a question! Well, I don't know what the significance is. It's a part of life. More particularly, it's a part of this young man's attitude. At the beginning, when he was just floating like anybody else, like a lot of young people, wondering what his role should be, he uses sex in a way that is appropriate in that kind of situation. Later on, when he gets involved in politics, his attitude changes quite considerably. The sex is not there just for titillation, if that's what you're worrying about. I think it plays an important part in the development of this character.

But how seriously should we take the revenge idea? Was Odili's sexual failure an isolating factor that led him into politics?
Well, people stumble into right causes in all kinds of ways. It seems to me perfectly legitimate to stumble into politics through failure in a love affair. If you take the view that politics is so important that one should only approach it through

training in a monastery or something, then that's not really life. It's not necessary to judge a man's action simply in terms of "well, he's only seeking revenge." He himself was honest enough to know that there was that element in his motivation, but soon there were other more worthwhile reasons. And I think I wouldn't quarrel with him at all for that.

Are characters like Jean and her husband in A Man of the People *characteristic of the African view of American men and women?*
I wonder why we must pin down things like this. This is one American couple. After all, we've been stereotyped in the past. Why shouldn't you be stereotyped? It's a possible American couple. Others have asked me whether they were real people. No, they're not real people. It's the kind of thing that could happen.

Is Nanga characteristic of political leadership in Africa?
He was characteristic of the leadership just before the military came into politics in Nigeria and characteristic of leadership in other places where the military did not come into politics. I would give you names, but I think I had better not. But if you look at the politics of Africa today, I think you'll find other countries where everything will be quite parallel to this book except the very end. In fact, two years ago the leader of an East African country I shall not name [Kenya] bought copies of this book and gave one to each government minister for Christmas.

What factors caused the emergence of politicians like Nanga?
Well, the colonial departure from the scene was not really a departure. I mean independence was unreal, and people like Nanga were actually used as front men, as puppets, by the former colonial power. As long as they could go about saying they were ministers, as long as they enriched themselves,

they were happy, and they would leave the real exploiter at his work. So I think in a very basic sense, characters like Nanga flourished because the colonial situation leading to the independence period in Africa made it possible. And it still happens; it's not a thing of the past.

Was it from the events in the Western Region of Nigeria prior to 1966 that you drew the political action of the novel? Or was it an anticipation of something that had not yet happened?

The novel was completed at least two years before January 1966. It was completed in '64. And the indication as to how politics was going to develop in Nigeria was there already. If you cared to look, I think the signs were everywhere, not only in the West. There were parallel events all over. The worst no doubt was in the West because that was the seat of the crisis. That was where the manipulation was the most blatant. But I think you could see signs everywhere.

Although there has been trouble in Nigeria between ethnic groups, you don't seem to make reference to any kind of tribal antagonism in your novels, particularly A Man of the People *where one might expect to see this portrayed.*

I hate the word tribe. Tribes were not really all that important, you know, in the past. However, it is not quite correct to say that I don't make reference to these antagonisms because I do. I can even refer to places where somebody loses a job or doesn't get a job and blames it on somebody from another tribe. But it was at that level; this didn't really become a terribly dangerous and explosive issue until it became a subject for political manipulation, especially since independence. There were rumbles before, but they were not more than you'd find anywhere else. It really got out of hand when you had politicians exploiting it, deliberately exploiting it to win elections. It's very easy for resentments to be exploited, and so we had explosions.

In addition to recording the past and current revolutions and changes that are going on, do African writers have any influence in determining Africa's future?

Yes, I think by recording what had gone on before, they were in a way helping to set the tone of what was going to happen. And this is important because at this stage it seems to me that the writer's role is more in determining than merely in reporting. In other words, his role is to act rather than to react. Today we are saying, "Well, let's not waste too much time explaining what we were and pleading with some people and telling them we are also human. Let us forget that; let us map out what we are going to be tomorrow." I think our most meaningful job today should be to determine what kind of society we want, how we are going to get there, what values we can take from the past, if we can, as we move along.

Often we think of creativity as something that has to come from a kind of contemplation, quiet or repose. How can you keep the artistic integrity of your writing while being so totally involved in the political situation?

I think there is a myth about creativity being something apart from life, but this is only a half truth. I can create, but of course not the kind of thing I created when I was at ease. I can't write a novel now; I wouldn't want to. And even if I wanted to, I couldn't. So that particular artistic form is out for me at the moment. I can write poetry—something short, intense, more in keeping with my mood. I can write essays. I can even lecture. All this is creating in the context of our struggle. At home I do a lot of writing, but not fiction, something more concrete, more directly related to what's going on. What I'm saying is that there are forms of creativity which suit different moments. I wouldn't consider writing a poem on daffodils particularly creative in my situation now. It would be foolish; I couldn't do it.

Are there any black American writers who've influenced you?
No, I don't like being influenced at all. There's been a lot of speculation over the years about who has influenced me, so I'm very, very cagey about saying anything on this because I don't know what you call being influenced. I have liked different writers at different times, some white, some black. But since you asked me about black American writers, I must admit I discovered them very late. What we were given to read at home when I was a child and went to school—all that we knew about black American writing—was Booker T. Washington's *Up from Slavery*. This was a prescribed text, approved reading. It was when I arrived in this country on a UNESCO fellowship in 1963 that I really got to know black American writers. Before that I had discovered people like Baldwin. I remember in Nigeria, after I read his *Go Tell it on the Mountain*, I went to the American Information Service in Lagos to borrow some of his books, and there was nothing in the library. There wasn't any Richard Wright; there wasn't any black writer in that library. So I made a fuss (this was in '61 or thereabouts) and they brought in some. When I came here in '63, I knew people like Baldwin, Wright, and Langston Hughes, and I met a whole range of younger people like John Williams and LeRoi Jones. But I recently discovered that even these are now old hat. I haven't been here for quite some time, and I have heard that there are newer figures. I mentioned Baldwin the other day as a militant writer, and people just laughed. So I am again out of touch.

What classics did you study in Nigeria as a student?
The Igbo translation of the Bible, John Bunyan's *Pilgrim's Progress*—that kind of thing, down to Hemingway and the others. I read everything I could lay my hands on. It was a very scattered kind of upbringing.

You mentioned Frantz Fanon a little while ago as a writer you admire. What other African writers do you admire?
I admire Camara Laye, Mongo Beti, Ferdinand Oyono, the Congolese poet Tchicaya U Tam'si. I admire Wole Soyinka, James Ngugi, Christopher Okigbo—our national poet who is dead. I could go on, but I think this is sufficient. There are a lot of people I admire.

What is your impression of Léopold Sédar Senghor?
I think he's a great poet. And I think that he was particularly important and valuable at one stage, maybe twenty years ago, in the whole development of black awareness. Today I'm not so sure that he's not almost anachronistic, both politically and even artistically. The younger generation of writers in West Africa—Senegalese and others—are not particularly enthused about Negritude, like Senghor and his group were. And many of them are particularly disenchanted with the politics of Senegal. If you want to see a neocolonial country, I think it's there without a doubt. To my mind he's almost a tragic figure—so very important in the past but today so out of date.

Do you have any idea what you might write about in the future?
I have no idea.

INDEX

Breinigsville, PA USA
06 October 2009
225308BV00001B/1/P